Hardships
in America

The Real Story
of Working Families

Heather Boushey
Chauna Brocht
Bethney Gundersen
Jared Bernstein

ECONOMIC POLICY INSTITUTE

About the authors

Heather Boushey is an economist at the Economic Policy Institute. She has previously conducted research on wages and employment, gender and racial wage inequalities, and social policy. Her current research is on welfare reform. She received her Ph.D. in economics from the New School for Social Research in New York City.

Chauna Brocht is a policy analyst at the Economic Policy Institute. Her research focuses on poverty measurement, low-wage labor markets, and living wage and minimum wage analysis. She coordinates EPI's outreach program and provides technical assistance to state and local advocates on living standards issues. She has an M.A. in public policy from the Humphrey Institute at the University of Minnesota.

Bethney Gundersen is a research fellow at the Economic Policy Institute. Her current research interests include the effect of labor unions and union organizing on the working poor. She has also conducted research on the impact of welfare reform on rural areas and American Indian communities. She received her masters in economics from Washington University in St. Louis and is a doctoral candidate in social work there.

Jared Bernstein is a labor economist at the Economic Policy Institute. His areas of research include income and wage inequality, technology's impact on wages and employment, low-wage labor markets and poverty, minimum wage analysis, and international comparisons. He has published extensively in popular and academic journals, and is the co-author of four editions of the book *The State of Working America*.

Copyright 2001

ECONOMIC POLICY INSTITUTE
1660 L Street NW, Suite 1200
Washington, DC 20036

http://epinet.org

ISBN: 0-944826-95-4

Hardships in America

Table of contents

Acknowledgments

We would like to thank the many people who provided insightful comments on this report, including Gregory Acs, Kurt Bauman, Sondra Beverly, Marcia Meyers, Bill Spriggs, Fasaha Traylor, and Eileen Appelbaum. We would also like to thank Matthew Walters, Jennifer Lake, and Danielle Gao for their assistance on the project and this report, Patrick Watson for overseeing its editing and publication, and Tom Kiley for helping to ensure a wide audience for its findings.

This project was funded by the Foundation for Child Development.

Executive summary

Policy makers in the United States have adopted the view that work is the solution to poverty, and the government's role is to promote employment rather than provide income support for poor families. For many families, however, work may not be enough to ensure a decent standard of living.

This report estimates the number of families who are not making ends meet. We examine the cost of living in every U.S. community and determine basic family budgets for various family types in each one. In all, over 400 separate basic family budgets for six family types are generated. We then count the number of working families in each state whose incomes fall below these basic budgets. Next we examine the hardships these families experience. Finally, we explore how the U.S. can create a social safety net that recognizes that work is not always enough to help families meet their basic needs.

The federal poverty line is traditionally used to measure whether families have incomes too low to enable them to meet basic needs. Yet most researchers now agree that a "poverty line" income is not sufficient to support most working families. "Basic family budgets," individualized for communities nationwide and for type of family, offer a realistic measure of how much income it takes for a safe and decent standard of living. In this report we focus on a subset of families: those with one or two adults and one to three children under 12. Among these kinds of families, we find:

- basic family budgets for a two-parent, two-child family range from $27,005 a year to $52,114, depending on the community. The national median is $33,511, roughly twice the poverty line of $17,463 for a family that size;
- nationally, 29% of families with one to three children under 12 fell below basic family budget levels for their communities in the late 1990s;
- over two-and-a-half-times as many families fall below family budget levels as fall below the official poverty line.

Families headed by single parents, young workers, minority workers, or workers with less than a high school degree are more likely to struggle to make ends meet. However, families not typically thought of as needy are also struggling. Of families with incomes below basic budget levels, half include a parent who works full time; nearly 60% are two-parent families. More than three-quarters are headed by a worker with a high school degree or more, and nearly half are headed by a worker over age 30. About one-third live in the suburbs, one-third in cities, and one-third in rural areas.

In examining the difficulties families face, we distinguish between two types of hardships. *Critical hardships* arise from the inability to meet basic needs such as food, housing, or medical care. Serious hardships arise when families can't afford preventive medical care, quality child care, or safe and affordable housing. Families that fall below basic family budget levels often lack the income needed to support a safe and decent living standard.

Using twice the national poverty line as a national proxy for the basic family budget, we found that in 1996:

* nearly 30% of families with incomes below twice the poverty line faced at least one critical hardship such as missing meals, being evicted from their housing, having their utilities disconnected, doubling up on housing, or not having access to needed medical care;
* over 72% of such families had at least one serious hardship, such as worries about food, missed rent or mortgage payments, reliance on the emergency room as the main source of medical care, or inadequate child care arrangements;
* families with incomes below the basic family budget level faced nearly the same incidence of critical and serious hardships as those with incomes below the poverty line.

We found that families at all income levels are struggling to meet their health care and child care needs. Families lacking private health insurance experience a variety of hardships. For example, families without health insurance are over twice as likely to miss meals and not pay their rent, mortgage, or utility bills as are other families with the same income, regardless of the amount of income they have.

Helping working families meet their basic needs requires a two-pronged approach. First, raising the minimum wage, removing barriers to unionizing, expanding the Earned Income Tax Credit, adopting pay equity policies, and increasing workforce development will increase family incomes. Second, investing in a social safety net of universal programs will help families meet basic needs.

The research reported here documents that families with incomes above the poverty line but below basic family budget levels experience as many hardships as poor families. Thus, policy solutions must be directed toward these families as well. Moreover, the market has priced basic items such as health care, child care, and housing above what many families can afford. It will take a social safety net to truly help families make ends meet.

Introduction

Policy makers in the United States have moved toward the conclusion that work is the solution to poverty. In this scenario, the government's role is to promote employment rather than provide income support for families. Recent policy changes, most importantly the welfare reform bill of 1996, embody this philosophy. In that legislation, Congress transformed welfare for poor families from a cash assistance program to one that is time limited and requires work from most recipients. But work may not offer the entire solution to poverty. Many families may not be able to make ends meet with only their wages to rely on even if they live above the official poverty threshold.

Researchers around the United States have begun to challenge the notion that work alone is the solution to poverty by asking the question, how much does a family need to earn in order to make ends meet? Researchers have also been documenting the kinds of hardships that poor and near-poor families experience. Looking at hardship measures reveals what happens to families that do not have enough income to meet their basic family budgets. Both of these strands of research point toward the kinds of policies that will enable working families to meet their basic needs without experiencing critical or serious hardships.

The first section of this report builds upon the concept of basic family budgets to determine the number of working families with incomes too low for a safe and decent living standard. These budgets, which calculate the costs for every major expense item, including housing, child care, health care, food, transportation, and taxes, reflect realistic costs faced by families. Using a consistent methodology, this report develops over 400 budgets covering six family types in every community in the U.S. Using the Current Population Survey, it then counts the number of families who fall below basic family budget levels and distinguishes between these families and families that fall below the official poverty line.

The findings in this report confirm what other researchers have found: many families do not meet their basic family budget. Twenty-nine percent of all families with one to two adults and one to three children under 12 have incomes below family budget levels. Families headed by single parents, young workers, minority workers, workers with less than a high school education, or less than full-time workers were more likely than other families to struggle to make ends meet. However, large majorities of families that are not typically thought of as the most needy, such as two-parent families, white families, families with a worker with a high school education or more, families with at least one full-time worker, and families headed by a worker over 30, were also struggling to get by.

The second section of this report uses "hardship measures" to specify the nature and level of material deprivation for families whose incomes falls below family budget levels. This analysis builds on previous research that documents the extent to which families experience hardships, but it expands the notion of hardships beyond those contemplated by the current research to include the goods and services that families need to help them make ends meet and balance their responsibilities as workers and parents. It distinguishes between two types of hardships. *Critical hardships* arise from the inability to meet basic needs, such as food, housing, or medical care. This kind of hardship indicates that a family's income level cannot support basic needs critical for survival. Working families suffer less critical but *serious hardships* when they lack the goods and services necessary to support a safe and decent standard of living. Serious hardships include lack of access to regular, preventive medical care; lack of accessible and quality child care; lack of affordable and stable housing; and worries about food.

Our findings confirm that the family budget levels are meaningful because families that fall below 200% of poverty (roughly equivalent to family budget levels) experience relatively high rates of critical and serious hardships. Indeed, critical and serious hardships are found not only among the poor. The near-poor (families between poverty and twice the poverty level) had similar rates of hardship as the poor. Families with incomes less than twice the poverty level had far more hardships than families with higher incomes, but even some families with incomes above twice the poverty threshold experienced hardships. Further, working full time does not necessarily insulate families from experiencing hardships.

The final section of this report identifies policies that expand the social safety net to help families meet basic needs. While policies that raise family incomes are crucial, there are other ways that the federal government can help ensure that families' needs are being met. If work were the only solution to poverty, then workers would not fall below family budget levels. Yet they do and, as a result, experience hardships. High-quality child care, access to quality, preventative health care, affordable housing, and safe transportation are currently out of reach for many families. The high cost of these goods and services necessary to the capacity to work results in many families falling short on meeting their food and other survival needs. A strengthened social safety net would alleviate these hardships and help working families make ends meet.

Chapter 1

Families that fall below basic family budget levels

Over the past several years, basic family budgets have been promoted by advocates and researchers as an alternative to the federal poverty line for measuring family well-being. Unlike the federal poverty line, basic family budgets use a market-basket approach. They identify budget items necessary for a working family to maintain a safe and decent standard of living, then determine how much it costs to provide each item at an adequate level. Basic family budgets are viewed by many as providing a more realistic picture of the income necessary for a family to achieve a safe and decent standard of living than do traditional poverty thresholds.

As the family budget methodology becomes more accepted, the next logical question is how many families subsist on incomes below family budget levels. This section addresses that question. The first part gives an overview of the critique of the official poverty measure and provides background on the family budget alternative. Next, the methodology for creating basic family budgets is discussed, and family budgets are presented for over 400 communities in the U.S. Finally, findings are presented on the number of families that fall below family budget levels.

The problem with the current poverty thresholds

Since the late 1960s, the official poverty thresholds produced by the U.S. Census Bureau have been the most universally accepted comparative measure of family well-being in the United States. However, there is general agreement that the current official poverty thresholds are outdated and inappropriate for measuring true economic hardship for families (Citro and Michael 1995). The poverty thresholds are constructed by costing out the U.S. Department of Agriculture's "thrifty food plan," adjusting it for family size and composition, and multiplying it by three.[1] The "1/3" rule was based on research in the 1960s that documented that families spent about that portion of their budget on food. The poverty threshold is updated each year based on the consumer price index, and there have been only minor changes to the way the thresholds are calculated since they were adopted.

There are numerous problems with the poverty threshold methodology. First, the assumption that families spend one-third of their income on food is outdated. Over time, the relative prices of the items that families consume have changed considerably, and families now spend more of their income on housing, health care, and transportation than they used to and less on food. In addition, even poor families now spend more on certain items, like child care, due to the increased number of mothers in the labor force. As a result of these changes, on average, families now spend less than one-fifth of their income on food (Bernstein, Brocht, and Spade-Aguilar 2000).

Second, the official poverty thresholds have fallen in relative terms. The failure to increase the poverty thresholds as real incomes have grown means that those who fall below the poverty line are worse off relative to the median family now than they were 30 years ago. When the poverty thresholds were first introduced, the threshold for a family of four—$16,530 in 1998 dollars— was 42% of the median income for that family size. By 1998, because of real growth in median family income, that value had fallen to 35.4% (Bernstein, Brocht, and Spade-Aguilar 2000).

There are also numerous other concerns about the adequacy of the poverty thresholds. For example, the poverty thresholds use a pre-tax definition of income and a post-tax definition of expenses; fail to account for geographic differences; exclude non-cash government benefits (such as food stamps, housing subsidies, free or reduced school lunches for children, and energy assistance) in the definition of resources; do not account for differences in child care and medical care expenses among families; and use inadequate equivalence scales (a mathematical formula for adjusting poverty thresholds for differences in family size and composition).

In the early 1990s, Congress, acknowledging that the current thresholds were inadequate, commissioned the National Research Council of the National Academy of Sciences to research the saliency of the thresholds and to propose alternatives. The council recommended basing the thresholds on the median expenditures of two-adult, two-child families on food, clothing, shelter, and utilities, plus a small amount for other incidentals. The council's other recommendations included changes to the equivalence scales; geographic adjustments to the thresholds; the addition of the value of non-cash government assistance (such as food stamps, housing subsidies, school lunches, and energy assistance) to the measure of income; and the subtraction of expenses such as taxes, costs associated with working (such as child care), and medical expenses (Citro and Michael 1995).

In analyses using "experimental poverty measures" based on the council's recommendations, the Census Bureau found that the percentage of people in poverty in 1998 increased from 12.7% under the current measure to a high of 15.4% under the experimental measures (depending on which version was used); also, using the experimental measures resulted in a lower rate of poverty for children and a higher rate of poverty for the elderly, compared to the current measures (Short, Iceland, and Garner 1999). The analysis also found lower poverty rates for female-headed households and higher poverty rates for married couples. Subsequent research found a higher rate of poverty than under the current measure among families in which adult members worked full time (Iceland 2000).

Basic family budgets

Basic family budgets measure the income a family requires to afford basic needs for a safe and decent standard of living. The family budget method differs significantly from the poverty thresholds in that it tabulates the costs of every major budget item a family needs, including housing, child care, health care, food, transportation and taxes, based on the composition of the family and where the family lives. The family budget method assumes that income comes from employment, and so it makes no assumptions about whether the family receives government assistance. Family budgets do, however, allow a determination of the amount of post-tax income a family needs.

Family budgets have a number of advantages over the poverty thresholds for evaluating the ability of a family to afford a safe and decent standard of living. First, family budgets are specific to a particular family type in a particular locality. Thus, for a family with two parents and one child under 6 in Minneapolis, the family budget method tabulates costs in Minneapolis, including local child care costs. Family budgets assume that all adults work; therefore, they account for child care costs that are specific to the child's age.

Basic family budgets are geographically specific for as many budget items as possible. In the U.S., the cost of living varies by region due to differences in local economies. For some budget items, such as food, there is no reliable data source for local costs. But for the items that vary the most by region, such as housing and child care, the use of locally specific data in basic family budgets makes them an accurate reflection of the costs faced by families.

The poverty thresholds are based on equivalence scales and do not account for geographic differences in the cost of living. Instead of tabulating the costs of goods and services needed based on the expenses of different family members, the poverty thresholds use a family of three as a basis and are multiplied by a scaled number to determine the threshold for different family types. Thus, the family budget methodology allows a more specific tabulation of a family's actual costs than do the poverty thresholds.

The family budget method also enables a discussion of the value of subsidies that families receive. Since the family budget measures costs, not income, subsidies can simply be subtracted from a family's costs. For example, to analyze the effects of child care subsidies, the value of these subsidies can be subtracted from total child care costs. Thus, the income a family needs declines in proportion to the value of the subsidy.

Similarly, taxes (and tax credits, such as the Earned Income Tax Credit) are tabulated into the income amount necessary to cover the family budget. For example, a two-parent, two-child family in Birmingham, Ala. that needs an after-tax income of $29,300 to meet all of its expenses needs $33,360 in pre-tax income.

Family budgets also differ from poverty thresholds in that they measure the income needed for a safe and decent standard of living, independent of government subsidies. While most poverty measures are viewed as a measure of deprivation, or the minimum necessary for survival, basic family budgets set a higher standard. For example, basic family budgets include the cost of *quality* child care, because they assume that families should not be expected to make their children worse off than if the mother remained at home.[2]

Family budget methodology

The first step in measuring the number of families whose incomes fall below basic family budget levels was to create a consistent set of budgets for the entire U.S. We created basic budgets for every metropolitan area in the country and a combined rural budget for each state using the detailed methodology outlined in Bernstein et al. (2000). Unlike other poverty measures, which use equivalence scales to extrapolate income levels for a large variety of family types, these budgets focus only on after-tax income for only six family types: single- and two-parent families with one, two, or three children all under the age of 12. These budgets cover 29% of the U.S. population and 71% of U.S. families with children under 12. The budgets assume that all adults work and that, therefore, child care is a necessity for all six family types.

We count families who fall below basic family budget levels using budgets for metropolitan statistical areas (MSAs) and one combined budget for rural areas per state. Creating a state or federal family budget would not give an accurate estimate, because there is much variation in the cost of living between various MSAs and between cities and rural areas even within a state. MSAs are the smallest geographic area for which data are available. We created a combined budget for rural areas in the state because creating a budget for each rural county in the country would involve creating hundreds of additional budgets.

Researchers around the country have already generated family budgets for specific communities. There are over 40 family budget studies that have been conducted for various communities around the country, each using a slightly different methodology.[3] However, we needed a methodologically consistent budget for every MSA and rural area in the country. Therefore, we created over 400 budgets for each family type, presented in Appendix F.

To create these budgets, we first determined the items necessary for a working family to maintain a safe and decent standard of living, then determined the cost of providing each item at an adequate level based on family composition. The cost estimates are based on the following sources (see Appendix A for a more detailed account of the methodology):

•   Food is based on the minimum amount a family needs to spend for food prepared at home, as recommended by the U.S. Department of Agriculture's "low-cost food plan."[4]

- Housing is based on a two-bedroom apartment (for families with one or two children) or a three-bedroom apartment (for families with three children) that costs no more than 40% of all structurally safe and decent housing in the community, as measured by the Department of Housing and Urban Development's fair market rents.

- Health care expenses are based on an amount that recognizes that not all families receive health insurance through their employers. We use a weighted average of the employee share of the premium for employer-sponsored health insurance (from the Bureau of Labor Statistics) and the premium costs for a non-group plan (from an online insurance quote service), plus the cost of out-of-pocket medical expenses (from a Lewin Group model).

- Transportation costs are based on average miles driven for work and other necessary trips. This amount takes into account different driving distances for cities, suburbs, and rural areas, from the Department of Transportation, and is based on the cost-per-mile estimates from the Internal Revenue Service.

- Child care expenses are based on center-based child care or family child care centers for 4- and 8-year-olds, as reported by the Children's Defense Fund.

- Other necessary expenses are based on the cost of telephone service as reported by the Federal Communications Commission, and the cost of clothing, personal care, household items, bank fees, union dues, reading materials, school supplies, and television as reported in Consumer Expenditure Survey data.

- Taxes include federal payroll taxes and federal, state, and local income taxes. This expense also takes into account funds received from the federal and state EITC and the Child and Dependent Care Tax Credit.

The budgets do not include the cost of restaurant meals, vacations, movies, or savings for education or retirement.

How do these budgets compare with other measures?

Table 1 presents a sample of budgets for one-parent, two-child families for eight areas (see Appendix F for the budgets for all six family types for every metropolitan area and a composite rural area). The budgets range from $21,989 in Hattiesburg, Miss., to $48,606 in Nassau-Suffolk County, N.Y. Comparing our budgets to other basic family budget estimates, we find small differences in overall levels due to slightly different methodologies (see Bernstein, Brocht, and Spade-Aguilar 2000 and epinet.org for a list of other family budget studies).

Among the over 400 family budgets created here, the lowest for a single parent with two children is in Hattiesburg, and it is 64% higher than the official

TABLE 1 Sample family budgets for eight areas, by month and year, 1999 (single parent, 4-year-old, 8-year-old)

	Little Rock-North Little Rock, Ark.	Los Angeles-Long Beach, Calif.	Hattiesburg, Miss.	Chicago, Ill.	Nassau-Suffolk, N.Y.	Seattle-Bellevue-Everett, Wash.	Houston, Texas	Rural Indiana
Housing	$497	$749	$398	$737	$1,105	$736	$601	$420
Food	351	351	351	351	351	351	351	351
Child care	525	786	459	722	975	734	556	637
Transportation	161	157	158	157	170	170	157	197
Health care	216	203	229	242	267	243	256	207
Other necessities	263	341	232	337	451	337	295	239
Taxes	139	316	5	397	731	306	153	167
Monthly total	2,151	2,903	1,832	2,942	4,051	2,878	2,369	2,218
Annual total	**$25,809**	**$34,839**	**$21,989**	**$35,307**	**$48,606**	**$34,534**	**$28,430**	**$26,618**
Percent of poverty threshold	192%	260%	164%	263%	362%	257%	212%	198%

* See Appendix F for the budgets for six family types for every MSA and a composite rural area.

Source: Authors' analysis.

poverty line. The highest, in Nassau-Suffolk, is 362% of poverty. Most family budgets range between 200% and 300% of poverty; budgets for 12 areas total more than 300% of poverty.

Number and shares of families falling below family budget levels

In order to count the number of families that fall below basic family budget levels, we used the U.S. Census Bureau's Current Population Survey. We combined data for the three years 1997-99 in order to generate a large enough sample size. We looked only at families with positive earnings and at families for the family types for which we created family budgets: families with one or two adults and one, two, or three children under 12. Our budgets assume that both parents work full time, so non-school-age children are assumed to be in child-care full time and school-age children to be in child care during after-school hours. Although all families in the sample worked during the period examined, not all families worked full time. To adjust for this, we reduced child care costs in proportion to the share of the year that family members worked.

We count the number of families that fell below the family budget levels by the MSA or rural budget levels. However, the sample sizes were too small to reliably estimate how many people fall below the budget levels by MSA or rural area. Therefore, we totaled the number of families that fall below family budget levels in all MSAs and in the rural area in each state, and are able to report totals by state (see Appendix B for more details on the methodology).

Nationally, over 4 million families with one to three children under 12 fell below basic family budgets in 1997-99 (see **Table 2**). These families comprise 14 million people, nearly 7 million adults and over 7 million children. Table 2 also compares the number of families in poverty compared to the number that fall below basic family budget levels; over two-and-a-half times more families fall below family budget levels than fall below the official poverty line. Thus, about 9 million persons in families with one to three children under 12 have incomes above the poverty line yet below the level required to meet their basic needs.

Table 3 compares the share of families with income below basic family budget levels to those whose income is below the poverty line and twice the poverty line. Over the period examined, 1997-99, the income of 28.9% of families with one to three children under 12 was below basic family budget levels, while just 10.1% were classified as poor. Thus, a much larger share of low-income working families are earning too little income to make ends meet than would be suggested by the national poverty statistics.

Families by demographics and work status
We can get a picture of the types of families most likely to fall below family budget levels by looking at Table 3 and **Table 4**. Families headed by single parents, young workers, or workers with less than a college education are the

TABLE 2 Numbers of families and persons below family budgets and poverty level

	Number below (000s)	
	Family budget	Poverty line
Families	4,229	1,485
Persons	14,154	4,926
White	7,011	2,042
African American	2,758	1,184
Hispanic	3,730	1,456
Other	655	244
Adults	6,686	2,175
Children	7,468	2,751
White	3,576	1,073
African American	1,580	729
Hispanic	1,958	809
Other	354	140

Source: Authors' calculations from the pooled 1997-99 March CPS.

Note: Sample is families with positive earnings, one to two parents, and one to three children under the age of 12.

most likely to be struggling to make ends meet. However, families not typically thought of as the most needy, such as two-parent families, white families, families with a high-school-educated worker, families with a full-time worker, and families headed by workers age 30 and over, are also struggling to get by.

Racial minorities face the greatest struggles making ends meet. As Table 3 shows, over 50% of black and Hispanic families and 28.5% of families in other racial categories (American Indians, Aleut Eskimos, Asians, Pacific Islanders, and others "unspecified") fall below family budget levels, compared to 20.3% of white families. However, as Table 4 shows, white families make up the majority (50.5%) of families that fall below family budget levels. Also, a greater share of white families fall below family budget levels than fall below poverty (50.5% vs. 43.6%). Thus, while racial minorities tend to dominate the ranks of the poor, a substantial portion of the near-poor are white families.

Since family income usually rises with the education level of the family head, families headed by a householder with lower levels of education are predictably more likely to fall below basic family budgets (Table 3). Families headed by a worker with less than a high school education are the most likely to fall below family budget levels (68.6%). However, as Table 4 shows, over three-fourths of families who fall below family budget levels are headed by a worker with at least a high school education, indicating that problems with meeting basic needs are not concentrated among families with the least-educated workers.

TABLE 3 Share of families with income less than family budgets and less than one or two times poverty threshold, by demographic characteristics

	Share of families below		
	Family budget	Poverty line	Twice poverty line
ALL	28.9%	10.1%	28.4%
Race/ethnicity*			
White	20.3	6.2	20.5
African American	52.1	22.3	50.2
Hispanic	56.3	21.5	54.1
Other	28.5	10.4	25.6
Education			
Less than high school degree	68.6	34.1	68.8
High school degree only	38.1	13.3	38.2
Some college	27.6	7.5	26.4
College degree	7.7	1.6	7.2
Age			
18-30	46.8	19.4	46.8
31-45	20.1	5.6	19.4
46+	21.6	6.6	21.0
Location			
City	39.3	15.0	36.6
Suburbs	21.7	6.1	19.5
Rural	32.8	13.1	38.3
Region			
Northeast	29.7	8.2	23.6
Midwest	23.4	9.1	24.7
South	30.0	11.5	32.5
West	32.0	10.7	29.6
Work status			
Full-time, full-year	20.9	3.9	19.9
Less than full-time, full-year	46.8	24.1	47.5
Family type			
One adult with one child	60.3	22.5	53.7
One adult with two children	75.3	34.5	67.8
One adult with three children	87.8	60.6	83.9
Two adults with one child	16.9	4.1	16.1
Two adults with two children	18.5	5.2	20.8
Two adults with three children	35.2	11.9	36.7

* White, African American, and Other exclude Hispanics.
Note: Sample is families with positive earnings, one to two parents, and one to three children under the age of 12.

Source: Authors' calculations from the pooled 1997-99 March CPS.

Young families (i.e., those headed by someone 30 or younger) were much more likely to fall below family budget levels than older families; as Table 3 shows, 46.8% of families headed by a worker age 18-30 fall below family budget levels,

TABLE 4   Distribution of families by family budget and poverty status

	Family budget	Poverty line	All
Race/ethnicity*			
White	50.5%	43.6%	71.7%
African American	21.8	26.6	12.1
Hispanic	23.5	25.6	12.1
Other	4.1	4.3	4.2
Total	100.0	100.0	100.0
Education			
Less than high school degree	23.9	33.9	10.1
High school degree only	39.1	38.9	29.6
Some college	29.0	22.4	30.3
College degree	8.1	4.8	30.1
Total	100.0	100.0	100.0
Age			
18-30	52.5	62.0	32.4
31-45	41.9	33.1	60.2
46+	5.6	4.9	7.5
Total	100.0	100.0	100.0
Location			
City	36.2	39.8	26.5
Suburbs	39.1	31.9	51.9
Rural	24.6	28.3	21.6
Total	100.0	100.0	100.0
Region			
Northeast	18.9	14.8	18.3
Midwest	19.1	21.2	23.6
South	36.9	40.3	35.5
West	25.1	23.8	22.6
Total	100.0	100.0	100.0
Work status			
Full-time, full-year	50.0	26.7	69.2
Less than full-time, full-year	50.0	73.3	30.8
Total	100.0	100.0	100.0
Family type			
One adult with one child	21.3	22.7	10.2
One adult with two children	15.7	20.5	6.0
One adult with three children	5.3	10.4	1.7
Two adults with one child	19.9	13.8	34.0
Two adults with two children	23.1	18.5	36.1
Two adults with three children	14.7	14.1	12.0
Total	100.0	100.0	100.0

Note: Sample is families with positive earnings, one to two parents, and one to three children under the age of 12.

Source: Authors' calculations from the pooled 1997-99 March CPS.

compared to about 20% of families headed by workers age 31 or older. As Table 4 shows, most families under family budget levels are headed by a young person (52.5%). The high share of young families falling below family budget levels may be explained by their lack of experience in the labor force, yet the fact that 47.5% of families with heads-of-household age 31-45 and 46 or older fall below basic family budget levels means that this problem cannot be explained only by time in the labor force.

Among the families in Tables 3 and 4 (all of which have positive earnings), there are two categories of work status in the paid labor market: those families headed by a full-time, full-year worker, and those headed by someone who worked less. This is an important distinction, since working families tend to depend on earnings as opposed to government transfer payments. Families with less than full-time, full-year workers are more likely to struggle to make ends meet. Nearly 47% of families with less than a full-time worker fall below family budget levels, compared to 20.9% of families with a full-time, full-year worker (Table 3). However, as Table 4 shows, families with a full-time worker are also struggling to make ends meet; half (50.0%) of families falling below family budget levels have a full-time full-year worker.

A clear majority of single-parent families have incomes below family budget levels; 75.3% of single-parent families with two children fall below family budget levels for their family type, as do 87.8% of single-parent families with three children. Two-parent families are much less likely to fall below family budget levels: only 18.5% of families with two parents and two children do so. However, as Table 4 shows, many two-parent families are struggling to make ends meet; 57.7% of families that fall below family budget levels are two-parent families.

Location, state, and region
A comparison of cities, suburbs, and rural areas shows that one-third or more of families in urban and rural areas fall below family budgets, compared to about a fifth of suburban families (Table 3). Surprisingly, however, the bulk of families falling below family budget levels live in the suburbs (Table 4). This distribution differs markedly from that of families in poverty, where 31.9% live in suburbs and 39.8% live in cities.

In terms of regions, families who fall below family budget levels also differ from families who fall below the poverty line. The percentage-point differences between the Northeast and Southern regions are smaller for basic family budgets than for poverty (0.3 points versus 3.3), largely due to the fact that basic family budgets reflect the lower price of certain budget components (e.g., housing, child care) in the South, while poverty thresholds do not capture this difference.[5]

Table 5 examines the percent and numbers of persons by state and region in families below basic family budgets levels. The smallest share of families falling below family budget levels is in the Midwest. While the South consistently has the highest regional poverty rates, this is not the case with the family budget

TABLE 5   Percent and number of persons in families with incomes less than family budgets, by state

State	Below family budgets	
	Percent	Number (000)
Northeast	28.6%	2,746
Maine	31.5	60
New Hamshire	34.7	77
Vermont	28.4	33
Massachusetts	27.9	293
Rhode Island	27.1	46
Connecticut	17.9	124
New York	37.5	1,247
New Jersey	21.0	332
Pennsylvania	23.7	535
Midwest	21.5%	2,628
Ohio	21.9	473
Indiana	17.8	208
Illinois	25.5	651
Michigan	20.2	380
Wisconsin	19.9	205
Minnesota	16.7	161
Iowa	20.9	103
Missouri	20.6	196
North Dakota	36.9	35
South Dakota	20.1	21
Nebraska	23.4	79
Kansas	24.3	116
South	28.5%	5,086
Delaware	27.8	38
Maryland	16.3	155
District of Columbia	41.9	26
Virginia	20.3	251
West Virginia	37.1	68
North Carolina	23.6	358
South Carolina	25.5	203
Georgia	29.0	410
Florida	29.7	751
Kentucky	29.9	211
Tennessee	32.6	391
Alabama	31.7	233
Mississippi	26.1	118
Arkansas	27.7	130
Louisiana	24.9	192
Oklahoma	25.5	136
Texas	34.0	1,414

TABLE 5 *(cont.)*   Percent and number of persons in families with incomes less than family budgets, by state

State	Below family budgets	
	Percent	Number (000)
West	31.6%	3,694
Montana	39.8	54
Idaho	39.1	96
Wyoming	23.4	12
Colorado	20.7	173
New Mexico	40.2	122
Arizona	35.0	337
Utah	30.7	130
Nevada	30.1	117
Washington	20.5	250
Oregon	36.0	251
California	33.1	2,007
Alaska	32.7	53
Hawaii	45.7	93
U.S.	27.6%	14,154

Note: Sample is families with positive earnings, one to two parents, and one to three children under the age of 12.

Source: Authors' calculations from the pooled 1997-99 March CPS.

thresholds, presumably due to price differences by region for the localized components of the budgets. For example, the rate at which family incomes fall below basic family budget levels in Louisiana was 24.9%, lower than the national average rate of 28.9%. Comparing poverty rates for all persons averaged over these same years (1997-99) yields a very different result: 18.2% for Louisiana versus 12.6% for the nation.[6]

The Western region had the largest share of families – 31.6% – falling below basic family budget levels. In four states in the region – Montana, Idaho, New Mexico, and Hawaii – approximately 40% of families had incomes below basic family budgets.

Figure A illustrates the shares of families falling below family budget levels and the poverty levels by region (the data are not specific enough to allow an examination at the state level).

Summary

Of the family types for whom we constructed basic family budgets, 28.9% fell below these income cutoffs, compared to 10.1% who fell below the poverty

FIGURE A   Family income below family budget and poverty, by region

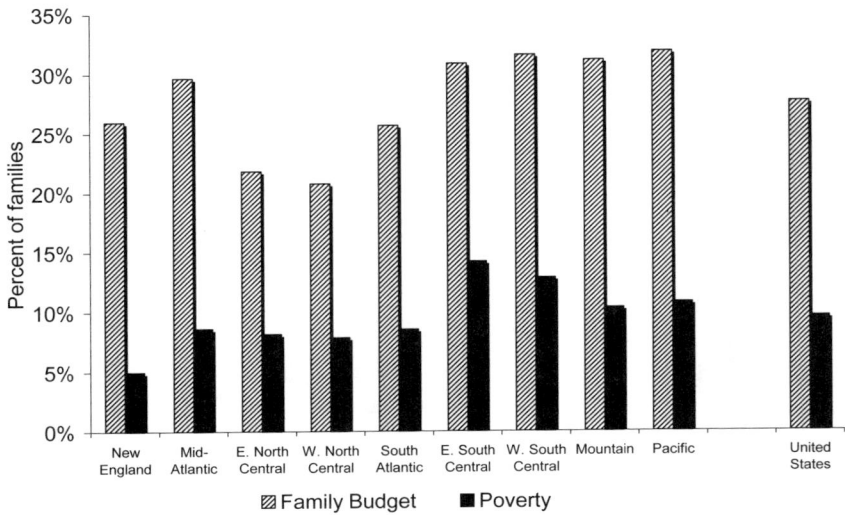

Note: Sample is families with positive earnings, one to two parents, and one to three children under the age of 12.

Source: Authors' calculations from the pooled 1997-99 March CPS.

threshold. We find that, while families with certain characteristics (single parents, minorities, and less-skilled workers) are at greatest risk, the majority of families that fall below family budget levels are white, two-parent families, where the breadwinner has at least a high school education. This analysis of families that fall below family budget levels suggests that a significant number are struggling to make ends meet. The next section of this report establishes this case by examining the extent to which income-constrained families face hardships.

Chapter 2

The hardships low-income families face

As documented in the previous section, 28.9% of working families with children had incomes below basic family budget levels in the late 1990s. But what exactly do these families do without?

To answer this question, we must document whether families are meeting their basic needs and whether those falling below basic family budgets are having more trouble than are families above basic family budgets. For this kind of analysis, we turn to recent innovations in measuring hardships. "Hardship indicators" were developed to address the inadequacies of traditional income-based poverty measures. They complement income-based measures of poverty by providing insight into the types of goods and services that poor families typically go without. Hardship indicators are not meant to be used alone, but rather in conjunction with more traditional, income-based measures of poverty.

Methods of measuring hardships

The measurement of hardships is typically accomplished via surveys with questions about food sufficiency, evictions, and adequate heating in cold-weather months. Unfortunately, it is sometimes difficult to ascertain whether the answers in these surveys indicate a genuine hardship or simply a family's preference or taste. Therefore, the kinds of questions asked and the way in which they are worded are important.

To help create accurate measures of hardship that reflect a family's actual deprivation, researcher Sondra Beverly (2000; 2001) proposed the use of material hardship variables. According to Beverly, material hardships should reflect basic standards of material adequacy, assessing consumption of only food, housing, utilities, medical care, clothing, and consumer durables. She further recommends that the indicators should measure the severity of hardships in an objective framework. The core set of hardship measures should consist of direct, rather than indirect, indicators, and they should indicate the cause of hardship as well as include composite indices and separate measures of hardship. Such a method should weed out families that may "choose" to experience certain hardships. For example, not having a telephone is often considered a material hardship. However, some families may choose not to have a telephone for personal reasons.

Alternatively, a wealthy person may not have paid the full amount of the rent or mortgage last month because he or she chose to spend the money on luxury goods instead. This person may not be experiencing a hardship in the same way as someone who did not pay the rent because he or she could not afford to. This, again, underscores the importance of question wording in the surveys.

The method used in this report expands on the notion of material hardships, which we refer to here as "critical" hardships, by looking as well at a broader array of "serious" hardships. Critical hardships explain the extent to which families fail to meet their basic needs for survival. In comparison, serious hardships explain the extent to which families lack the goods, services, and financial ability to maintain employment and a stable, healthy home environment. The concept of serious hardships includes lack of access to regular and preventive medical care, low-quality and insufficient-quality child care, the inability to pay housing bills, and unreliable transportation.[7]

The method used here for choosing variables that measure critical hardships involved looking to previous literature on material hardship. The critical hardship measures we use come from existing research on basic needs and material hardship (Beverly 2000; Bauman 1998; Mayer and Jencks 1989). These variables measure the extent to which households go without the very basic necessities: food, housing, and health care. We selected those questions that have been tested for validity in terms of their measure of hardship; those that, to the extent possible, were objective measures of hardship; and those that measured material rather than financial hardship. This last criteria was due to the fact that we wanted the critical hardship measures to demonstrate the extent to which households experience material deprivation, not the extent to which they are having financial difficulties.

The serious hardship measures used here are new to the hardship literature, so we created our own method in selecting these measures. The selection process was similar to the selection of critical measures in the sense that it required objective measures. For these measures we focused on financial hardship rather than material hardship, because we wanted to determine the extent to which households are having trouble meeting their needs even though they may or may not actually experience material deprivation. In addition, we searched for variables that would measure the stability and health of the household. As with critical hardships, we relied for these variables on external criteria of how the measure affected health and stability.

Hardship indicators

Data and sample
Hardships fall under four broad categories: food insecurity, insufficient access to health care, housing problems, and inadequate child care. To understand whether or not families are living with hardships, it is necessary to know whether basic needs under these categories are being met. This requires the use of surveys with detailed questions about how families meet their basic needs. Given the

specific and invasive nature of the questions, the primary difficulty with measuring hardships is the availability and consistency of appropriate data.

There are two national surveys that ask questions about family hardships—the Survey of Income and Program Participation (SIPP) and the National Survey of American Families (NSAF). These surveys ask families questions about whether they "go without" and experience material deprivation. This report uses both the SIPP and the NSAF in its analysis. The questions asked in the two surveys are not identical, but the use of both surveys allows an expansion of the measures of hardship. **Table 6** presents the questions selected from the two datasets. (See Appendix C for a detailed description of the data. A complete analysis of these issues can be found in Gundersen and Boushey 2001.)

While the SIPP and NSAF have their strengths and weaknesses, the nature and structure of the NSAF makes it a better survey from which to study hardships. The SIPP is a panel dataset focused on income, employment, and participation in government programs. The hardship questions are the last set of questions asked in the last month of the panel. As with all panel datasets, attrition is a problem in the SIPP. Since attrition tends to occur among low-income respondents, and these respondents are more likely to experience hardship, the SIPP measures may underestimate the extent of hardship. The NSAF, on the other hand, is a cross-sectional survey of the experiences of families that focuses on a number of hardships and family-stress indicators. The cross-sectional nature of this survey eliminates attrition bias. Additionally, the NSAF survey focuses exclusively on well-being, perhaps prompting respondents to give more thoughtful or detailed answers to hardship questions. Given the NSAF's advantages in this regard, we focus on those results. The SIPP results are presented in the tables in order to demonstrate the similarity of the results across measures of hardship.

Unfortunately, data constraints prevent us from matching basic family budgets directly to the NSAF data.[8] Further, our family budgets were tabulated only for six family types, covering only a small proportion of the total U.S. population. In order to generate a large-enough sample to estimate hardships reliably, we use 200% of poverty instead of family budgets for the analysis of hardships. In the previous section, we documented that family budgets correspond closely with 200% of the poverty level: 87% of families living below family budget levels also live below 200% of poverty. Further, using the Current Population Survey, we found that the proportion of families below the family budget level in the nation as a whole closely corresponds to the proportion below 200% of poverty: 28.9% of families fall below basic family budgets, while 28.4% of families fall below 200% of poverty. We also found that the proportion of families experiencing particular hardships was similar using the two thresholds. (See Appendix D.) Thus, the 200%-of-poverty threshold is a good approximation of basic family budgets for use in the hardship analysis.

Our sample for the analysis of hardships is individuals in families with positive income that are headed by an adult age 18-64.[9] These households may

TABLE 6   Critical vs. serious hardships

	Data set	Question
Food		
Critical hardships		
Not enough food to eat*	SIPP	Which of the following statements best describe the amount of food eaten in your household: enough food to eat, sometimes not enough to eat, or often not enough to eat.
Missed meals	NSAF	In the last 12 months, since (name of current month) of last year, did you or other adults in your family ever cut the size of your meals or skip meals because there wasn't enough money for food?
Serious hardships		
Don't have the kind of food the family would like to eat	SIPP	Do you have enough and the kind of food you want to eat, or do you have enough but not always the kind of food you want to eat?
Worry about having enough food	NSAF	For these statements, please tell me whether the statement was often, sometimes or never true for (you/your family) in the last 12 months... "(I/we) worried whether (my/our) food would run out before (I/we) got money to buy more."
Housing		
Critical hardships		
Evicted	SIPP	In the past 12 months, has there been a time when your household was evicted from your home/apartment for not paying the rent or mortgage?
Utilities disconnected	SIPP	In the past 12 months, has there been a time when your household did not pay the full amount of the gas, oil, or electricity bills?
Doubling up with friends or family	NSAF	During the last 12 months, did you or your children move in with other people, even for a little while because you could not afford to pay your mortgage, rent, or utility bills?
Serious hardships		
Unable to make housing or utility payments	NSAF	During the last 12 months, was there a time when (you/you and your family) were not able to pay your mortgage, rent, or utility bills?
Telephone disconnected	NSAF	During the last 12 months, has your household ever been without telephone service for more than 24 hours?
Health care		
Critical hardships		
Did not receive necessary medical care	NSAF	During the past 12 months, did [you/(SPOUSE/PARTNER)] or (insert names of children) not get or postpone getting medical care or surgery when [you/(he/she/they)] needed it?

TABLE 6 *(cont.)* Critical vs. serious hardships

	Data set	Question
Serious hardships		
Emergency room is main source for health care	NSAF	What kind of place is it that [you usually go (SPOUSE/ PARTNER/CHILD) usually goes] to for health care needs? Is it…[VALUE 2: Hospital Emergency Room]
No health insurance	NSAF	Derived variable from current health insurance coverage label: private, public, or uninsured.
Child care		
Child cares for self	NSAF	During the last month did (child) take care of (himself/ herself) {or stay alone with (his/her) brother or sister who is under 13 years old} on a regular basis even for a small amount of time?
Child not in after-school or enrichment activities	NSAF	No question. Label: Child is NOT involved in any activities
Inadequate adult-to-child ratio in child care facility	NSAF	{For the program you use most}, About how many adults usually supervise the children in (CHILD's) room or group? —————————OVER————————— About how many children are usually in (CHILD's) room or group at this center or program?

or may not have children, but we exclude households with only one adult and no children. For the NSAF, the weighted sample consists of 233 million persons. The descriptive tables of hardship presented in this report use persons as the unit of analysis. That is, the tables indicate the proportion and number of persons in households experiencing hardship. The unit of analysis in the regressions is the social family (NSAF) or household (SIPP). That is, the percentages indicate the probability of a family/household experiencing hardship based on family/ household characteristics.

Critical hardships and serious hardships

Food inadequacy
To go without sufficient food is the most basic critical hardship. We measure food insufficiency in terms of not having enough to eat or missing meals sometimes or often. These measures are based on questions that have been tested for validity: families who report food insufficiency have been found to have lower food expenditures and lower intake of calories and nutrients (Rose and Oliveira 1997). A serious food hardship is less severe in that the family may not actually go without food, but it does not have the kind of food it feels it needs or it worries about food intake.

Living with food hardship

As she weighs bunches of purple grapes or rings up fat chicken legs at the supermarket where she works, Fannie Payne cannot keep from daydreaming.

"It's difficult to work at a grocery store all day, looking at all the food I can't buy," Mrs. Payne said. "So I imagine filling up my cart with one of those big orders and bringing home enough for all my kids."

Instead, she said that she and her husband, Michael, a factory worker, routinely go without dinner to make sure their four children have enough to eat. They visit a private hunger center monthly for three days' worth of free groceries, to help stretch the $60 a week they spend on food.

"We're behind on all of our bills," Mrs. Payne said. "We don't pay electricity until they threaten a cut-off. To be honest, I'm behind two months on the mortgage – that's $600 a month. We owe $800 on the water bill and $500 for heat."

The Euclid Hunger Center helped her seek aid from her parish, St. William's Catholic Church. But it hurt that three cars broke down in six months.

"They all died and we had to get Mike to work, so we bought a good used car we can't afford," she said.

The first thing to go was money for food for herself and her husband.

"Some nights Mike and I eat our kid's leftovers, and when we don't have any money for milk I feed the kids soup for breakfast," she said.

—From "Millions Eligible for Food Stamps Aren't Applying," by Elizabeth Becker, The New York Times, February 26, 2001. Reprinted by permission.

The variables that went into determining a critical food hardship include:

- whether a respondent missed meals sometimes or often in the last 12 months (from the NSAF).
- whether a respondent sometimes or often did not have enough food to eat (from the SIPP).

The variables that went into determining a serious food hardship include:

- whether a family worries that food will run out before it can buy more (NSAF).
- whether a family lacked the kinds of food it liked to eat (SIPP).

Housing problems

In accordance with Beverly's work (2000; 2001), critical housing hardships are defined as the consequences of not paying housing bills. Eviction, utility disconnection, and moving in with others because a family could not pay its bills constitute critical housing hardships. Serious housing hardships, on the other hand, measure a family's ability to afford housing or utility bills; these families may not have actually experienced a critical hardship such as an eviction in the past year, but they still struggle to pay their housing bills. Losing telephone service would be considered a serious hardship because, while a telephone is necessary for finding and keeping a job, it is not an immediate critical need.

The variables that went into determining a critical hardship in housing include:

- whether there was a time in the past 12 months that an individual was evicted from his or her household for nonpayment of mortgage or rent (SIPP).

- whether a family moved in with others because it could not afford to pay its mortgage, rent, or utility bill (NSAF).
- whether there was a time in the past 12 months that an individual's household had its utility service disconnected because the household did not pay the utility bill (SIPP).

The variables that went into determining a serious hardship in housing include:

- whether there was a time in the past 12 months that an individual's household was not able to pay the mortgage, rent, or utility bill (NSAF).
- whether there was a time in the past 12 months that an individual's household did not have telephone service because payments were not made to the telephone company (NSAF).

Insufficient access to health care
A critical hardship in health care occurs when, in the past 12 months, any individual in the family did not get or postponed necessary medical care. As Beverly (2000) notes, some consider this measure to be subjective, because respondents are asked to evaluate whether they "need" to see the doctor. However, we agree with others, such as Mayer and Jencks (1989), who argue that not being able to see a doctor when you feel you need to (whether you objectively need to see one or not) is a hardship.

While critical hardships involve immediate medical needs, the survey question gauging serious health care hardships inquires about access to preventative care. Having health insurance is a key element in one's ability to access preven-

---

Living with housing hardship

Hector Cuatepotzo, a waiter at the upscale Miramar Hotel in Santa Monica, Calif., lives in a tiny, one-bedroom apartment with his wife, Maria, 6-year-old daughter, Ashley, and infant son, Bryan. All four sleep in the same small room, with Bryan's crib nestled in one corner and Ashley's bed in another.

Cuatepotzo earns about $20,000 a year in salary and tips (equal to about $10 an hour, almost twice the minimum wage). But with $625 a month in rent and another $80 for monthly gas and electricity, the Cuatepotzos spend more than 40 percent of their income for housing. Cuatepotzo works from 6 a.m. to 2 p.m. and travels 40 miles round-trip to work each day because rents in buildings closer to his job are even higher.

Since Maria took time off from her job in a restaurant to have the baby, they have received several eviction notices for late payment.

Cuatepotzo is thinking about getting a second job, but that would mean rarely seeing his children. Cuatepotzo, who has worked at the Miramar since arriving from Mexico 10 years ago, would like to own his own home someday. "It's my dream," he says. But he can't imagine how he'll ever get there when his family lives paycheck to paycheck.

—From "America's Workers Can't Pay the Rent," by Peter Dreier, America @ Work, February 2000. Reprinted by permission.

Living with health care hardship

In 1997, Steve Ducharme was carrying plasterboard when he heard something pop in his arm and felt something strange in his armpit. It was his biceps muscle, which had snapped and then sprung back into his armpit like a recoiling window shade.

That started the worst of bad times for Mr. Ducharme, a carpenter in this southern Maine town: unemployment, bankruptcy, a repossessed car, the works.

The bankruptcy showed his vulnerability. After his biceps snapped, he needed an operation, and without insurance that meant $6,000 out of pocket. He could not work at full strength for months. The bills piled up until the pile toppled over. For a while, when Lisa was pregnant with Nick, she would put off prenatal doctor's appointments because under her insurance plan she had to pay for them herself and then be reimbursed, and she lacked the cash. "That was an awful, awful time," she said.

—From "Working Hard, Doing Well, Less Than Excited About Bush's Tax Plan," by Carey Goldberg, The New York Times, April 8, 2001. Reprinted by permission.

tative care. Therefore, one serious hardship is whether anyone in the family lacks health insurance. However, even families with health insurance can still lack access to preventative care, either because their plans do not cover it or they cannot afford the out-of-pocket costs (Beverly 2000). To determine whether families are actually accessing preventative care, we consider whether or not they use an emergency room as their usual source of health care. Families who rely primarily on emergency room services for health care do not receive adequate preventative care, and the care they do receive is episodic, non-comprehensive, and lacks the benefit of a continuous relationship with a physician (Weissman and Epstein 1994). As a result, these families are classified as experiencing serious hardships.

A family experienced a critical hardship in health care if:

- in the past 12 months any individual in the family did not get or postponed necessary medical care (NSAF).

A family experienced a serious health care hardship if:

- any individual in the family does not have health insurance (NSAF).
- any individual in the family used the emergency room as his or her usual place of health care (NSAF).

Inadequate child care
There are no critical hardships for child care because it is not considered an immediate basic need. Lack of adequate child care is, however, considered a serious hardship because it has long-term consequences for the family's well-being. A serious hardship in child care occurs if the parent experiences the hardship for any child in the household.

Measuring serious child care hardships involves an assessment of quality of care. Many researchers believe that child care quality has important effects on both the short- and long-term well-being of children (Vandell and Wolfe 2000). When using these measures, we assume that families are providing the best-quality child care they can afford. We apply our criteria to both in-home and center-based care.

There are two ways to measure child care quality. The first is to measure the child care process through the observation of the child care setting. The second is through examining structural measures that are related to the quality of care, such as the child-to-adult ratio, the group size, and caregiver education and training. These structural measures of quality have been shown to be correlated with process measures of quality and have been shown to be related to concurrent (short-term) and long-term child outcomes (Vandell and Wolfe 2000). Due to the limitations of the data, we are able to use only structural measures of child care quality. The structural measures provide an indication of the adequacy of the family's child care, but are not sufficient to truly measure child care quality.

The structural measure of child care quality we use is child-to-adult ratio. We measure child care quality (reported in the NSAF) by the child-to-adult ratio in the child care setting, based on the

---

Living with child care hardship

Dale Russakoff, writing in *The Washington Post* ("Burdened Families Look for Child-Care Aid," July 6, 2000), chronicled the child care challenges faced by Kathy and Warren Popino of Metuchen, N.J.

When Warren was in the military, the family enjoyed subsidized child care for their son, Matthew. Seventy-five dollars a month bought infant care by a trained and licensed family child care provider.

When Warren left the military, the Popinos were unable to find affordable, licensed child care, so they put their son, by then a toddler, in the care of an unlicensed family child care provider. After Matthew began to display behavioral problems, the family moved him to a more expensive KinderCare Learning Center. The arrangement was out of their price range, though, and so the Popinos relied on credit cards to make ends meet.

Ultimately, the Popino's found more affordable, high-quality child care at the YWCA, where they now send their one-and-a-half-year-old son, Gillian, and Matthew (for after-school care) for $800 a month. However, the family still struggles to pay for their child care costs, and relies on credit cards to finance their child care arrangements.

---

recommendations of the American Academy of Pediatrics and the American Public Health Association. These recommendations range from three children to one adult for children one year or younger to 12 children for every adult for 9- to 12-year-olds.

For school-age children, we look at the type of non-school care a child receives, which has been shown to influence a variety of aspects of a child's well-being (Capizzano, Adams, and Tout 2000). We use two measures of quality: whether the child cares for himself or herself and whether the child is involved in activities. Children who care for themselves during non-school hours are placed at a greater risk for physical and psychological harm and are at a greater risk for being victims of crime. Self-care has also been linked to poor school performance, behavioral problems, and an increased chance of engaging in risky behaviors such as smoking, alcohol and drug use, sexual activity, and crime. Children involved in extracurricular activities and enrichment programs have been shown to perform better in school and to adjust better socially.

The variables used to determine if a family is experiencing a serious child care hardship include:

- whether the child-to-adult ratio is less than that recommended by the American Academy of Pediatrics and the American Public Health Association (American Public Health Association and American Academy of Pediatrics 1992) (NSAF).
- whether a child has cared for himself or herself in the past month or stayed alone with a sibling under 13 years old (NSAF).
- whether a child was involved in any enrichment activities (NSAF).

Hardships indices
To compare the proportion of families experiencing hardships, we construct two hardship indices. The index of critical hardships includes:

- whether anyone in the family goes without necessary medical care (NSAF and SIPP),
- whether anyone in the family did not have enough to eat sometimes or often (NSAF and SIPP), or
- whether the family has been either evicted and/or had utilities disconnected (SIPP) or whether the family doubled-up with friends or family (NSAF) because it could not afford its housing payments.

The index of serious hardships includes:

- whether a family worries that food will run out before it can buy more (NSAF) or whether a family lacked the kinds of food it liked to eat (SIPP).
- whether there was a time in the past 12 months that an individual's household was not able to pay the mortgage, rent, or utility bill (NSAF and SIPP).
- whether there was a time in the past 12 months that an individual's household did not have telephone service because payments were not made to the telephone company (NSAF and SIPP).
- whether any individual in the family does not have health insurance (NSAF and SIPP).
- whether any individual in the family used the emergency room as his or her usual place of health care (NSAF and SIPP).
- whether the child-to-adult ratio is less than that recommended by the American Academy of Pediatrics and the American Public Health

Association (American Public Health Association and American Academy of Pediatrics 1992) (NSAF).

- whether a child has cared for himself or herself in the past month or stayed alone with a sibling under 13 years old (NSAF and SIPP).
- whether a child was involved in any enrichment activities (NSAF).

Both indices are unweighted and merely count the number of critical and serious hardships that a family experiences.

Analysis: critical and serious hardships

The most basic questions about families that experience hardships concern what types of families are subject to these difficulties and whether families are able to escape hardships through employment. To address these questions, we examine whether critical and serious hardships are more likely to occur in families with low family income, single-parent families, and families that do not have a full-time worker. Access to health insurance is also explored separately as an indicator of whether families are able to meet their basic needs. In our analysis, we present both descriptive statistics and results from regression analyses. For each category, we first examine the descriptive statistics, then examine whether our findings hold once we account for the different characteristics of families. Throughout our discussion, we refer only to the NSAF results because they provide a higher degree of confidence (although we provide SIPP results as well for comparison).

How common are hardships?
Hardships, both critical and serious, are more common among families living below 200% of poverty than among those above (**Table 7** and **Figure B**). We find that 29% of families below the poverty threshold and 25% of families between 100% and 200% of poverty experience critical hardships. The similarity of the results for poor and near-poor families substantiates the family budget analysis. The family budgets reveal that the poverty threshold provides insufficient income for families to meet basic needs, since most budgets were approximately 200% of poverty. This is also the case for serious hardships. Families living above poverty but still below the average family budget level are unable to avoid hardships to the same extent as non-poor families.

Some hardships are more common than others, but families living below 200% of poverty are two to three times as likely as families living above 200% of poverty to experience each of the specific critical and serious hardships (**Table 8**). There is an exception in our measure of child care: poor families do not have consistently higher proportions of child care hardship relative to higher-income families. Our measures of child care hardships are limited in that we are unable to measure child outcomes, relative child care costs, or relative quality of the child care environment. However, the fact that the child care hardships that we are able to measure are similar across family income suggests that, of

TABLE 7   Proportion of persons in families experiencing hardships

	NSAF proportion		SIPP proportion	
	One or more hardships	Two or more hardships	One or more hardships	Two or more hardships
Critical hardships				
All	15.8%	2.5%	9.2%	1.9%
Below 100% poverty	29.4	6.8	28.6	6.5
Between 100% and				
200% poverty	24.5	4.6	17.4	4.1
Above 200% poverty	10.7	0.9	4.4	0.6
Serious hardships				
All	45.4	19.7	17.9	3.8
Below 100% poverty	74.1	44.1	46.1	15.3
Between 100% and				
200% poverty	63.2	33.9	32.4	6.2
Above 200% poverty	30.1	8.5	10.1	1.4

Sources: Authors' calculations from the 1993 SIPP (for calendar year 1995) and 1997 NSAF (for calendar year 1996).

FIGURE B   Proportion of people in families experiencing hardships by poverty status

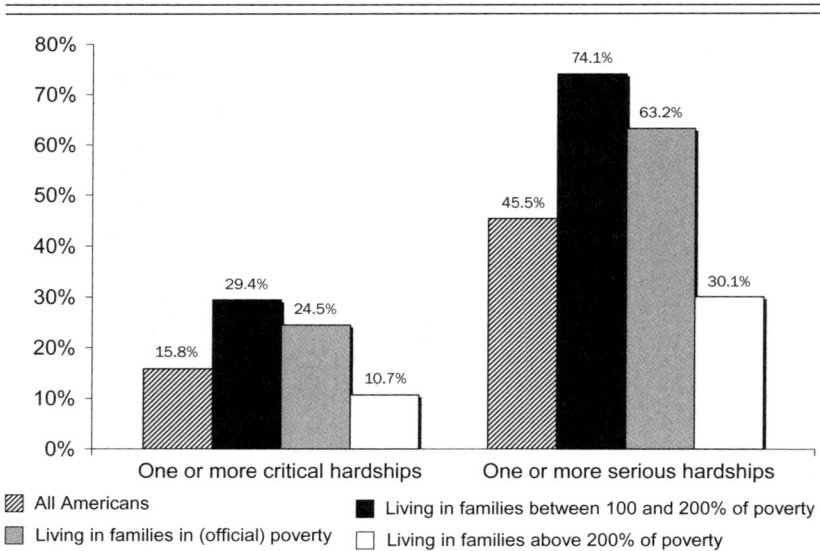

Source: Authors' calculations from 1997 NSAF (for calendar year 1996).

TABLE 8   Proportion of persons living in families with incomes above and below 200% of poverty and experiencing hardships

	Below 200% poverty	Above 200% poverty
Critical hardships		
Food insecurity		
Not enough food to eat*	12.6%	1.6%
Missed meals	17.5	3.4
Insufficient health care		
Did not receive necessary medical care	12.7	8.0
Housing problems		
Evicted*	1.1	0.1
Utilities disconnected*	4.1	0.6
Doubling up with friends or family	2.4	0.3
Serious hardships		
Food insecurity		
Kind of food*	28.8	8.4
Worried about having enough food	41.1	11.0
Insufficient health care		
Emergency room is main source of care	7.3	2.3
No health insurance coverage	35.9	9.9
Housing problems		
Unable to make housing or utility payments	25.0	7.8
Telephone disconnected	10.4	3.0
Inadequate child care		
Child cares for self	5.1	6.8
Child not in after-school or enrichment activities	21.2	8.5
Inadequate adult-to-child ratio in child care facility	6.0	8.5

*Data for these variables come from the SIPP.

Sources: Authors' calculations from the 1993 SIPP (for calendar year 1995) and 1997 NSAF (for calendar year 1996).

all our measured hardships, child care hardships are the least likely to be affected by family income. Overall, food insecurities are the most common hardships: 17.5% of families living below 200% of poverty missed meals, and over 40% worried about food.

What kinds of families experience hardships?
Single-parent families have more difficulties reaching family budget levels, and these families are also more likely to experience the most hardships (**Table 9**). Again, food insecurities were the most common critical and serious hardships: 23% of families with only one adult missed meals and 57% worried about food. Not all hardships were most prevalent among single-parent families, however,: using the emergency room as the main source of care and not having a child in activities were more prevalent among families with more than one adult. In general, having two adults leads to lower rates of hardship relative to having one adult, but having three adults does not necessarily do so.

Table 10 shows the results from an ordered logit regression that allows us to calculate adjusted probabilities for the incidence of critical hardships. (See Appendix E for a detailed description of our method and regression analysis.) The regression takes into account differences across families, including family income within poverty grouping; age, race, and education of the household head; marital status; age of children; and geographic location. The variables that are statistically significant in the regression are whether the family had income above or below 200% of poverty, health insurance coverage, race of household head, whether there was a child between the ages of 6 and 17, and whether a married couple headed the family. By presenting the predicted probability of experiencing hardships from the regression analysis, Table 10 allows us to look at the proportion of families experiencing any critical hardships, holding all else constant.

Table 10 shows that, although race is significant, African American and white families have about the same probability of experiencing one or more critical hardships. Hispanic families, on the other hand, are more likely than white or black families to experience hardships. Education was not significant in the NSAF regressions (although it was significant in the SIPP regressions), but the probability of experiencing hardships is greater for families headed by someone with less education.

In terms of family type, Table 10 shows that single-mother families are at higher risk of experiencing critical hardships relative to families that are not headed by single mothers. However, holding all else constant, single-mother families living under 200% of poverty are more likely than those living above 200% of poverty to experience hardships. The former has a 36% probability of experiencing any critical hardships, compared to a 18% probability for the latter. This indicates that it is not family type alone that determines deprivation but rather family composition combined with poverty status. Poor single mothers experience more critical hardships, but this appears to be a function of their low incomes, rather than just the absence of a partner.

Do working families have more or fewer hardships?
The family budget analysis found that families without a full-time worker had more trouble reaching their budget level. These families are also more likely to

**TABLE 9   Proportion of persons in families with income below 200%
of poverty and experiencing hardships, by family composition**

	One adult with children	Two adults with children	Three adults with children
Critical hardships			
Food insecurity			
Not enough food to eat*	17.2%	12.3%	14.6%
Missed meals	22.9	14.9	16.7
Insufficient health care			
Did not receive necessary medical care	15.0	12.5	8.8
Housing problems			
Evicted*	1.9	1.1	0.6
Utilities disconnected*	6.1	4.4	3.1
Doubling up with friends or family	4.6	2.1	2.4
Serious hardships			
Food insecurity			
Kind of food*	28.8	30.6	29.1
Worried about having enough food	57.3	42.3	43.6
Insufficient health care			
Emergency room is main source of care	5.1	6.5	7.2
No health insurance coverage	26.1	38.8	43.8
Housing problems			
Unable to make housing or utility payments	33.5	28.9	29.6
Telephone disconnected	16.6	11.5	15.5
Inadequate child care			
Child cares for self	6.4	5.5	3.0
Child not in after-school or enrichment activities	22.7	19.5	24.6
Inadequate adult-to-child ratio in child care facility	9.4	5.8	3.5

*Data for these variables come from the SIPP.

Sources: Authors' calculations from the 1993 SIPP (for calendar year 1995) and 1997
NSAF (for calendar year 1996).

TABLE 10   Predicted probability of families experiencing critical hardships

	All		Below 200% of poverty		Above 200% of poverty	
	One or more critical hardships	Two or more critical hardships	One or more critical hardships	Two or more critical hardships	One or more critical hardships	Two or more critical hardships
NSAF						
All	14.4%	2.1%	26.8%	4.4%	10.2%	1.3%
Full-time employee	11.9	1.7	24.2	3.8	9.8	1.3
Not full-time employee	19.7	3.1	28.4	4.7	11.3	1.5
Black*	14.8	2.2	24.5	3.8	8.6	1.1
White*	13.6	2.0	26.9	4.4	10.3	1.4
Hispanic*	20.6	3.3	29.0	4.8	12.0	1.6
Single mother	30.7	5.4	35.9	6.5	17.8	2.5
Married*	11.0	1.5	21.3	3.2	8.6	1.1
Less than high school degree	19.1	3.0	28.1	4.6	11.1	1.5
High school degree	14.6	2.1	25.0	4.0	9.8	1.3
Some college	14.6	2.2	27.6	4.6	10.9	1.5
College degree	11.1	1.5	23.7	3.7	9.6	1.3
Child 5 or under	16.9	2.6	26.7	4.3	8.9	1.2
Child 6 - 17*	18.9	3.0	30.3	5.2	11.6	1.6
Private health insurance*	10.1	1.3	17.8	2.5	8.8	1.1
Public health insurance*	24.0	3.8	29.1	4.7	14.1	1.9
No health insurance*	29.8	5.0	36.2	6.4	21.4	3.1
SIPP						
All	8.3%	1.6%	20.6%	4.4%	4.1%	0.7%
Full-time employee	5.4	1.0	15.6	3.1	3.7	0.6
Not full-time employee	14.0	2.9	23.9	5.2	5.4	0.9
Black*	11.9	2.4	20.0	4.1	4.1	0.7
White*	7.0	1.3	20.2	4.3	4.0	0.7
Single mother*	19.2	4.1	24.5	5.3	5.3	0.9
Married*	5.9	1.1	16.7	3.4	3.5	0.6
Less than high school degree*	20.2	4.3	25.7	5.6	7.2	1.3
High school degree*	11.1	2.2	21.1	4.5	5.3	0.9
Some college*	8.3	1.6	19.3	4.0	4.7	0.8
College degree*	3.4	0.6	11.5	2.2	2.6	0.4
Child 5 or under	10.1	2.0	19.7	4.1	3.8	0.6
Child 6 - 17*	11.1	2.3	22.1	4.8	4.7	0.8
Private health insurance*	4.5	0.8	11.3	2.0	3.3	0.6
Public health insurance*	26.6	5.8	28.0	6.1	10.3	1.9
No health insurance*	21.0	4.5	28.2	6.2	11.9	2.2

* Significant at the one percent level (relative to not having that characteristic).

Sources: Authors' calculations from the 1993 SIPP (for calendar year 1995) and 1997 NSAF (for calendar year 1996).

FIGURE C   Proportion of people in families below 200% of poverty experiencing hardships, by work status

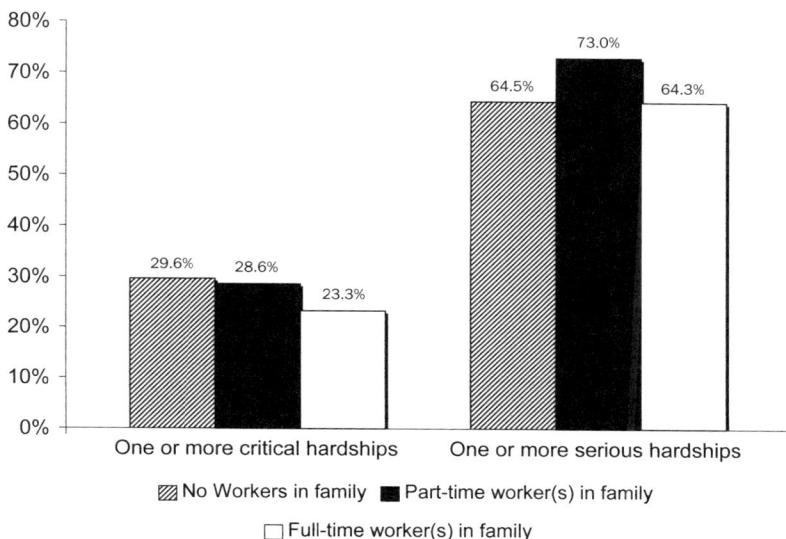

Source: Authors' calculations from 1997 NSAF (for calendar year 1996).

experience hardships. Families below 200% of poverty without a worker experience higher rates of critical hardships than families with a full-time worker (**Figure C**). However, having a worker does not ensure that a family escapes hardships: while 30% of families with no worker experience one or more critical hardships, 29% of families with a part-time worker and 23% of families with a full-time worker experience one or more critical hardships. The rate of serious hardships experienced in families below 200% of poverty is virtually identical across families with and without a worker.

The kinds of hardships experienced are similar among families below 200% of poverty by work status (**Table 11**). Surprisingly, some serious hardships are more prevalent among families that do some work (a family member working less than full time), relative to families that do not work or who have a family member working full time. For example, families that do not have a worker were less likely to go without health insurance (22%), relative to families with a part-time worker (43%) and families with a full-time worker (35%).

When we look at the adjusted probabilities (Table 10), we find that having a full-time worker in the family reduces a family's chances of experiencing any hardships, although this is more likely for families living above 200% of poverty (10%) than below (25%). Thus, families that have a full-time worker and are able to lift their incomes above the family budget level are more likely to avoid

TABLE 11   Proportion of persons in families with incomes below 200% of poverty and experiencing hardships, by work status of family

	Not working	Working part time	Working full time
Critical hardships			
Food insecurity			
Not enough food to eat*	15.1%	14.3%	10.1%
Missed meals	21.7	18.8	14.6
Insufficient health care			
Did not receive necessary medical care	13.2	14.1	11.3
Housing problems			
Evicted*	1.4	1.1	0.9
Utilities disconnected*	3.5	4.6	3.9
Doubling up with friends or family	2.4	2.9	1.9
Serious hardships			
Food insecurity			
Kind of food*	29.6%	29.8%	27.8%
Worried about having enough food	47.3	44.1	36.0
Insufficient health care			
Emergency room is main source of care	6.7	8.3	6.8
No health insurance coverage	22.3	43.4	35.4
Housing problems			
Unable to make housing or utility payments	21.1	29.1	23.0
Telephone disconnected	9.8	12.9	8.5
Inadequate child care			
Child cares for self	4.2	4.7	5.5
Child not in after-school or enrichment activities	25.1	21.6	20.3
Inadequate adult-to-child ratio in child care facility	6.1	6.4	5.7

*Data for these variables come from the SIPP.

Sources: Authors' calculations from the 1993 SIPP (for calendar year 1995) and 1997 NSAF (for calendar year 1996).

hardships than are families with a full-time worker who cannot lift their incomes that high.

Health insurance
The lack of health insurance is both a hardship and a strong predictor of experiencing other hardships. High proportions of families go without health insurance, more so for families living below 200% of poverty (36%) than those

TABLE 12   Proportion of persons in families with incomes below 200% of poverty and experiencing hardships, by health insurance status of family

	Private health insurance	Public health insurance	Uninsured
Critical hardships			
Food insecurity			
Not enough food to eat*	10.0%	20.7%	8.7%
Missed meals	10.8	25.2	22.9
Insufficient health care			
Did not receive necessary medical care	10.1	12.3	16.5
Housing problems			
Evicted*	0.8	1.5	1.8
Utilities disconnected*	2.9	7.4	3.1
Doubling up with friends or family	0.9	3.7	3.8
Serious hardships			
Food insecurity			
Kind of food*	25.2%	39.9%	27.2%
Worried about having enough food	26.0	58.0	48.6
Insufficient health care			
Emergency room is main source of care	3.4	5.7	14.7
Housing problems			
Unable to make housing or utility payments	16.0	30.5	30.8
Telephone disconnected	6.8	13.7	12.9
Inadequate child care			
Child cares for self	5.5	4.4	5.1
Child not in after-school or enrichment activities	16.5	23.8	25.9
Inadequate adult-to-child ratio in child care facility	6.9	7.1	4.5

*Data for these variables come from the SIPP.

Sources: Authors' calculations from the 1993 SIPP (for calendar year 1995) and 1997 NSAF (for calendar year 1996).

above (10%). **Table 12** shows that, among families living below 200% of poverty, those without private health insurance are more likely to have health-related hardships. Families that receive Medicaid are generally more likely to experience hardships overall, relative to families that have no health insurance at all, except for health-related hardships, which families without health insurance are more likely to experience. This is probably due to selection bias; that is, within the group of families living below 200% of poverty, Medicaid families are, on average, poorer than families without health insurance at all since, in order to get Medicaid, an adult must often either be on public assistance or have recently left public assistance for employment. "Working poor" adults are, in most states, left without health insurance coverage even though they have only marginally higher incomes.

The correlation of hardships and health insurance status holds even when accounting for other variations among families. Table 10 shows that one of the largest predictors of a family experiencing any hardships is whether or not it has health insurance.[10] Families with private health insurance are unlikely to experience critical hardships—only 4% of all such families experience at least one critical hardship and only 1% have two or more. This is true across poverty status: families with private health insurance who have incomes below 200% of poverty have just an 11% probability of experiencing any critical hardships, only slightly higher than for the overall population. However, families without private health insurance (both public and no insurance at all) are highly likely to experience critical hardships.

Having health insurance in and of itself may not be the most important reason why families experience hardships. As shown in Table 12, families are just as likely to have health-related hardships as to have other hardships. What this indicates is that families who have access to health insurance may be in a less-precarious economic position. A family without insurance may be foregoing it because it is too expensive and would prevent the family from meeting other, more immediate, basic needs (such as housing, for example). A family without health insurance, however, could be thrown into financial turmoil if a health crisis—even a relatively small one—were to occur.

Hardships across location
Location plays an important role in determining the probability that a family will experience critical and serious hardships. **Table 13** shows the proportion of hardships experienced by families living below 200% of poverty in 13 states. There is a wide distribution of hardships across states. Overall, Texas has the highest proportion of families experiencing hardships in three of the categories, making it the worst performer. Families in California were the most likely to miss meals: 21% of families below 200% of poverty missed meals compared to only 17% of such families nationwide. Using the emergency room as the main source of care also has a wide range: in Alabama, 12% of families living below 200% of poverty had this hardship compared to only 8% nationally.

Hardships also vary considerably by region (**Figures D-G**). There are no clear trends across the regions. In terms of food insecurity, there are very little differences by region. Doubling-up is lowest in New England, but the inability to pay rent or having the telephone disconnected is relatively high there. West South Central has high housing hardship in most indicators. Access to health care is best in New England and the Mid-Atlantic regions, where skipping

TABLE 13 **Proportion of persons living in families with income below 200% of poverty and experiencing hardships by state**

	Ala.	Calif.	Colo.	Fla.	Mass.	Mich.	Minn.	Miss.	N.J.	N.Y.	Texas	Wash.	Wis.	U.S.
Critical hardships														
Food insecurity														
Missed meals	14.4%	21.4%	18.3%	17.4%	18.8%	15.2%	16.1%	17.2%	19.7%	19.2%	18.8%	19.3%	15.0%	17.5%
Insufficient health care														
Did not receive necessary medical care	12.0	9.9	15.4	14.3	14.1	12.8	12.8	10.6	12.2	9.5	11.7	14.8	11.7	12.7
Housing problems														
Doubling up with friends or family	1.5	3.3	1.9	2.0	1.9	3.3	1.8	2.8	2.5	2.1	2.6	2.5	1.4	2.4
Serious hardships														
Food insecurity														
Worried about having enough food	43.1	44.5	40.0	39.3	39.1	36.2	35.6	48.0	40.7	42.0	49.0	41.4	34.5	41.1
Insufficient health care														
Emergency room main source of care	12.4	8.5	5.5	8.7	7.5	6.4	4.2	9.6	6.6	6.8	7.6	2.1	4.5	7.3
No health insurance coverage	34.9	43.3	36.3	39.0	30.5	27.3	19.6	37.0	33.6	33.2	49.2	30.1	26.1	35.9
Housing problems														
Unable to make housing/utility pmts.	27.8	22.5	19.9	25.0	26.9	25.4	24.6	28.3	29.5	29.4	29.9	22.7	23.5	25.0
Telephone disconnected	13.5	9.4	7.8	13.0	9.7	9.4	8.1	16.5	10.1	11.3	16.2	11.7	8.8	10.4
Inadequate child care														
Child cares for self	2.6	2.4	6.7	4.3	5.3	5.6	8.1	5.2	4.7	4.8	5.7	5.0	8.8	5.1
Child not in after-school or enrichment activities	23.1	23.8	21.5	18.7	22.0	21.2	18.0	23.6	19.9	23.3	24.7	19.0	18.4	21.2
Inadequate adult-to-child ratio in child care facility	5.4	4.9	5.1	5.7	7.9	5.6	9.6	4.7	7.3	4.8	4.1	7.2	5.3	6.0

Sources: Authors' calculations from the 1997 NSAF (for calendar year 1996).

FIGURE D   Health care hardships across regions for persons living in families with incomes below 200% of poverty

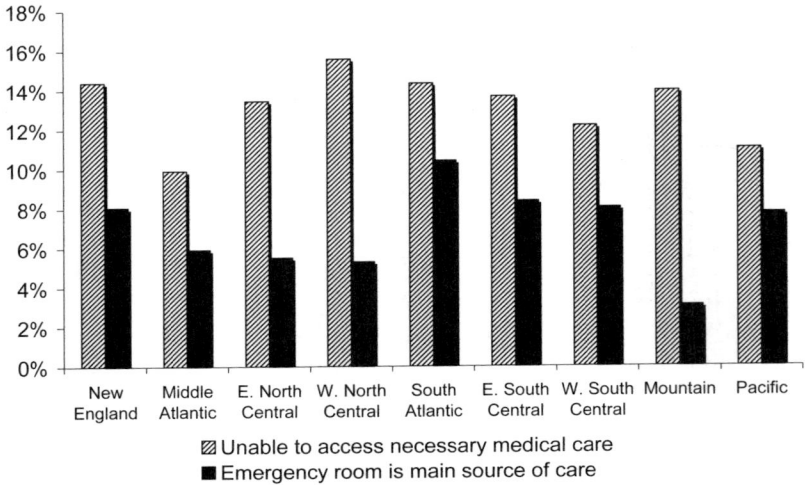

☒ Unable to access necessary medical care
■ Emergency room is main source of care

Source: Authors' analysis of NSAF 1997 data (for calendar year 1996).

FIGURE E   Housing hardships across regions for persons living in families with incomes below 200% of poverty

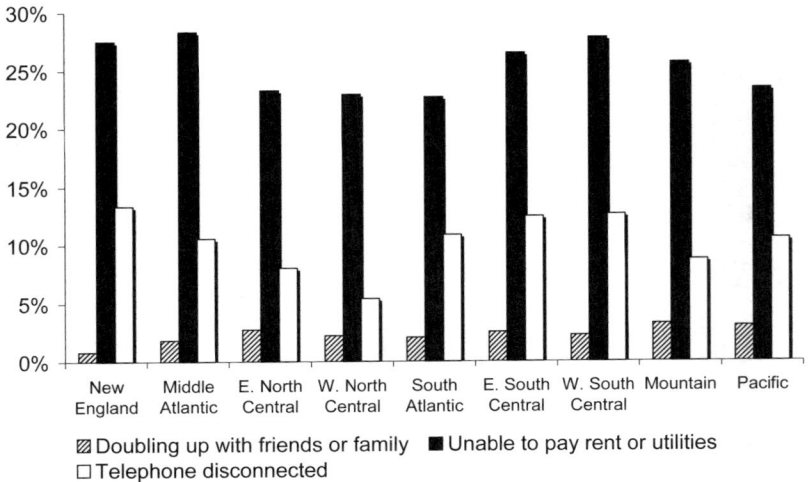

☒ Doubling up with friends or family   ■ Unable to pay rent or utilities
☐ Telephone disconnected

Source: Authors' analysis of NSAF 1997 data (for calendar year 1996).

FIGURE F   Food insecurity across regions for persons living in families with incomes below 200% of poverty

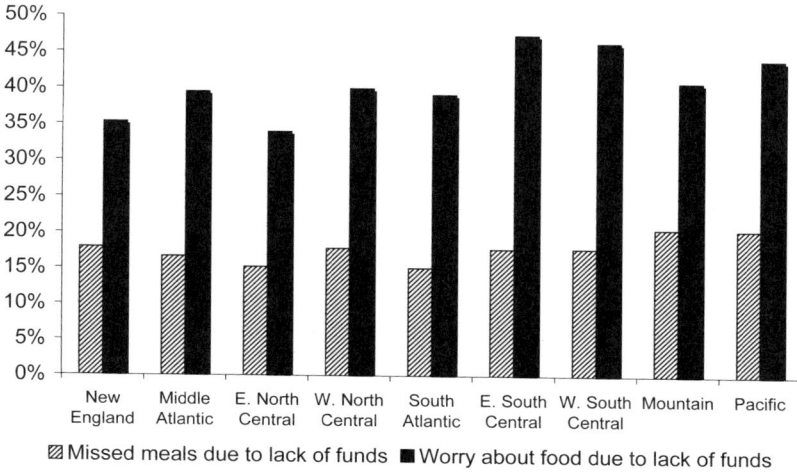

☒ Missed meals due to lack of funds   ■ Worry about food due to lack of funds

Source: Authors' analysis of NSAF 1997 data (for calendar year 1996).

FIGURE G   Inadequate child care across regions for persons living in families with incomes below 200% of poverty

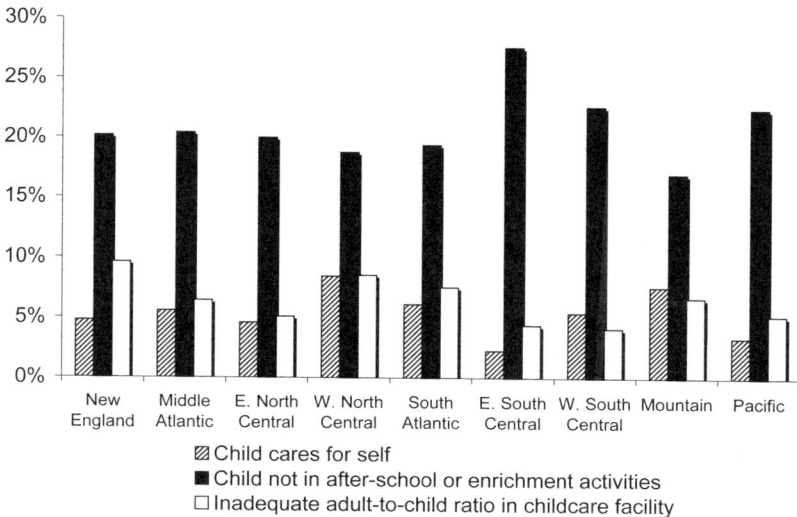

☒ Child cares for self
■ Child not in after-school or enrichment activities
☐ Inadequate adult-to-child ratio in childcare facility

Source: Authors' analysis of NSAF 1997 data (for calendar year 1996).

necessary medical care is relatively low or average. The Mountain region has the highest proportion of families skipping necessary medical care, but it also has the lowest proportion using the emergency room as its main source of care.

Summary

What predicts hardships? Both critical and serious hardships are more common among families living below 200% of poverty, indicating that families living under the family budget level experience more hardships than families living above this level. This substantiates the family budgets analysis and documents that families below the family budget level suffer real consequences of not being able to make ends meet. Other strong predictors are being a single parent and not having private health insurance. Having a member of the family employed full-time in the labor market is also important, but the social safety net—as indicated by health insurance—is key. This points to the need for policies that strengthen the safety net and make it easier for parents, especially single mothers, to balance work and family.

Compared to other nations, families in the United States are more likely to enter into poverty because of a change in family structure. Specifically, divorce is far more likely to leave families (single mothers and children) in poverty than it does in other nations (Directorate for Education, Employment, Labour, and Social Affairs 2001). This is consistent with the finding here that single-parenthood increases the probability of experiencing hardships.

Employment matters, but work is not enough to enable families to escape hardship. Employment reduces hardship to the extent that it is full time and year round, but families below 200% of poverty with a full-time worker still experience high rates of hardship. Moreover, underemployed households tend to experience greater hardship than do unemployed and other non-working households. These results confirm earlier findings by Bauman (1998) regarding the extent of housing hardship among households with an employed household head: he found that an employed head of household significantly reduced the prevalence of not paying rent, being evicted, not paying utilities, and not having a telephone. The findings here build on these results by showing that it is not only an employed household head that matters but also that the household head be a full-time, year-round worker. We show that this is important for housing hardship as well as broader definitions of hardship, including the lack of goods and services working families need to maintain employment.

We also find, in confirmation of other research (Bauman 1998), that private health insurance coverage is highly correlated with the nonexistence of hardship among families above and below poverty. The relationship between private health insurance coverage and well-being remains significant even after controlling for employment status and income level. Private health insurance coverage helps to provide families with stable access to health care. However, beyond its influence on health well-being, private health insurance coverage also raises other aspects of well-being, including food, housing, and child care.

This may suggest that access to health insurance is a proxy for a stable home and work environment beyond that described by income, work status, and demographics. It is also indicative of the dire financial consequences that can occur for families who must go without health insurance. A medical emergency can be a devastating financial drain and require families to choose between buying food, paying the rent, or seeing the doctor.

Child care is an area in which many American families experience hardships. Poor families do not appear to be worse off relative to higher-income families in terms of their ability to find child care centers with the recommended number of children relative to adults. Further, families living above 200% of poverty are just as likely as poor families to have children 13 or younger home alone or cared for by young siblings. The structural measures of child care adequacy used here show that families across the income spectrum struggle with child care, yet poorer families may still have less access to high-quality, enriching child care relative to other families.

This section confirms that basic family budgets are a useful indicator for measuring whether families are able to attain a safe and decent standard of living. Families that are unable to reach this income level are more likely to experience hardships, regardless of work status. Families need help bridging the gap between the incomes they earn in the labor market and the income they need to meet their basic needs.

Chapter 3

Policies to help families meet basic needs

The analysis of hardships indicators above show that significant numbers of families are struggling to meet their needs in basic areas such as food, health care, child care, and housing. Helping families meet these basic needs requires a two-pronged approach. The first is to help families increase their wages and incomes through policies such as raising the minimum wage, removing barriers to unionizing, expanding the EITC, adopting pay equity policies, and promoting workforce development programs. By raising a family's after-tax income, a family's ability to afford these basic services will be enhanced.

• **Minimum wage.** Raising family income through increasing the minimum wage and adopting living wage policies is one way to help families meet their needs. Families with a minimum wage worker face twice the level of hardships as do families without a minimum wage worker. The inflation-adjusted minimum wage is now 24% lower than it was in 1979, meaning that minimum wage workers' incomes are falling further behind what a family needs to get by and will continue to do so unless Congress acts to raise the minimum wage. Living wage ordinances, which have been adopted in over 50 communities around the country, help raise the incomes of thousands of workers. A living wage is defined as what a family would need to earn in order to support itself at the poverty line. These ordinances typically apply only to businesses that have contracts with the government or receive economic development funds. Campaigns are currently under way in about 70 communities to adopt living wage policies.
• **Unions.** An important approach to helping families meet their needs is through removing obstacles that make it difficult for workers to obtain union representation. Unionized workers have higher wages; greater access to health insurance, pension plans, and paid family leave; and increased job security (Freeman and Medoff 1984). Currently, unions are devoting increased resources to organizing workers who need unions the most (for example, janitors and home health aids). Organizing workers is difficult, however, given current labor laws. To help remove some of the barriers workers face when trying to organize a union, national labor relations law should be changed in accordance with the recommendations in the recent report by Human Rights Watch, *Unfair Advantage*

(Human Rights Watch 2000). For example, penalties for employers who violate workers' rights should be significantly strengthened so as to provide a meaningful deterrent to unlawful conduct. Employees should be able to choose whether they wish to be represented by unions through methods that are not subject to manipulation by employers, such as card check agreements, and access rules should be changed to ensure that workers considering whether to join a union have a full and fair opportunity to hear the union's arguments in favor of unionization and not just the employer's views. Statutory exclusions that deny labor law protections to agricultural workers, domestic workers, and "independent" contractors who actually work in a dependent relationship with a single employer should be eliminated, as should state laws that categorize welfare recipients employed in workfare programs as "trainees," and therefore exclude them from organizing and bargaining protection. In general, the laws should be revised to ensure that all workers who want to organize and bargain collectively – including temporary workers, part-time workers, and others in nonstandard work arrangements – have that right, except where their predominant function is truly managerial or supervisory.

- **Tax credits.** Such tax credits as the EITC and the Child Tax Credit are another way to boost family income. The Child Tax Credit was recently expanded from $500 to $1,000 per child, and is now refundable for families earning more than $10,000 a year (meaning that families can get a tax refund). This expansion means that the credit will now help approximately 17 million more children (Bhargava 2001). Proposals to expand the EITC include the Universal Unified Tax Credit, which would expand the benefits working families receive by restructuring and combining the EITC with other tax benefits available to families with children (Cherry and Sawicky 2000).

- **Pay equity.** Policies that promote equal pay for men and women would also increase family income. The gender-wage ratio (women's wages as a percentage of men's) among full-time, full-year workers is 81%. The Paycheck Fairness Act would amend the Fair Labor Standards Act to eliminate discrimination that leads to pay inequities; it would do so by enhanced enforcement of the equal pay requirements. A second bill, the Fair Pay Act, would require employers to pay equal wages to women and men performing comparable jobs. Comparable worth policies require that firms give equal pay to workers with jobs with comparable skill requirements and responsibilities. Comparable worth legislation has been introduced in 28 states and is pending in another three. If the current comparable worth legislation proposed in many states were to become law, there is great potential for it to reduce the wage gap and especially benefit low-wage workers, while not causing an excessive burden on employers.

- **Economic and workforce development.** Family income can also be raised through economic development and workforce development programs that give workers access to better jobs. Economic development and workforce development funds must be steered toward programs that ensure that new jobs pay at least a living wage, and that job training candidates are trained for jobs that have a career path that will enable them to support their families.

These interventions to raise family income are crucial to helping the poorest of the poor, and they will help many families meet some of their most crucial daily survival needs. But for many workers, wage-based policies alone may not go far enough to enable them to meet all their basic needs. This may be especially true for single parents. For example, for a single mother with two children in Los Angeles to make an income equivalent to the family budget level, she would have to earn $16.75 an hour, an amount that may be above her earnings capacity. Even with the EITC, she may still not be able to meet her basic needs.

The second approach, therefore, requires increasing the investment in a social safety net. The single mother in Los Angeles needs nearly $17 an hour so that she can buy health care, child care, housing, and transportation. As the hardships results show, both poor families and near-poor families face difficulties affording these basic items.

The need for an expanded social safety net

Historically, the U.S. has had two separate safety nets – one for those who work in the paid labor force and one for those who care for children. The safety net for non-workers has been dismantled due to welfare reform; poor mothers are no longer able to stay home to raise their children and are now required to work. These former welfare recipients are joining the ranks of the working poor, who face a safety net that is not made for today's families.

The safety net for workers is based on a model that assumes one full-time male worker. This model does not work for today's families, which in most cases include a working mother; today, children are as likely to live with a working mother as they are to live with a working father (Hartmann 2001). The unemployment compensation system excludes many part-time workers, such as those with child-rearing responsibilities, because they don't earn enough working part time to become eligible for unemployment insurance. The U.S. lacks a comprehensive system of paid leave for new parents, which means significant income losses for families with young children. Decades after women entered the workforce in great numbers, the nation still lacks a child care system that meets the needs of working parents. Finally, the nation still relies on private employers to provide health insurance for all but the very indigent, leaving 44 million Americans uninsured every year (Kaiser Commission on Medicaid and the Uninsured 2000).

This lack of a social safety net puts basic items such as health care, child care, paid time off work for family needs, housing, transportation, and food out of reach for many families. For example:

- **Health care.** As the hardships indicators here show, families without health insurance are vulnerable not only to health-related hardships but to hardships in the areas of food and housing as well. Health insurance in the U.S. is primarily provided through employers. However, 37% of workers do not have health insurance through their employers (Mishel, Bernstein, and Schmitt 2001). Lack of employer-provided health insurance is even more severe for low-wage workers; in 1998, only 30% of workers in the lowest wage fifth had employer-provided insurance, compared to 82% of workers in the highest fifth (Mishel, Bernstein, and Schmitt 2001). Even if low-wage workers are offered employer-sponsored health insurance, their plans often include higher co-payments and deductibles and are more likely to require sizable employee contributions for premiums for family coverage (Agency for Health Care Policy and Research 1997). If a working-poor family is not offered employer-based health care or cannot afford the plan offered, in most cases it cannot rely on government assistance for health coverage. In the typical state, a parent in a family of three earning over $7,992 (59% of the poverty line) is not eligible for Medicaid coverage (Guyer and Mann 1999). According to the family budget research here, a non-group health insurance plan for a two-parent, two-child family would cost an average of $350 a month.

• **Child care.** Families at all income levels experience difficulties in affording quality child care, primarily due to its high cost. As a Children's Defense Fund study shows, in all but one state the average cost of child care in a child care center is more than the annual cost of tuition at a public college (Schulman 2000), putting quality child care out of the reach of many families. A single-parent family in Hartford, Conn. living at the basic family budget level would need to spend 31% of its income to afford quality child care for two children under 8. Currently, federal and state programs reach few families with child care needs; tax credits are too low to help families with child care costs, Head Start serves less than half of eligible children (Blank, Schulman, and Ewen 1999), and only about one in 10 eligible families receives assistance through the Child Care and Development Fund (U.S. Department of Health and Human Services 1999).

Furthermore, child care quality is inadequate. A report from the National Institute of Child Health and Human Development estimates that only 11% of child care programs for children under 4 are rated as "excellent" (Gornick and Meyers 2001). Poor-quality child care has been shown to have negative effects on both short-term and long-term child outcomes (Vandell and Wolfe 2000). One reason for poor-quality child care is low pay for child care workers. Despite increased federal funding for child care over the past decade, wages for child care workers stagnated, resulting in continued problems with recruiting and retraining qualified teachers (Whitebrook, Howes, and Phillips 1998).

• **Housing.** Many families face problems finding affordable housing. This is not an individual problem but rather is related to problems of urban sprawl, which is a manifestation of continuing racial and economic inequities. Sprawl is defined as "random unplanned growth characterized by inadequate accessibility to essential land uses such as housing, jobs, and public services" (Bullard, Johnson, and Torres 2001). The effects of sprawl, such as disparities between urban and suburban schools and urban infrastructure decline (Bullard, Johnson, and Torres 2001), create incentives for families to move to suburban areas with high housing costs that they can't afford. Sprawl also contributes to a lack of affordable housing by encouraging gentrification, which is the replacement of housing and buildings that accommodate the poor (usually people of color) with upscale housing and services for middle class residents (usually whites) (Bullard, Johnson, and Torres 2001). Furthermore, U.S. housing policy favors middle class homeowners over low-income renters; in 1999, mortgage and interest payment deductions for homeowners totaled $63 billion, three times the size of HUD's budget (Dreier 2000).

• **Transportation.** Sprawl also has severe consequences for working families in the areas of transportation. Sprawl creates a spatial mismatch between where jobs are located and where low-income residents live (Bullard, Johnson, and Torres 2001). This mismatch makes relying on public transportation difficult, and families living in areas with severe sprawl face higher transportation costs (Surface Transportation Policy Project 2000). The problems families face in finding affordable housing and transportation options are exacerbated by government policies that encourage sprawl, such as inadequate spending on public transit in favor of more roads, and tax subsidies for suburban employment centers (Bullard, Johnson, and Torres 2001).

• **Food.** Forty-one percent of families worried about affording food in 1996. Families facing food shortages are also struggling to pay other bills; they sometimes fall short on food as they struggle to meet their rent or mortgage payments, pay unexpected medical bills, or keep their children in child care so they can remain employed. Addressing food insecurity and hunger is therefore linked to helping families meet their other needs.

Policies that can help meet a family's needs

The combination of low wages and lack of a safety net puts working families in a bind. The patchwork of current policies in the areas of health care, child care, and housing are not meeting families needs. Even tax credits for child care, vouchers for low-income housing, and employer-sponsored health insurance, all of which which rely on the market for provision of services, leave many families with unmet needs. Moreover, current policies affect people differently based on their attachment to the labor force (e.g., full-time vs. part-time work).

Helping all families meet their basic needs requires a federal solution. The purpose of the "devolution" of responsibility for the safety net was to give states the flexibility to experiment in providing services. But as the research here shows, hardships persist in every state and region in the country. After several years of experimentation, it is time to implement the best practices on a national level.

Therefore we recommend the following policies:

• **Universal health care.** In order for all families (including those without children) to be able to meet their basic needs, universal health insurance must be a long-range policy goal. Multiple studies show that the most efficient way to provide health insurance to everyone is through a national health insurance (NHI) program, which would provide health insurance to every American and would be similar to an expanded and improved version of Medicare. Under a proposal by Physicians for a National Health Program, the NHI would provide operating budgets to hospitals and clinics (Physicians for a National Health Program 2001). Physicians could be reimbursed by NHI on a fee-for-service basis or become salaried employees of group practices, hospitals, or clinics. PNHP's proposal would eliminate the high overhead, profits, and marketing costs of the medical industry by eliminating insurance companies and converting investor-owned facilities to non-profit status. This plan would save at least $150 billion annually, which would fully offset the costs of expanded and improved coverage for the uninsured and under-insured (Physicians for a National Health Program 2001).

• **Universal child care.** Helping families meet the basic need of quality, affordable child care will require a coordinated, federally funded universal child care program. The U.S. needs to develop a child care system that gives all families, regardless of income, access to certified, age appropriate, educational child care. While many families may still choose to have a friend or relative care for their children, this is becoming less of an option as more women, including grandmothers, are in the paid labor force. Additionally, all child care workers, whether they provide center-based or family child care, need a wage that will allow them to meet their basic needs as well.

While there is not a consensus on how to implement a more comprehensive system of child care, several proposals have been advanced. They differ on the ages of children served, whether they would be universal or targeted to lower-income families, whether they should be provided by the public sector as an extension of the school system or by a voucher system for existing sources of child care, and whether they emphasize improving quality (through raising wages and other measures) or expanding access. Regardless, these proposals would require a significant increase in funds. Sawhill (1999) proposes a high-quality program of preschool for 3- and 4-year-olds for families with incomes of less than $30,000 a year, at a cost of $30 billion annually. Folbre (2000) estimates that to expand this to all 3- and 4-year-olds would cost $50 billion in addition to the $11 billion currently spent on child care. (Helburn and Bergmann (forthcoming) propose a system of vouchers to a combination of nonprofit, for-profit, and public agencies to provide child care for all age groups, including infants, toddlers, and school-age children. They estimate that, with no improvements to quality, such a system would cost $50 billion annually.

Even though creating a system of high-quality child care would be a costly endeavor, benefits could accrue to society at large, not just the families receiving child care. For example, according to one estimate, expanding Head Start would pay for itself in short-term cost savings for health and educational costs and long-term savings in terms of increased educational attainment and earnings for participants (Currie 2001).

•   **Paid family leave.** Paid family leave is another important component to helping families meet their child care needs. A federal program of paid family leave, modeled on either the unemployment insurance or temporary disability systems already in place, would ensure that all U.S. workers would have access to the same family leave options. This system could be paid for through a federal payroll tax, and could be administered federally or by the states. Estimates for providing paid family leave for birth or adoption range from $11 to $28 per worker a year, while covering other family leave circumstances would cost about $22 per worker per year (Lovell and Rahmanou 2000).

•   **Equitable housing and transportation policies.** Solutions to both sprawl and affordable housing must take into account the effects of transportation policies on equitable housing and vice versa. Smart growth policies that don't address affordable housing needs lead to rising housing costs that squeeze low-income families, resulting in overcrowding as the supply of affordable housing dwindles. Affordable housing policies that don't address sprawl result in isolated affordable housing units far from jobs and social networks. One policy that addresses both housing and transportation needs is "transit-led development," where mixed use, high-density development is created near transit hubs. Another policy is reforming urban zoning laws to allow for job creation near transit hubs. Increased funding for public transit that is spent equitably and targeted toward transit that helps low-income residents get to jobs is also needed. To ensure that housing and transportation policies benefit low-income as well as upper-income communities, low-income communities must be involved in the planning process.

Another step in providing affordable housing is to shift the bias of U.S. housing policy away from middle-class homeowners to low-income families and increase the total funds available for affordable housing. The National Low Income Housing Coalition is spear-heading an effort to create a National Affordable Housing Trust Fund. The goal of the fund is to use excess Federal Housing Administration and Ginnie Mae revenue as the primary source of revenue to produce, rehabilitate, or preserve 1.5 million units of affordable housing by 2010, estimated to cost $75 billion over 10 years (National Housing Trust Fund Campaign 2001).

The current patchwork of programs to help families meet basic needs fails to cover millions of families. To truly address the needs of working families requires a real investment in a social safety net to help both the poorest, most vulnerable families as well as the near poor who are struggling to get by.

Conclusion

Millions of working families do not have incomes high enough to meet their basic needs, and families that fall below basic family budget levels suffer critical and serious hardships. The findings point to the conclusion that, for many families, employment is insufficient to ensure that they can make ends meet and avoid hardship. If work were the solution to poverty, then workers would be meeting their basic family budgets. But they don't and, as a result, experience hardships. A strengthened social safety net is essential for giving families a boost that their work can't.

In her most recent book, Barbara Ehrenreich became a low-wage worker and experienced many of these hardships first hand. She concluded:

> It is common, among the nonpoor, to think of poverty as a sustainable condition—austere, perhaps, but they get by somehow, don't they? They are "always with us." What is harder for the nonpoor to see is poverty as acute distress: The lunch that consists of Doritos or hot dog rolls, leading to faintness before the end of the shift. The "home" that is also a car or a van. The illness or injury that must be "worked through," with gritted teeth, because there's no sick pay or health insurance and the loss of one day's pay will mean no groceries for the next. These experiences are not part of a sustainable lifestyle, even a lifestyle of chronic deprivation and relentless low-level punishment. They are, by almost any standard of subsistence, emergency situations. And that is how we should see the poverty of so many millions of low-wage Americans—as a state of emergency. (Ehrenreich 2001, 214)

This report substantiates this critique: working families need work supports to make ends meet. There is a critical role for government to play in insuring that families are able to avoid hardships and meet their basic needs. The extension of health care, child care, and affordable housing to all families will be important steps in this direction.

Appendix A

Family budgets
methodology

Housing. Housing costs are based on the Department of Housing and Urban Development's fair market rents (FMRs). FMRs are based on the 40th percentile rents for "privately owned, decent, [structurally] safe, and sanitary rental housing of a modest (non-luxury) nature with suitable amenities" (Federal Register 1994, quoted in Bernstein, Brocht, and Spade-Aguilar 2000). FMRs for metropolitan statistical areas were used for metropolitan areas, and an average (weighted by population) of FMRs for rural counties in a state was used for rural areas. Two-bedroom apartments were used for families with one to two children, and three-bedroom apartments for families with three children, based on HUD guidelines (Department of Housing and Urban Development 1991). Fair market rents are available at www.huduser.org/datasets/fmr.html.

Food. Food costs are based on the Department of Agriculture's "low-cost food plans." The USDA food plans represent the amount families need to spend to achieve nutritionally adequate diets. The age groups used in this report are males and females age 20-50 and children age 3-5, 6-8, and 9-10. Food cost estimates are the same for the whole nation (the Bureau of Labor Statistics found that food costs vary little by region; see Bernstein, Brocht, and Spade-Aguilar 2000). USDA food plans are available at www.usda.gov/cnpp/using3.htm.

Child care. Child care costs are the average cost per state at child care centers.[11] Costs are for 4-year-olds for one-child families, one 4-year-old and one school-age child for two-child families, and a 4-year-old and two school-age children for three-child families.

While ideally we would like to have used child care costs by county, no consistent data source for child care by county is available. Therefore, we used average child care costs by state. Most state averages are from the Children's Defense Fund's "The High Cost of Child Care Puts Quality Care Out of Reach for Many Families" (http://www.childrensdefense.org/). We used Table A-4 for the statewide average for a 4-year-old and Table A-10 for the statewide average for a school-age child.

When the statewide average for a particular state was listed as "not available," we used an average of urban and rural costs (Tables A-2 and A-3 for 4-year-olds and A-8 and A-9 for school-age children) weighted by the urban and rural populations in those states.

The following is a list of states where costs for 4-year-olds were based on a weighted average of urban and rural costs: Alabama, Arizona, Georgia, Illinois, Montana, New Jersey, New York, Pennsylvania, Tennessee, and Utah.

The following is a list of states where costs for school-age children were based on a weighted average of urban and rural costs: Alabama, Arizona, Georgia, Illinois, Kentucky, Montana, New Jersey, New York, Pennsylvania, Tennessee, and Utah.

If data were also unavailable for urban and rural areas in the state, we used the Children's Defense Fund Report, *Child Care Challenges* (1998, http://www.childrensdefense.org/). We used the statewide average for the state and inflated the dollar amount, which was in 1997 dollars, to 1999 dollars. The following is a list of states for which data were obtained from the *Challenges* report: Massachusetts (both 4-year-olds and school age), Vermont (school age only), New Mexico (4-year-olds only), and Hawaii (school age only).

Data for school-age child care costs in New Mexico and all data for the District of Columbia were not available in any CDF data source. In these cases, we contacted researchers in New Mexico and D.C. to obtain survey results.[12]

Transportation. Transportation costs are based on the costs of owning and operating a car. We derived these costs from the average miles driven per person for the size of the metropolitan area (from the Nationwide Personal Transportation Survey[13]). Thus, transportation costs vary by the size of the metropolitan area (or whether the area is rural).

Costs per mile are from the IRS cost-per-mile rate, which includes the cost of gas, insurance, vehicle registration fees, maintenance, and depreciation (http://www.irs.ustreas.gov/prod/forms_pub/pubs/p4630401.htm.).

We included only costs for non-social trips (work, school, church, and errands) for the first adult and costs for work trips for the second adult. According to the National Personal Transportation survey, 28% of trips are work related and 41% are for other non-social trips.

The formula for deriving transportation costs is:

[.69 (non soc trips 1st adult) * Average Miles/MSA * .325 (IRS cost/mile)]
* [.28 (work trips 2nd adult) * Average Miles/MSA * .325 (IRS cost/mile)]

Health care. In calculating health care costs, we took into account the fact that 40% of families do not receive health insurance through their employers. We assumed that any workers who do not have health insurance through their employers or through Medicaid would purchase health insurance through a non-group plan. Thus, health care costs are based on a weighted average of the costs of employer-provided health insurance and the cost of purchasing a non-group plan. We used the same cost of health insurance for the whole state, as we found that non-group plans did not vary significantly within states.

Premium costs for a non-group plan were obtained from two online health insurance quote firms, www.ehealthinsurance.com and www.quotesmith.com. Both of these sites provide quotes from major providers for non-group health plans. Quotes are based on ages of family members and zip codes. We assumed parents were 33 and the children were age 4, 8, and 10. We selected the plan closest to a $500 deductible and a $20 co-pay. We used a zip code from an urban area in the state; we found that using zip codes for different areas in the state did not change the cost of the plans significantly.

For the employee cost for premiums for employer-sponsored insurance, we used the average employee cost for premiums for family health insurance plans for each state. These data were obtained from the Medical Expenditure Panel Survey (http://www.meps.ahcpr.gov/mepsdata/ic/1997/Index297.htm, table II.D.2.).

Out-of-pocket costs are from "Hidden From View: The Growing Burden of Health Care Costs" from Consumer's Union (Table 9), inflated to 1999 dollars. For the weights for whether families have health insurance through an employer, we use the percentage of families with incomes between $20,000 and $30,000 who receive health insurance from their employer, the percentage who have Medicaid, and the percentage that are covered by neither and therefore would have to purchase a non-group plan. For the weighted average for two-parent families, the formula is:

0.59 * employer-sponsored premium + 0.08 * $0 (no premium cost for Medicaid) + 0.33 * non-group premium + out-of-pocket costs.

For one-parent families, the formula is:

0.61 * employer-sponsored premium + 0.08 * $0 (no premium cost for Medicaid) + 0.31 * non-group premium + out-of-pocket costs.

Other necessities. The cost of other necessities includes the cost of telephone, clothing, personal care expenses, household supplies, reading materials, school supplies, union dues, bank fees, television, music, and toys. Bernstein, et al. (2000) derives these costs from the Federal Communications Commission and the Consumer Expenditure Survey, and calculates that these costs are 31% of housing and food costs. Thus, we derive the cost of other necessities by taking 31% of the housing and food costs for the area and family type.

Taxes. Citizens for Tax Justice (CTJ) computed the taxes for the tax year 1999. Taxes include federal personal income taxes, federal Social Security and Medicare payroll taxes (direct worker payments only) equal to 7.65% of pretax wages, and state income taxes. Local income taxes are included in two states where they are applicable across the entire state (Maryland and Michigan). Sales and property taxes are not included in the tax category because sales taxes are included in the cost of other necessities and property taxes are included in the cost of housing.

CTJ calculated taxes based on the after-tax incomes necessary to meet basic needs (i.e., after-tax family budget levels). It calculated the pretax incomes necessary for families to achieve this after-tax income.

The taxpayer family types are married couples with one, two, or three children, filing jointly for federal income taxes and single parents with one, two, or three children filing as head of household federally.

We assume all income is from wages, none of the adults is elderly, all families are renters, and all couples have two wage earners (with one earner making 68.6% of the total wages).

For the dependent care tax credit, we assume that (1) all families have the maximum amount of dependent care expenses ($2,400 for one eligible child; $4,800 for two or more eligible children), and (2) all children are under 13 years old and thus "eligible" for purposes of the dependent care credit.

Taxes are based on the standard deduction for both federal and state income tax purposes. No adjustments are taken in computing adjusted gross income for federal income taxes. Likewise, no adjustments are taken for state income tax purposes, except in states that allow an adjustment for federal income taxes paid (Alabama, Iowa, Louisiana, Missouri, Montana, North Dakota, Oklahoma, Oregon, and Utah), an adjustment for dependent care expenses (Idaho, Indiana, Massachusetts, Maryland, Michigan, South Carolina, and Virginia), a second-earner adjustment (Maryland and North Dakota), or an earned income exclusion (Maryland and West Virginia).

A note about metropolitan statistical areas. Many MSAs include areas from two or more states. Families living in the same MSA but in different states will pay different state taxes. Therefore, we calculated separate budgets for the parts of the MSA in each state.

For example, the Washington, D.C. MSA includes the District of Columbia and portions of Maryland, Virginia, and West Virginia. Therefore we calculated budgets for the MSA in D.C. and the three states. When we calculated the number of families thsat fall below family budget levels, we used both the MSA code and the state code to identify which budget should be used.

Housing and transportation costs are based on the costs for the MSA, so these costs remain the same across states. For food, health care, and child care we used the same average for the whole state, so these items will vary in the same MSA depending on the state.

Appendix B

CPS methodology

The results for Tables 2-5 and Figure A are derived from the March Current Population Survey (CPS), a nationally representative survey by the U.S. Bureau of the Census. The CPS has extensive information on income levels and family composition, and is the source for our national poverty statistics. It also has geographic indicators, enabling us to link families to budgets specific to their locales.

In order to generate large enough samples, we combined data for the three years 1997-99 (since the income data from the CPS is retrospective to the prior year, these are survey years 1998-2000). Our family budgets were constructed in 1999 dollars, thus we put the 1997 and 1998 incomes in 1999 dollars for the analysis. The budgets are constructed for six family types: one- and two-parent families, with positive earnings, with one to three children less than 12 years old. Our pooled CPS's yielded an unweighted sample of 21,000 families of these types consisting of 75,000 persons. For example, if a single parent worked half the year, we reduced the family budget by one half the annual child care amount. In families with two adults, if one worked full time while the other reported no work, we reduced the budget by the full amount of child care, under the assumption that the non-working adult could provide child care. However, if the second adult worked half the year, we reduced the budget by half the child care amount.

We constructed budgets for every MSA and for one combined rural area in each state. The CPS provides MSA identifiers for families, with the exception that a small minority of cases suppress the identifier for reasons of confidentiality. These cases were deleted from our analysis since we could not assign them a budget. Families not in an MSA who resided in a rural area were assigned the non-MSA budget for their state.

The CPS allows for fairly complex evaluations of family relations. For example, the file allows the identification of households with subfamilies. Such households contain more than one family (a family is defined as two or more persons related by blood, adoption, or marriage), either related or unrelated to the primary family.

For our purposes, the important question is the extent to which such families share resources and expenditures, information which is not available in the file. For example, it is impossible to identify whether a subfamily is contributing to rent or food costs. Our solution is to assign the budgets to families with the relevant number of adults and children, without strict reference to family status (e.g., whether a couple is married or cohabitating), and with a maximum of two adults and three children in the household. For example, consider two different family types: one, a family with two adult parents and one child under 12; and second, a family with an adult brother and sister and one foster child. These were both assigned the budget for two adults, one child. However, if the first family also had the child's grandparent in the home, we deleted the case from our study, since we do not have budgets for this family type. In most cases, treating married couples and cohabitating couples the same is consistent with our methodology in constructing family budgets; for all items except taxes it doesn't matter whether the adults are married or not (but for our tax calculations we assumed the two adults are married).

In our racial/ethnic analysis, Hispanics are a separate category, not comingled with other racial groups (in much Census analysis Hispanics can also be included in other racial groups).

Appendix C

Hardships data

We use two datasets for our analysis, the National Survey of American Families (NSAF) and the Survey of Income and Program Participation (SIPP). We selected variables that have comparable definitions across the two datasets to compare critical and serious hardships experienced by families in the two surveys. The NSAF provides annual cross-section data, while the SIPP has the advantage of using months as the time period of analysis and is longitudinal, although we make use of it only as a cross-sectional database. The SIPP provides data on hardships for calendar year 1995, while the NSAF provides data for calendar year 1996.

NSAF. The NSAF is a survey of the economic, health, and social characteristics of children, adults under the age of 65, and their families with data for 1997. The sample is representative for 13 states (Alabama, California, Colorado, Florida, Massachusetts, Michigan, Minnesota, Mississippi, New Jersey, New York, Texas, Washington, and Wisconsin). For each family with children, one child was selected randomly from the family's children under six (if there were any) and one from the family's children age 6-17 (if there were any). These children are referred to as "focal children." This rule was applied to households, not just families, so if there were two families in the household there were still no more than two focal children chosen. The adults sampled fall under two categories: an adult most knowledgeable (MKA) about the focal child and his or her spouse/partner, called the non-most knowledgeable adult. The weighted estimates from the data are of the population of MKA, or adults other than primary caregivers age 18-64.

SIPP. The SIPP is a multipanel, longitudinal survey of the civilian, non-institutional population in the United States. Respondents are interviewed every four months and the data are compiled such that one can examine the respondents' economic circumstances by month. The SIPP data for this study came from wave 9 of the 1993 panel. This wave refers to a four-month period in 1995. Information on income, demographics, and program participation came from the core wave and longitudinal files, while information on critical and serious hardships came primarily from the topical module associated with wave 9.

The two surveys have significant differences that may lead to discrepancies in measuring hardships. First, the thematic focus of the two surveys differs, and respondents may therefore react to questions differently. The primary purpose of the SIPP is to collect income, employment, and program participation of the respondents. In contrast, the purpose of the NSAF is to collect information on well-being. This difference may lead the NSAF respondents to be more attuned to their experiences with hardship than are the SIPP respondents. Second, attrition and survey exhaustion may lead to different hardship results across the two surveys. The NSAF does not, by definition, have a problem with attrition, but the SIPP does. The hardship questions are asked in the last wave of the SIPP panel, and therefore respondents may either be exhausted or choose not to answer those questions or may have already dropped out of the survey. Those who drop out are more likely to have characteristics associated with hardships than those who do not (Lamas, Tin, and Eargle 1994). Third, the timing of the two surveys and the period over which respondents had to recall information differs. The SIPP asks respondents to recall their experiences with hardships over the past four to 12 months. The NSAF interviewed people from February to December 1997 and asks respondents questions about the experiences in 1996.

Sample. We exclude families that have negative or missing family income. Prior research has shown that families with negative income have very different characteristics than other "poor" families because they are mostly small-family-business owners. In the NSAF, family income is taken for 1996 and is blurred to protect confidentiality, but it is not top-coded.[14] In the SIPP, family income is the sum of total household income over the past 12 months.

The universe for our analysis is families or households headed by an adult between the ages of 18 and 64 with positive family income.[15] In our descriptive analysis, we use person-weights. Thus, we examine the number of people who live in a household or family that experiences critical and serious hardships. Due to the longitudinal nature of the SIPP, between 15% and 25% of the survey was not interviewed in each month, due to attrition and new sample members added into the panel. Households are not categorically deleted from our sample if they missed some months of the survey, although there will be missing data for those months they were not interviewed.

Variables. The unit of analysis for the hardship variables differs across the two surveys. In the NSAF, the hardships questions are asked at the "social family" level, while, in the SIPP, they are asked at the household level. In the NSAF, unrelated individuals who are in a personal relationship with an adult in the family are considered part of the family, as are all persons related by blood in the household. These unrelated individuals and the family they are associated with make up a social family. In contrast, the 1993 panel of the SIPP does not indicate whether unrelated individuals are in a relationship with an adult in the household. Given these constraints, when looking at family type we create four categories

TABLE A1.1   Family composition for SIPP and NSAF samples

	SIPP proportion	NSAF proportion	Percentage-point difference (SIPP – NSAF)
One adult with children	8.1%	8.6%	-0.5
Two adults with children	42.4	41.9	0.5
Three or more adults with children	15.3	12.0	3.3
Households without children	34.3	37.5	-3.2

Sources: Authors' calculations from the 1993 SIPP (for calendar year 1995) and 1997 NSAF (for calendar year 1996).

of family/households that are as similar as possible across the two surveys: (1) one adult and one (or more) children; (2) two adults and one (or more) children; (3) three adults and one (or more) children; and (4) adult(s) only. As Table A1.1 shows, the percentage of persons in each family/household category is similar across the two surveys, suggesting that the social family definition in the NSAF closely approximates the household definition in the SIPP.

The definition of poverty in the NSAF is whether the annual family income for 1996 falls above or below 200% of the poverty threshold. In the SIPP, the poverty threshold is a bit more complicated. The SIPP household poverty variable is an annual poverty level that changes with each month because it is adjusted for inflation. This is summed over the past 12 months and divided by 12 to get the average poverty level over the course of the year. To determine if the household falls above or below 200% of poverty, we divide the household income variable by twice the average poverty threshold.

For the regression analysis we construct other variables, which are measured at the family level in the NSAF and the household level in the SIPP. Race and education refer to the characteristics of the oldest adult in the family/household. Race is measured as four mutually exclusive categories: white (non-Hispanic), African American (non-Hispanic), Hispanic, and other (non-Hispanic). Education is measured in five mutually exclusive categories: not a high school graduate, high school graduate, some college or two-year degree, four-year college degree, and graduate work. An immigrant family/household is one in which any family/household member is an immigrant. All employment-related questions refer to the job in which the respondent worked the most hours.

The unit of analysis for the regression analysis is family or household, given that hardship questions are asked at this level. The NSAF provides only person or family weights, and the hardship questions in the SIPP can only be used with person or household weights. This may lead to differences in results across the two surveys. (See Gundersen and Boushey 2001 for a complete discussion.)

Appendix D

Family budgets vs. 200% of poverty

We compared the critical and serious hardships experienced by families falling under both 200% of poverty and family budgets using the SIPP data. These results are shown in **Tables A2.1** and **A2.2**. We find that both critical and serious hardships are nearly identical for samples below the two thresholds.

TABLE A2.1 Critical hardships for households in family-budget definition, living below family budget level and living below 200% of poverty

	Living below family budget level	Living below 200% of poverty
Food insecurity		
Not enough food	12.6%	12.9%
Insufficient health care		
Didn't receive nec. medical care	11.0	11.5
Housing problems		
Evicted	1.6	1.7
Utilities disconnected	4.4	4.5

TABLE A2.2 Serious hardships for families in family-budget definition, living below family budget level and living below 200% of poverty

	Living below family budget level	Living below 200% of poverty
Food insecurity		
Kind of food	28.3%	29.0%
Insufficient health care		
Emergency room is main source of care	5.0	4.8
Housing problems		
Didn't pay rent or mortgage	15.3	15.7
Didn't pay utilities	22.5	23.3
Didn't pay rent or mortgage and/or utilities	27.9	28.9
Telephone disconnected	10.2	10.6
Inadequate child care		
Child cares for self	1.3	1.4

Sources: Authors' calculations from the 1993 SIPP (for calendar year 1995).

Appendix E

Analytic method

To predict the probability that a family suffers a critical hardship, we regress the critical hardship index on employment status, poverty status, and demographic controls.

Econometrics

The model is estimated as an ordered logit regression. This kind of model is appropriate when the dependent variable represents an ordinal ranking. Our dependent variable ranks the severity of hardships faced by a family by counting the number of critical hardships they experience. This model is a direct generalization of the ordinary two-outcome logit model.

The model is based on the following equation:

$$y = \beta'X + \varepsilon$$

Where y^* is the latent index that is unobserved; X are the independent variables; and β are the estimated coefficients. What we observe is:

$$y = 0 \text{ if } y^* <= 0$$
$$y = 1 \text{ if } 0 < y^* <= \mu_1$$
$$y = 2 \text{ if } \mu_1 < y^* <= \mu_2$$
$$y = 3 \text{ if } \mu_2 < y^* <= \mu_3$$

The μ_i (commonly referred to as "cut-points") are the unknown parameters estimated with β. The probability of observing an outcome corresponds to the probability that the estimated linear function ($\beta'X$) plus random error (ε) is within the range of the cut-points estimated for the outcome. We assume that ε is normally distributed across observations.

To generate estimates of the probability of an outcome, we estimate the coefficients, β, together with the cut-points, μ, across the possible outcomes. In our regression, the outcomes range from 0 to 3 because a family can have zero, one, two, or three critical hardships.

One difficulty with the ordered logit model is that the marginal effects of the regressors on the probabilities are not equal to the coefficients. Therefore, we report the predicted probabilities, comparing across dummy variables.[16]

Regression analysis

Our dependent variable counts the number of critical hardships a family suffers. We measure critical hardships as whether anyone in the family goes without necessary medical care, whether anyone in the family must skip meals sometimes or often (NSAF) or go without sufficient food (SIPP), whether the family has been either evicted (SIPP) or doubled-up with friends or family (NSAF) because it could not afford its housing payments, or whether the family has had its utilities disconnected because it could not pay its bills (SIPP). This variable takes the values zero, one, two, or three in the estimates from the NSAF and also four in the estimates from the SIPP.

Our independent variables include three measures of labor market outcomes. We include a poverty status dummy variable that indicates whether a family has income below 200% of poverty. We also include the log of family income. To account for whether the family is participating in the labor market, we include a dummy variable indicating whether the family has a full-time worker.

We also include a set of demographic controls in the list of independent variables. A family's race and education are taken from that of the oldest adult in the household. In cases where there are two (or more) adults of the same age, we take the higher educational attainment level of the adults and the race of the female adult. If there is not a female adult, we take the race to be the minorities' race.[17] An immigrant household includes all households with any family member born outside the U.S. Health insurance coverage indicates whether a family has private insurance, public insurance, or no health insurance. There are indicators for whether there are children under age 5 or between 6 and 17, as well as whether it is a single-parent family or whether the parents are married. There are also dummies for the nine Census regions. All regressions use the family-level weights, and the unit of analysis is the family.

Our results are based on the predicted probabilities from the estimated regressions. To calculate the predicted probabilities, all variables are set to their sample means except the variable in question and the category it describes. The variable in question is set to one, and the rest of the variables in that category are set to zero. For example, for the category of race, to calculate the probabilities for those who are "white," that variable is set to one, the other three race variables are set to zero, and the rest of the variables are set to their sample means.

Table A3.1 shows the means for the variables included in the regressions. **Tables A3.2** and **A3.3** shows the regression results. As noted above, the coefficients on ordered logit models do not provide marginal probabilities; therefore we generate predicted probabilities for our variables of interest to interpret these regression results.

TABLE A3.1 NSAF and SIPP regression sample means

	NSAF		SIPP	
	No. observations	Mean	No. observations	Mean
Dependent variable				
Number of material				
hardships experienced	38,097	0.175	14,812	0.09
Demographics				
Age of head	38,097	42.008	11,744	43.225
Race of head	38,097	1.458	11,740	1.421
Number of children below 5	38,097	0.252	14,812	0.199
Number of children 6 - 17	38,097	0.412	14,812	0.336
Female-headed family	38,097	0.087	14,812	0.157
Married	38,097	0.683	14,812	0.653
Anyone in family is immigrant	38,097	0.11	14,812	0.115
Highest grade completed of head	37,891	2.819	14,811	2.863
State dummies	38,097	5.041	14,787	5.023
Health insurance	32,243	1.415	14,812	1.35
Income and employment				
Log of family income	37,780	10.461	14,812	10.377
Dummy for above/below				
200% of poverty	26,649	0.267	14,381	0.296
Any family members				
employed full time	38,097	0.693	14,812	0.535

TABLE A3.2   NSAF Regressions

| Ordered logit estimates | Number of obs=20,482 |
| Wald chi2(26)=472.130 |
| Prob > chi2=0.000 |
| Log likelihood = -9109.4557 | Pseudo R2=0.073 |

Number of material hardships experienced	Coefficients	Robust standard error	z	P>|z|	95% confidence interval	
Dummy for below 200% of poverty	0.629	0.118	5.330	0.000	0.398	0.860
Log of family income	-0.062	0.052	-1.180	0.237	-0.163	0.040
Any family member employed full-time	0.061	0.094	0.640	0.520	-0.124	0.245
Public health insurance	0.692	0.124	5.590	0.000	0.449	0.934
No health insurance	1.005	0.106	9.450	0.000	0.796	1.213
(Private health insurance omitted)						
Age of head	-0.004	0.003	-1.190	0.233	-0.011	0.003
Race of head is African American	-0.395	0.122	-3.230	0.001	-0.635	-0.156
Race of head is Hispanic	-0.006	0.132	-0.040	0.965	-0.265	0.253
Race of head is other	-0.348	0.210	-1.660	0.097	-0.759	0.063
(White omitted)						
Number of children below 5	-0.093	0.105	-0.890	0.375	-0.298	0.112
Number of children 6 - 17	0.218	0.082	2.650	0.008	0.057	0.380
Female-headed family	0.167	0.137	1.220	0.224	-0.102	0.435
Married	-0.402	0.102	-3.960	0.000	-0.601	-0.203
Anyone in family is immigrant	-0.168	0.133	-1.260	0.209	-0.429	0.094
Highest grade completed of head is high school/GED	-0.087	0.117	-0.740	0.459	-0.317	0.143
Highest grade completed of head is some college	0.037	0.106	0.340	0.730	-0.171	0.244
Highest grade completed of head is college (4 year)	0.006	0.146	0.040	0.965	-0.279	0.292
Highest grade completed of head is more than 4 year college	0.089	0.151	0.590	0.554	-0.207	0.385
(Less than high school omitted)						
Middle Atlantic	-0.075	0.176	-0.430	0.669	-0.419	0.269
East North Central	0.055	0.191	0.290	0.772	-0.320	0.431
West North Central	0.161	0.228	0.710	0.480	-0.286	0.609
South Atlantic	0.029	0.190	0.150	0.879	-0.343	0.400
East South Central	0.031	0.215	0.140	0.886	-0.391	0.453
West South Central	0.108	0.192	0.560	0.575	-0.269	0.485
Mountain	0.174	0.232	0.750	0.453	-0.281	0.629
Pacific	0.115	0.179	0.640	0.522	-0.237	0.467
(New England omitted)						
_cut1	1.294	0.599			(Ancillary parameters)	
_cut2	3.483	0.607				
_cut3	6.249	0.699				

Number of material hardships experienced	Probability	Observed
0	Pr(xb+u<_cut1)	0.854
1	Pr(_cut1<xb+u<_cut2)	0.125
2	Pr(_cut2<xb+u<_cut3)	0.019
3	Pr(_cut3<xb+u)	0.001

Table A3.3: SIPP Regressions

Ordered logit estimates	Number of obs=11,364
	Wald chi2(26)=912.690
	Prob > chi2=0.000
Log likelihood = -3287.25	Pseudo R2=0.138

Number of material hardships experienced	Co-efficients	Robust standard error	z	P>|z|	95% confidence interval	
Dummy for below 200% of poverty	0.764	0.121	6.300	0.000	0.526	1.001
Log of family income	-0.269	0.080	-3.370	0.001	-0.426	-0.113
Any family member employed full-time	-0.157	0.101	-1.550	0.120	-0.356	0.041
Public health insurance	0.771	0.153	5.040	0.000	0.471	1.071
No health insurance	1.042	0.109	9.540	0.000	0.828	1.256
(Private health insurance omitted)						
Age of head	-0.008	0.004	-2.060	0.039	-0.015	0.000
Race of head is African American	-0.257	0.138	-1.860	0.062	-0.528	0.013
Race of head is Hispanic	0.070	0.136	0.520	0.604	-0.195	0.336
Race of head is other	-0.707	0.282	-2.510	0.012	-1.259	-0.155
(White omitted)						
Number of children below 5	-0.062	0.100	-0.620	0.538	-0.257	0.134
Number of children 6 - 17	0.394	0.085	4.630	0.000	0.227	0.561
Female-headed family	-0.360	0.144	-2.500	0.013	-0.643	-0.077
Married	-0.396	0.101	-3.920	0.000	-0.594	-0.198
Anyone in family is immigrant	-0.124	0.143	-0.870	0.385	-0.405	0.156
Highest grade completed of head is high school/GED	-0.094	0.127	-0.740	0.461	-0.343	0.156
Highest grade completed of head is some college	-0.162	0.132	-1.220	0.221	-0.421	0.097
Highest grade completed of head is college (4 year)	-0.651	0.171	-3.800	0.000	-0.986	-0.315
Highest grade completed of head is more than 4 year college	-0.599	0.217	-2.760	0.006	-1.024	-0.174
(Less than high school omitted)						
Middle Atlantic	0.245	0.240	1.020	0.307	-0.226	0.716
East North Central	-0.148	0.245	-0.600	0.546	-0.627	0.332
West North Central	0.179	0.264	0.680	0.498	-0.338	0.696
South Atlantic	0.467	0.236	1.980	0.048	0.004	0.930
East South Central	-0.315	0.275	-1.140	0.252	-0.855	0.224
West South Central	-0.226	0.262	-0.870	0.387	-0.739	0.286
Mountain	0.463	0.259	1.790	0.074	-0.045	0.970
Pacific	0.372	0.240	1.550	0.121	-0.098	0.843
(New England omitted)						
_cut1	-0.360	0.893			(Ancillary parameters)	
_cut2	1.462	0.897				
_cut3	2.866	0.915				
_cut4	5.253	1.040				

Number of material hardships experienced	Probability	Observed
0	Pr(xb+u<_cut1)	0.918
1	Pr(_cut1<xb+u<_cut2)	0.066
2	Pr(_cut2<xb+u<_cut3)	0.012
3	Pr(_cut3<xb+u<_cut4)	0.004
4	Pr(_cut4<xb+u)	0.000

Appendix F

Family budgets for 400 U.S. communities

The family budget tables, for six family types (one parent with one, two, or three children and two parents with one, two, or three children) appear following page 72.

Endnotes

1. The thrifty food plans have been found to be too low for a family to afford a nutritionally adequate diet (Bernstein, Brocht, and Spade-Aguilar 2000).

2. However, most family budgets use a set of conservative assumptions by not including items such as restaurant meals, vacations, movies, or savings for education or retirement.

3. For a review of 19 family budget studies see Bernstein, Brocht, and Spade-Aguilar (2000) and www.epinet.org for a current list of family budget studies.

4. The thrifty food plans, which are the basis for the official poverty measures, are not normally used for family budgets, since they have been found to be too low for a family to afford a nutritionally adequate diet (Bernstein, Brocht, and Spade-Aguilar 2000). Thus, the slightly more generous low-cost food plans are used instead.

5. The same finding is seen in the Census Bureau's implementation of the NAS method of measuring poverty. Note that these regional results differ from those shown in Table 4 because the latter examine person, not family, rates.

6. See U.S Bureau of the Census, P60-210, p. xii.

7. We do not have a measure for transportation hardship in our data. We could have included the lack of a vehicle, but this is an inadequate measure for two reasons. First, even families with vehicles could be driving an unsafe vehicle or lack car insurance. Second, in the few cities with adequate public transportation systems, lack of a vehicle is not a hardship.

8. Due the nature of the NSAF data, we are unable to calculate the number of children under 12 within families.

9. Due to the large sample sizes of the two surveys, tests of significance (t-tests) of the sample properties show that the two surveys are drawn from statistically different populations. Thus, very small differences in a proportion show up as statistically different. We focus on differences that are substantive in comparing a proportion with a particular outcome.

10. Tests of this result show that this is not merely because the critical hardships index measures whether a family needed to go to the doctor but did not go. The probability of missing meals and doubling-up were also significantly affected by the presence of health insurance.

11. Except for Vermont, for which costs for child care centers were unavailable. The cost of family child care homes were used instead.

12. In New Mexico, we contacted Disa Lindgren, YWCA Cariño director of CCR&R Services. She provided the "YWCA Cariño 2000 Annual Child Care Rate Survey," which listed the full-time, weekly child care rate for school-age children in Child Care Centers. This number was broken down into a corresponding hourly rate and then recalculated using the CDF school-age formulation (3.5 hours per day for 180 days a year and eight hours per day for 71 days a year).

   In the District of Columbia, we contacted Deborah Lyons, director of the Center for Applied Research and Urban Policy. She provided "Table 24: Comparison of Daily Full Time Rates for Child Care Services." Using the CDF formulation for 4-year-old child care (five days per week, 52 weeks per year), we multiplied the daily rate for 4-year-olds to find a weekly rate and then a yearly rate. To find the school-age rate we divided the school-age daily rate by eight to find an hourly rate and then recalculated using the CDF formulation.

13. Average miles per person from http://www-cta.ornl.gov/npts/1990/fat/index.html, tables 4.23 and 4.26 (average miles per person was derived by multiplying average trip length and number of trips per person from Table 4.26 and private trips from Table 4.23 for the appropriate MSA size).

14. The various components of income are top-coded, but this does not significantly affect the distribution of income (Converse et al. 2000).

15. Less than 1% of SIPP households were headed by someone less than 18 years old. They were dropped from the sample.

16. See Greene (1993, 672-6).

17. This is a small number of observations (51 cases in the NSAF) and should not affect outcomes.

References

Agency for Health Care Policy and Research. 1997. *Trends in Personal Health Care Expenditures, Health Insurance, and Payment Sources, Community Based Population, 1997-1995.* Washington, D.C.: Agency for Health Care Policy and Research.

American Public Health Association, and American Academy of Pediatrics. 1992. *National Health and Safety Performance Standards: Guidelines for Out-of-Home Child Care Programs.* Arlington, Va.: National Center for Education in Maternal and Child Health.

Bauman, Kurt. 1998. *Direct Measures of Poverty as Indicators of Economic Need.* Washington, D.C.: U.S. Bureau of the Census.

Beverly, Sondra. 2001. Measures of Material Hardship: Rationale and Recommendations. *Journal of Poverty* 5 (1).

Beverly, Sondra. 2000. Using Measures of Material Hardship to Assess Well-Being. *Focus.*

Bernstein, Jared, Chauna Brocht, and Maggie Spade-Aguilar. 2000. *How Much Is Enough? Basic Family Budgets for Working Families.* Washington, D.C.: Economic Policy Institute.

Bhargava, Deepak. 2001. *A Silver Lining in Cloudy Washington, DC.* Washington, D.C.: National Campaign for Jobs and Income Support.

Blank, Helen, Karen Schulman, and Danielle Ewen. 1999. *State Prekindergarten Initiatives, 1998-1999.* Washington, D.C.: Children's Defense Fund.

Boushey, Heather, Chauna Brocht, and Bethney Gunderson. 2001. *Going Without: Hardships Faced by Minimum Wage Families.* Issue Brief. Washington, D.C.: Economic Policy Institute.

Bullard, Robert, Glenn Johnson, and Angel Torres. 2001. *Race, Equity, and Smart Growth.* Atlanta, Ga.: Environmental Justice Resource Center.

Capizzano, Jeffrey, Gina Adams, and Kathryn Tout. 2000. *Child Care Patterns of School-Age Children with Employed Mothers.*

Cherry, Robert, and Max Sawicky. 2000. *Giving Tax Credit Where Credit Is Due.* Briefing Paper. Washington, D.C.: Economic Policy Institute.

Citro, Constance F., and Robert T. Michael, eds. 1995. *Measuring Poverty: A New Approach*. Washington, D.C.: National Academy Press.

Converse, Nate, Robin McCullough-Harlin, Adam Safir, Fritz Scheuren, Jeanne Yang, Dan Nooter, and Hongwei Zhang. 2000. *1997 NSAF Social Family Public Use File Documentation and Codebook with Undercount-Adjusted Weights*. Washington, D.C.: Urban Institute.

Currie, Janet. 2001. "Early Childhood Education Programs." *Journal of Economic Perspectives* 15(2): 213-38.

Directorate for Education, Employment, Labour, and Social Affairs. 2001. *Employment Outlook 2001*: Organization for Economic Cooperation and Development.

Dreier, Peter. 2000. "Why America's Workers Can't Pay the Rent." *Dissent,* Summer, pp. 38-44.

Ehrenreich, Barbara. 2001. *Nickel and Dimed: On (Not) Getting By in America*. New York, N.Y.: Metropolitan Books.

Folbre, Nancy. 2000. "Universal Child Care: It's Time." *The Nation*, July 3.

Freeman, R.B., and J.L. Medoff. 1984. *What Do Unions Do?* New York: Basic Books.

Gornick, Janet, and Marcia Meyers. 2001. "Support for Working Families: What the United States Can Learn From Europe." *American Prospect,* January 1-15.

Greene, William H. 1993. *Econometric Analysis*. Second Edition. New York, N.Y.: Macmillan.

Gundersen, Bethney, and Heather Boushey. 2001. *A New Approach to Measuring Poverty: Testing the Reliability of Hardship Indicators*. Technical Paper. Washington, D.C.: Economic Policy Institute.

Guyer, Jocelyn, and Cindy Mann. 1999. *Employed But Not Insured*. Washington, D.C.: Center on Budget and Policy Priorities.

Hartmann, Heidi. 2001. "Economic Security for Women and Children—What Will It Take?" In R. Borosage and R. Hickey, eds., *The Next Agenda: Blueprint for the New Progressive Movement.* Boulder, Colo.: Westview Press.

Helburn, Suzanne, and Barbara Bergmann. Forthcoming. *The Future of Child Care: What Should be Done?* New York, N.Y.: St. Martin's Press.

Human Rights Watch. 2000. *Unfair Advantage.* New York, N.Y.: Human Rights Watch.

Iceland, John. 2000. *Poverty Among Working Families: Findings From Experimental Poverty Measures*. Washington, D.C.: U.S. Census Bureau.

Kaiser Commission on Medicaid and the Uninsured. 2000. *Uninsured in America: A Chart Book*. Menlo Park, Calif.: Kaiser Family Foundation.

Lamas, E., J. Tin, and J. Eargle. 1994. *The Effect of Attrition on Income and Poverty Estimates From the Survey of Income and Program Participation*. Washington, D.C.: U.S. Bureau of the Census.

Lovell, Vicki, and Hedieh Rahmanou. 2000. *Paid Family and Medical Leave: Essential Support for Working Women and Men*. Washington, D.C.: Institute for Women's Policy Research.

Mayer, S.E., and C. Jencks. 1989. "Poverty and the Distribution of Material Hardship." *Journal of Human Resources* 24: 99-113.

Mishel, Lawrence, Jared Bernstein, and John Schmitt. 2001. *The State of Working America 2000/2001*. Ithaca, N.Y.: ILR Press.

National Housing Trust Fund Campaign. 2001. *Policy Workgroup Recommendations*. Washington, D.C.: National Low Income Housing Coalition.

Physicians for a National Health Program. 2001. *Proposal of the Physicians' Working Group for Single-Payer National Health Insurance*. Chicago, Ill.: Physicians for a National Health Program.

Rose, Donald. 1999. Economic determinants and dietary consequences of food insecurity and hunger in the U.S. *Journal of Nutrition* 129 (2S): 517S-20S.

Sawhill, Isabel. 1999. *Investing in Children*. Washington, D.C.: Brookings Institute.

Schulman, Karen. 2000. *The High Cost of Child Care Puts Quality Care Out of Reach for Many Families*. Washington, D.C.: Children's Defense Fund.

Short, Kathleen, John Iceland, and Thesia Garner. 1999. *Experimental Poverty Measures*. Washington, D.C.: U.S. Census Bureau.

Surface Transportation Policy Project. 2000. *Driven to Spend*. Washington, D.C.: Surface Transportation Policy Project.

U.S. Department of Health and Human Services (DHHS). 1999. *National Study of Child Care for Low-Income Families*. Washington, D.C.: DHHS.

U.S. Department of Housing and Urban Development (HUD). 1991. *Public Housing Occupancy Handbook*. Washington, D.C.: HUD.

Vandell, Deborah Lowe, and Barbara Wolfe. 2000. *Child Care Quality: Does It Matter and Does It Need to be Improved?* Washington, DC: U.S. Department of Human Services.

Weissman, Joel, and Arnold Epstein. 1994. *Falling Through the Safety Net*. Baltimore, Md.: Johns Hopkins University Press.

Whitebrook, Marcy, Carolee Howes, and Deborah Phillips. 1998. *Worthy Work, Unlivable Wages*: Washington, D.C.: Center for the Child Care Workforce.

TABLE A4.1 Basic family budgets for one parent, one child, 1999

State	Area name	Housing	Food	Child care	Trans.	Health care	Other necess.	Taxes	Total	Annual total
						Monthly expenses				
AK	Anchorage	$ 773	$ 230	$ 616	$ 148	$ 231	$ 311	$ 379	$ 2,687	$32,241
AK	Rural	783	230	616	197	231	314	397	2,768	33,212
AL	Anniston	381	230	295	158	269	189	72	1,593	19,114
AL	Birmingham	481	230	295	161	269	220	175	1,830	21,956
AL	Decatur	436	230	295	158	269	206	128	1,721	20,647
AL	Dothan	394	230	295	158	269	193	83	1,621	19,453
AL	Florence	429	230	295	158	269	204	121	1,705	20,455
AL	Gadsden	364	230	295	158	269	184	63	1,562	18,739
AL	Huntsville	518	230	295	148	269	232	205	1,895	22,745
AL	Mobile	482	230	295	161	269	221	176	1,832	21,984
AL	Montgomery	496	230	295	148	269	225	183	1,845	22,140
AL	Tuscaloosa	482	230	295	158	269	221	173	1,826	21,915
AL	Columbus (Ala. portion)	464	230	295	148	269	215	148	1,768	21,219
AL	Rural	360	230	295	197	269	183	80	1,612	19,348
AR	Fayetteville-Springdale-Rogers	506	230	325	148	201	228	133	1,772	21,259
AR	Fort Smith (Ark. portion)	404	230	325	158	201	196	41	1,555	18,664
AR	Jonesboro	397	230	325	158	201	194	37	1,542	18,507
AR	Little Rock-North Little Rock	497	230	325	161	201	225	134	1,773	21,281
AR	Pine Bluff	450	230	325	158	201	211	78	1,652	19,826
AR	Memphis (Ark. portion)	530	230	325	170	201	235	181	1,873	22,473
AR	Texarkana (Ark. portion)	458	230	325	158	201	213	91	1,675	20,104
AR	Rural	368	230	325	197	201	185	38	1,544	18,532
AZ	Flagstaff	594	230	353	158	203	255	199	1,991	23,896
AZ	Phoenix-Mesa	634	230	353	170	203	268	249	2,106	25,273
AZ	Tucson	603	230	353	161	203	258	213	2,020	24,245
AZ	Yuma	563	230	353	158	203	246	170	1,922	23,062
AZ	Las Vegas (Ariz. portion)	693	230	353	170	203	286	307	2,242	26,900
AZ	Rural	495	230	353	197	203	225	133	1,835	22,018
CA	Bakersfield	508	230	476	161	195	229	163	1,961	23,533
CA	Chico-Paradise	564	230	476	158	195	246	211	2,079	24,942
CA	Fresno	500	230	476	161	195	226	157	1,944	23,329
CA	Los Angeles-Long Beach	749	230	476	157	195	303	329	2,438	29,258
CA	Merced	538	230	476	158	195	238	189	2,023	24,277
CA	Modesto	572	230	476	148	195	248	211	2,080	24,960
CA	Oakland	861	230	476	170	195	338	384	2,654	31,848
CA	Orange County	871	230	476	170	195	341	389	2,672	32,063
CA	Redding	519	230	476	158	195	232	170	1,979	23,752
CA	Riverside-San Bernardino	597	230	476	157	195	256	238	2,148	25,780
CA	Sacramento	613	230	476	170	195	261	265	2,210	26,515
CA	Salinas	746	230	476	148	195	302	324	2,421	29,055
CA	San Diego	729	230	476	170	195	297	324	2,421	29,055
CA	San Francisco	1,167	230	476	170	195	433	532	3,203	38,431
CA	San Jose	1,139	230	476	170	195	424	517	3,151	37,813
CA	San Luis Obispo-Atascadero-Paso Robles	727	230	476	158	195	297	319	2,401	28,809
CA	Santa Barbara-Santa Maria-Lompoc	867	230	476	148	195	340	379	2,634	31,613
CA	Santa Cruz-Watsonville	954	230	476	158	195	367	424	2,803	33,633
CA	Santa Rosa	829	230	476	148	195	328	361	2,567	30,798
CA	Stockton-Lodi	592	230	476	161	195	255	236	2,144	25,727
CA	Vallejo-Fairfield-Napa	753	230	476	148	195	305	327	2,433	29,201
CA	Ventura	793	230	476	161	195	317	349	2,520	30,239
CA	Visalia-Tulare-Porterville	506	230	476	148	195	228	154	1,936	23,232
CA	Yolo	664	230	476	158	195	277	290	2,289	27,464
CA	Yuba City	488	230	476	158	195	222	145	1,913	22,957
CA	Rural	564	230	476	197	195	246	235	2,142	25,702
CO	Boulder-Longmont	766	230	451	148	223	309	422	2,548	30,576
CO	Colorado Springs	623	230	451	148	223	264	348	2,287	27,447
CO	Denver	664	230	451	170	223	277	379	2,395	28,735
CO	Fort Collins-Loveland	656	230	451	158	223	275	371	2,363	28,352
CO	Grand Junction	515	230	451	158	223	231	251	2,058	24,697
CO	Greeley	582	230	451	158	223	252	326	2,221	26,649
CO	Pueblo	540	230	451	158	223	239	278	2,118	25,410
CO	Rural	567	230	451	197	223	247	339	2,254	27,051
CT	Bridgeport	703	230	568	148	204	289	353	2,495	29,940

TABLE A4.1 Basic family budgets for one parent, one child, 1999

		Monthly expenses								Annual
State	Area name	Housing	Food	Child care	Trans.	Health care	Other necess.	Taxes	Total	total
CT	Danbury	905	230	568	158	204	352	445	2,861	34,333
CT	Hartford	692	230	568	170	204	286	356	2,506	30,066
CT	New Haven-Meriden	785	230	568	161	204	315	392	2,655	31,854
CT	New London-Norwich (Conn. portion)	723	230	568	148	204	295	362	2,530	30,357
CT	Stamford-Norwalk	1,106	230	568	148	204	414	549	3,218	38,620
CT	Waterbury	735	230	568	158	204	299	370	2,563	30,759
CT	Worcester (Conn. portion)	632	230	568	148	204	267	323	2,372	28,459
CT	Rural	705	230	568	197	204	290	370	2,563	30,761
DC	Washington (D.C. portion)	820	230	650	157	260	325	667	3,109	37,309
DE	Dover	613	230	413	158	256	261	328	2,259	27,104
DE	Wilmington-Newark (Del. portion)	671	230	413	161	256	279	363	2,373	28,481
DE	Rural	579	230	413	197	256	251	326	2,251	27,016
FL	Daytona Beach	580	230	340	148	244	251	160	1,953	23,436
FL	Fort Lauderdale	698	230	340	170	244	288	277	2,247	26,962
FL	Fort Myers-Cape Coral	578	230	340	148	244	250	159	1,949	23,386
FL	Fort Pierce-Port St. Lucie	657	230	340	148	244	275	227	2,121	25,448
FL	Fort Walton Beach	500	230	340	158	244	226	97	1,794	21,533
FL	Gainesville	536	230	340	158	244	237	130	1,875	22,496
FL	Jacksonville	569	230	340	170	244	248	165	1,966	23,591
FL	Lakeland-Winter Haven	479	230	340	148	244	220	74	1,734	20,809
FL	Melbourne-Titusville-Palm Bay	566	230	340	148	244	247	149	1,923	23,077
FL	Miami	702	230	340	170	244	289	279	2,254	27,046
FL	Naples	732	230	340	158	244	298	287	2,288	27,457
FL	Ocala	500	230	340	158	244	226	97	1,794	21,533
FL	Orlando	678	230	340	170	244	281	261	2,205	26,459
FL	Panama City	500	230	340	158	244	226	97	1,794	21,533
FL	Pensacola	500	230	340	148	244	226	91	1,779	21,346
FL	Punta Gorda	616	230	340	158	244	262	199	2,049	24,582
FL	Sarasota-Bradenton	654	230	340	161	244	274	232	2,135	25,620
FL	Tallahassee	603	230	340	148	244	258	181	2,004	24,043
FL	Tampa-St. Petersburg-Clearwater	584	230	340	170	244	252	177	1,998	23,975
FL	West Palm Beach-Boca Raton	715	230	340	170	244	293	284	2,276	27,309
FL	Rural	514	230	340	197	244	231	137	1,892	22,709
GA	Albany	431	230	379	158	233	205	132	1,766	21,190
GA	Athens	517	230	379	158	233	231	226	1,973	23,677
GA	Atlanta	688	230	379	157	233	284	385	2,355	28,262
GA	Augusta-Aiken (Ga. portion)	503	230	379	148	233	227	204	1,923	23,071
GA	Columbus (Ga. portion)	464	230	379	148	233	215	159	1,827	21,920
GA	Macon	504	230	379	148	233	227	205	1,925	23,100
GA	Savannah	524	230	379	148	233	234	226	1,972	23,668
GA	Chattanooga (Ga. portion)	510	230	379	148	233	229	211	1,939	23,270
GA	Rural	429	230	379	197	233	204	161	1,832	21,978
HI	Honolulu	863	230	420	161	195	339	496	2,703	32,433
HI	Rural	955	230	420	197	195	367	568	2,932	35,181
IA	Cedar Rapids	494	230	459	158	211	224	220	1,996	23,951
IA	Davenport-Moline-Rock Island (Iowa portion)	477	230	459	148	211	219	191	1,935	23,225
IA	Des Moines	551	230	459	148	211	242	277	2,118	25,411
IA	Dubuque	455	230	459	158	211	212	173	1,898	22,775
IA	Iowa City	567	230	459	158	211	247	308	2,180	26,154
IA	Sioux City (Iowa portion)	509	230	459	158	211	229	239	2,035	24,415
IA	Waterloo-Cedar Falls	430	230	459	158	211	204	136	1,828	21,938
IA	Omaha (Iowa portion)	578	230	459	161	211	250	322	2,211	26,535
IA	Rural	419	230	459	197	211	201	165	1,882	22,583
ID	Boise City	540	230	312	148	240	239	166	1,874	22,489
ID	Pocatello	417	230	312	158	240	200	32	1,588	19,057
ID	Rural	450	230	312	197	240	211	103	1,742	20,903
IL	Bloomington-Normal	551	230	433	158	225	242	283	2,122	25,459
IL	Champaign-Urbana	589	230	433	158	225	254	322	2,210	26,523
IL	Chicago	737	230	433	157	225	300	398	2,480	29,762
IL	Decatur	447	230	433	158	225	210	182	1,885	22,617
IL	Kankakee	546	230	433	158	225	240	278	2,110	25,323
IL	Peoria-Pekin	553	230	433	148	225	243	278	2,110	25,316
IL	Rockford	559	230	433	148	225	244	283	2,123	25,477

TABLE A4.1 Basic family budgets for one parent, one child, 1999

State	Area name	Housing	Food	Child care	Trans.	Health care	Other necess.	Taxes	Total	Annual total
IL	Davenport-Moline-Rock Island (Ill. portion)	477	230	433	148	225	219	203	1,936	23,229
IL	St. Louis (Ill. portion)	501	230	433	170	225	226	245	2,031	24,375
IL	Springfield	510	230	433	158	225	229	244	2,030	24,357
IL	Rural	392	230	433	197	225	193	155	1,825	21,903
IN	Bloomington	631	230	394	158	194	267	330	2,204	26,444
IN	Elkhart-Goshen	533	230	394	158	194	236	230	1,975	23,705
IN	Evansville-Henderson (Ind. portion)	489	230	394	148	194	223	182	1,860	22,314
IN	Fort Wayne	501	230	394	148	194	226	193	1,887	22,639
IN	Gary	620	230	394	161	194	263	322	2,184	26,213
IN	Indianapolis	545	230	394	170	194	240	254	2,028	24,336
IN	Kokomo	525	230	394	158	194	234	223	1,957	23,488
IN	Lafayette	583	230	394	158	194	252	281	2,092	25,100
IN	Muncie	434	230	394	158	194	206	133	1,748	20,977
IN	South Bend	556	230	394	148	194	244	249	2,014	24,173
IN	Terre Haute	427	230	394	158	194	204	126	1,732	20,787
IN	Louisville (Ind. portion)	498	230	394	161	194	226	199	1,902	22,823
IN	Cincinnati (Ind. portion)	531	230	394	170	194	236	238	1,993	23,916
IN	Rural	420	230	394	197	194	201	148	1,785	21,420
KS	Lawrence	541	230	468	158	231	239	256	2,123	25,474
KS	Topeka	494	230	468	158	231	224	208	2,013	24,161
KS	Wichita	521	230	468	161	231	233	238	2,082	24,983
KS	Kansas City (Kan. portion)	534	230	468	170	231	237	259	2,129	25,552
KS	Rural	408	230	468	197	231	198	147	1,879	22,551
KY	[HUD FMR] Gallatin County	429	230	303	158	252	204	119	1,694	20,332
KY	[HUD FMR] Grant County	404	230	303	158	252	196	76	1,618	19,420
KY	Lexington	521	230	303	148	252	233	212	1,898	22,779
KY	Louisville (Ky. portion)	498	230	303	161	252	226	198	1,867	22,404
KY	Owensboro	406	230	303	158	252	197	78	1,623	19,476
KY	[HUD FMR] Pendleton County	399	230	303	158	252	195	70	1,607	19,281
KY	Evansville-Henderson (Ky. portion)	489	230	303	148	252	223	174	1,819	21,822
KY	Cincinnati (Ky. portion)	531	230	303	170	252	236	240	1,962	23,542
KY	Clarksville-Hopkinsville (Ky. portion)	443	230	303	158	252	209	134	1,727	20,729
KY	Huntington-Ashland (Ky. portion)	437	230	303	148	252	207	120	1,696	20,354
KY	Rural	374	230	303	197	252	187	75	1,618	19,411
LA	Alexandria	438	230	325	158	235	207	50	1,642	19,709
LA	Baton Rouge	467	230	325	161	235	216	82	1,716	20,593
LA	Houma	413	230	325	158	235	199	30	1,590	19,077
LA	Lafayette	400	230	325	148	235	195	21	1,554	18,650
LA	Lake Charles	553	230	325	158	235	243	165	1,908	22,897
LA	Monroe	451	230	325	158	235	211	65	1,674	20,088
LA	New Orleans	520	230	325	170	235	232	143	1,855	22,265
LA	[HUD FMR] St James Parish	414	230	325	158	235	200	31	1,592	19,099
LA	Shreveport-Bossier City	486	230	325	148	235	222	91	1,737	20,842
LA	Rural	370	230	325	197	235	186	24	1,567	18,800
MA	Barnstable-Yarmouth	831	230	616	158	308	329	583	3,054	36,649
MA	Boston (Mass. portion)	906	230	616	157	308	352	622	3,191	38,290
MA	Brockton	695	230	616	148	308	287	508	2,791	33,494
MA	Fitchburg-Leominster	614	230	616	158	308	262	469	2,656	31,871
MA	Lawrence (Mass. portion)	708	230	616	148	308	291	515	2,815	33,781
MA	Lowell (Mass. portion)	737	230	616	148	308	300	530	2,868	34,419
MA	New Bedford	628	230	616	158	308	266	477	2,682	32,180
MA	Pittsfield	560	230	616	158	308	245	441	2,557	30,682
MA	Springfield	649	230	616	161	308	272	489	2,725	32,698
MA	Worcester (Mass. portion)	632	230	616	148	308	267	475	2,676	32,107
MA	Providence-Fall River-Warwick (Mass. portion)	662	230	616	170	308	276	500	2,762	33,144
MA	Rural	697	230	616	197	308	287	529	2,864	34,370
MD	Baltimore	628	230	439	170	207	266	414	2,355	28,260
MD	[HUD FMR] Columbia	885	230	439	158	207	346	554	2,818	33,816
MD	Cumberland (Md. portion)	497	230	439	158	207	225	226	1,982	23,781
MD	Hagerstown	495	230	439	158	207	225	222	1,976	23,707
MD	Washington (Md. portion)	820	230	439	157	207	325	516	2,695	32,340
MD	Wilmington-Newark (Md. portion)	671	230	439	161	207	279	434	2,421	29,052
MD	Rural	565	230	439	197	207	246	389	2,273	27,275

TABLE A4.1 Basic family budgets for one parent, one child, 1999

State	Area name	Housing	Food	Child care	Trans.	Health care	Other necess.	Taxes	Total	Annual total
ME	Bangor	543	230	408	158	359	240	319	2,256	27,067
ME	Lewiston-Auburn	495	230	408	158	359	225	265	2,138	25,661
ME	Portland	641	230	408	158	359	270	376	2,442	29,299
ME	Portsmouth-Rochester (Maine portion)	710	230	408	158	337	291	405	2,538	30,461
ME	Rural	543	230	408	197	359	240	335	2,312	27,738
MI	Ann Arbor	698	230	470	161	181	288	401	2,428	29,138
MI	Benton Harbor	497	230	470	158	181	225	243	2,004	24,042
MI	Detroit	634	230	470	157	181	268	365	2,305	27,663
MI	Flint	521	230	470	148	181	233	261	2,044	24,526
MI	Grand Rapids-Muskegon-Holland	559	230	470	170	181	244	318	2,173	26,073
MI	Jackson	502	230	470	158	181	227	250	2,017	24,206
MI	Kalamazoo-Battle Creek	530	230	470	148	181	235	270	2,065	24,774
MI	Lansing-East Lansing	597	230	470	148	181	256	339	2,222	26,663
MI	Saginaw-Bay City-Midland	502	230	470	148	181	227	239	1,997	23,961
MI	Rural	433	230	470	197	181	205	207	1,923	23,077
MN	Duluth-Superior (Minn. portion)	459	230	588	158	224	213	147	2,019	24,228
MN	Minneapolis-St. Paul (Minn. portion)	666	230	588	170	224	278	348	2,504	30,045
MN	Rochester	569	230	588	158	224	248	281	2,296	27,556
MN	St. Cloud	491	230	588	158	224	223	188	2,101	25,212
MN	Fargo-Moorhead (Minn. portion)	550	230	588	158	224	242	271	2,262	27,140
MN	Grand Forks (Minn. portion)	536	230	588	158	224	237	249	2,221	26,652
MN	La Crosse (Minn. portion)	461	230	588	158	224	214	150	2,024	24,288
MN	Rural	444	230	588	197	224	209	174	2,065	24,781
MO	Columbia	475	230	343	158	192	218	92	1,707	20,489
MO	Joplin	388	230	343	158	192	191	19	1,521	18,252
MO	Kansas City (Mo. portion)	534	230	343	170	192	237	168	1,874	22,486
MO	St. Joseph	393	230	343	158	192	193	22	1,530	18,363
MO	St. Louis (Mo. portion)	501	230	343	170	192	226	129	1,792	21,505
MO	Springfield	435	230	343	148	192	206	40	1,594	19,129
MO	Rural	368	230	343	197	192	185	24	1,539	18,463
MS	Biloxi-Gulfport-Pascagoula	479	230	282	148	216	220	36	1,611	19,326
MS	Hattiesburg	398	230	282	158	216	195	(2)	1,476	17,716
MS	Jackson	504	230	282	148	216	227	61	1,668	20,015
MS	Memphis (Miss. portion)	530	230	282	170	216	235	106	1,769	21,229
MS	Rural	375	230	282	197	216	187	2	1,489	17,869
MT	Billings	501	230	361	158	260	226	215	1,950	23,402
MT	Great Falls	491	230	361	158	260	223	205	1,927	23,125
MT	Missoula	504	230	361	158	260	227	218	1,957	23,485
MT	Rural	470	230	361	197	260	217	214	1,949	23,386
NC	Asheville	538	230	325	158	226	238	172	1,887	22,638
NC	Charlotte-Gastonia-Rock Hill (N.C. portion)	551	230	325	170	226	242	196	1,940	23,284
NC	Fayetteville	476	230	325	148	226	219	95	1,719	20,627
NC	Goldsboro	429	230	325	158	226	204	45	1,616	19,394
NC	Greensboro--Winston-Salem--High Point	550	230	325	170	226	242	195	1,938	23,255
NC	Greenville	525	230	325	158	226	234	158	1,856	22,269
NC	Hickory-Morganton	488	230	325	148	226	222	108	1,747	20,968
NC	Jacksonville	460	230	325	158	226	214	86	1,698	20,380
NC	Raleigh-Durham-Chapel Hill	645	230	325	170	226	271	299	2,166	25,997
NC	Rocky Mount	429	230	325	158	226	204	45	1,616	19,394
NC	Wilmington	602	230	325	158	226	258	243	2,041	24,497
NC	Norfolk-Va Beach-Newpt News (N.C. portion)	576	230	325	170	226	250	223	2,000	23,995
NC	Rural	428	230	325	197	226	204	84	1,693	20,318
ND	Bismarck	503	230	377	158	197	227	167	1,858	22,298
ND	Fargo-Moorhead (N.D. portion)	550	230	377	158	197	242	218	1,971	23,652
ND	Grand Forks (N.D. portion)	536	230	377	158	197	237	203	1,937	23,249
ND	Rural	274	230	377	197	197	156	(8)	1,422	17,067
NE	Lincoln	525	230	313	161	202	234	35	1,699	20,390
NE	Omaha (Neb. portion)	578	230	313	161	202	250	85	1,819	21,829
NE	Sioux City (Neb. portion)	509	230	313	158	202	229	10	1,650	19,803
NE	Rural	405	230	313	197	202	197	(38)	1,505	18,056
NH	Manchester	677	230	480	158	274	281	318	2,417	29,006
NH	Nashua	774	230	480	158	274	311	355	2,581	30,976
NH	Portsmouth-Rochester (N.H. portion)	710	230	480	158	274	291	330	2,473	29,675

TABLE A4.1 Basic family budgets for one parent, one child, 1999

State	Area name	Housing	Food	Child care	Trans.	Health care	Other necess.	Taxes	Total	Annual total
							Monthly expenses			
NH	Boston (N.H. portion)	906	230	480	157	274	352	405	2,804	33,649
NH	Lawrence (N.H. portion)	708	230	480	148	274	291	327	2,457	29,488
NH	Lowell (N.H. portion)	737	230	480	148	274	300	338	2,506	30,076
NH	Rural	683	230	480	197	274	283	332	2,478	29,736
NJ	Atlantic-Cape May	739	230	438	148	216	300	352	2,423	29,072
NJ	Bergen-Passaic	878	230	438	170	216	343	418	2,693	32,315
NJ	Jersey City	776	230	438	161	216	312	372	2,504	30,044
NJ	Middlesex-Somerset-Hunterdon	960	230	438	170	216	369	453	2,835	34,021
NJ	Monmouth-Ocean	879	230	438	170	216	344	418	2,695	32,336
NJ	Newark	820	230	438	170	216	325	393	2,593	31,111
NJ	Trenton	810	230	438	148	216	322	382	2,546	30,548
NJ	Vineland-Millville-Bridgeton	692	230	438	158	216	286	335	2,354	28,246
NJ	Philadelphia (N.J. portion)	722	230	438	157	216	295	348	2,405	28,859
NM	Albuquerque	584	230	341	161	233	252	208	2,009	24,103
NM	Las Cruces	436	230	341	158	233	206	53	1,656	19,877
NM	Santa Fe	740	230	341	158	233	301	336	2,339	28,062
NM	Rural	427	230	341	197	233	204	77	1,708	20,500
NV	Las Vegas (Nev. portion)	693	230	405	170	229	286	290	2,303	27,641
NV	Reno	708	230	405	148	229	291	289	2,300	27,599
NV	Rural	623	230	405	197	229	264	264	2,213	26,552
NY	Albany-Schenectady-Troy	601	230	654	161	267	257	375	2,546	30,548
NY	Binghamton	498	230	654	158	267	226	320	2,353	28,230
NY	Buffalo-Niagara Falls	507	230	654	170	267	228	330	2,387	28,640
NY	Dutchess County	877	230	654	148	267	343	518	3,037	36,440
NY	Elmira	490	230	654	158	267	223	311	2,332	27,988
NY	Glens Falls	565	230	654	158	267	246	355	2,475	29,701
NY	Jamestown	480	230	654	158	267	220	306	2,314	27,771
NY	Nassau-Suffolk	1,105	230	654	170	267	414	703	3,543	42,513
NY	New York	891	230	654	157	267	347	529	3,075	36,899
NY	Newburgh (N.Y. portion)	712	230	654	148	267	292	431	2,734	32,812
NY	Rochester	606	230	654	170	267	259	382	2,568	30,819
NY	Syracuse	569	230	654	161	267	248	359	2,487	29,845
NY	Utica-Rome	489	230	654	148	267	223	306	2,317	27,807
NY	Rural	541	230	654	197	267	239	358	2,487	29,840
OH	Akron	554	230	358	161	179	243	154	1,879	22,546
OH	Canton-Massillon	472	230	358	148	179	217	35	1,640	19,674
OH	Cincinnati (Ohio portion)	531	230	358	170	179	236	139	1,843	22,112
OH	Cleveland-Lorain-Elyria	594	230	358	170	179	255	201	1,987	23,848
OH	Columbus	553	230	358	170	179	243	160	1,893	22,717
OH	Dayton-Springfield	542	230	358	161	179	239	142	1,851	22,214
OH	Hamilton-Middletown	566	230	358	148	179	247	156	1,884	22,606
OH	Lima	448	230	358	158	179	210	21	1,604	19,247
OH	Mansfield	433	230	358	158	179	205	14	1,577	18,925
OH	Steubenville-Weirton (Ohio portion)	419	230	358	158	179	201	8	1,553	18,637
OH	Toledo	528	230	358	161	179	235	124	1,815	21,780
OH	Youngstown-Warren	439	230	358	161	179	207	18	1,592	19,100
OH	Huntington-Ashland (Ohio portion)	437	230	358	148	179	207	13	1,572	18,858
OH	Parkersburg-Marietta (Ohio portion)	417	230	358	158	179	200	8	1,550	18,596
OH	Wheeling (Ohio portion)	419	230	358	158	179	201	8	1,553	18,637
OH	Rural	428	230	358	197	179	204	30	1,626	19,513
OK	Enid	398	230	313	158	210	195	22	1,525	18,296
OK	Lawton	469	230	313	158	210	217	80	1,676	20,110
OK	Oklahoma City	468	230	313	170	210	216	89	1,697	20,360
OK	Tulsa	520	230	313	161	210	232	136	1,803	21,630
OK	Fort Smith (Okla. portion)	404	230	313	158	210	196	25	1,536	18,427
OK	Rural	364	230	313	197	210	184	19	1,517	18,199
OR	Eugene-Springfield	597	230	410	148	245	256	330	2,217	26,598
OR	Medford-Ashland	601	230	410	158	245	257	343	2,244	26,926
OR	Portland-Vancouver (Ore. portion)	645	230	410	158	245	271	373	2,331	27,977
OR	Salem	568	230	410	148	245	247	274	2,122	25,467
OR	Rural	522	230	410	197	245	233	264	2,101	25,207
PA	Allentown-Bethlehem-Easton	669	230	514	161	178	279	385	2,415	28,980
PA	Altoona	431	230	514	158	178	205	198	1,914	22,962

TABLE A4.1 Basic family budgets for one parent, one child, 1999

State	Area name	Monthly expenses								Annual total
		Housing	Food	Child care	Trans.	Health care	Other necess.	Taxes	Total	
PA	Erie	441	230	514	148	178	208	201	1,920	23,035
PA	Harrisburg-Lebanon-Carlisle	559	230	514	161	178	244	326	2,212	26,546
PA	Johnstown	439	230	514	158	178	207	206	1,931	23,177
PA	Lancaster	576	230	514	148	178	250	333	2,228	26,740
PA	Philadelphia (Pa. portion)	722	230	514	157	178	295	407	2,503	30,035
PA	Pittsburgh	495	230	514	170	178	225	270	2,082	24,981
PA	Reading	544	230	514	148	178	240	300	2,153	25,839
PA	Scranton--Wilkes-Barre--Hazelton	480	230	514	161	178	220	250	2,032	24,386
PA	Sharon	439	230	514	158	178	207	206	1,931	23,177
PA	State College	624	230	514	158	178	265	361	2,329	27,946
PA	Williamsport	441	230	514	158	178	208	208	1,936	23,230
PA	York	544	230	514	148	178	240	300	2,153	25,839
PA	Newburgh (Pa. portion)	712	230	514	148	178	292	400	2,473	29,681
PA	Rural	458	230	514	197	178	213	255	2,044	24,530
RI	Providence-Fall River-Warwick (R.I. portion)	662	230	530	170	260	276	391	2,520	30,239
RI	New London-Norwich (R.I. portion)	723	230	530	148	260	295	412	2,598	31,180
RI	Rural	828	230	530	197	260	328	480	2,853	34,237
SC	Charleston-North Charleston	534	230	312	161	201	237	107	1,781	21,373
SC	Columbia	544	230	312	161	201	240	117	1,805	21,657
SC	Florence	470	230	312	158	201	217	36	1,623	19,472
SC	Greenville-Spartanburg-Anderson	483	230	312	161	201	221	51	1,659	19,904
SC	Myrtle Beach	549	230	312	158	201	241	120	1,811	21,727
SC	Sumter	433	230	312	158	201	205	11	1,550	18,601
SC	Augusta-Aiken (S.C. portion)	503	230	312	148	201	227	65	1,686	20,233
SC	Charlotte-Gastonia-Rock Hill (S.C. portion)	551	230	312	170	201	242	136	1,842	22,104
SC	Rural	425	230	312	197	201	203	22	1,589	19,073
SD	Rapid City	553	230	342	158	224	243	132	1,881	22,571
SD	Sioux Falls	591	230	342	158	224	254	164	1,962	23,545
SD	Rural	435	230	342	197	224	206	56	1,689	20,272
TN	Chattanooga (Tenn. portion)	510	230	341	148	205	229	75	1,738	20,854
TN	Clarksville-Hopkinsville (Tenn. portion)	443	230	341	158	205	209	23	1,607	19,286
TN	Jackson	462	230	341	158	205	214	38	1,648	19,772
TN	Johnson City-Kingsport-Bristol (Tenn. portion)	447	230	341	148	205	210	20	1,600	19,203
TN	Knoxville	468	230	341	161	205	216	45	1,666	19,990
TN	Memphis (Tenn. portion)	530	230	341	170	205	235	106	1,817	21,804
TN	Nashville	626	230	341	170	205	265	191	2,029	24,342
TN	Rural	365	230	341	197	205	184	1	1,523	18,275
TX	Abilene	479	230	316	158	241	220	63	1,706	20,467
TX	Amarillo	443	230	316	158	241	209	29	1,625	19,504
TX	Austin-San Marcos	699	230	316	170	241	288	262	2,206	26,470
TX	Beaumont-Port Arthur	474	230	316	148	241	218	52	1,679	20,152
TX	Brazoria	619	230	316	158	241	263	185	2,011	24,132
TX	Brownsville-Harlingen-San Benito	532	230	316	148	241	236	100	1,803	21,638
TX	Bryan-College Station	553	230	316	158	241	243	127	1,867	22,401
TX	Corpus Christi	552	230	316	148	241	242	120	1,849	22,189
TX	Dallas	718	230	316	157	241	294	269	2,224	26,693
TX	El Paso	527	230	316	161	241	235	104	1,813	21,761
TX	Fort Worth-Arlington	588	230	316	170	241	253	164	1,962	23,548
TX	Galveston-Texas City	562	230	316	158	241	245	134	1,886	22,632
TX	Houston	601	230	316	157	241	257	166	1,968	23,619
TX	Killeen-Temple	522	230	316	148	241	233	92	1,782	21,382
TX	Laredo	485	230	316	158	241	222	67	1,718	20,619
TX	Longview-Marshall	439	230	316	158	241	207	26	1,617	19,403
TX	Lubbock	499	230	316	158	241	226	79	1,748	20,978
TX	McAllen-Edinburg-Mission	418	230	316	161	241	201	15	1,582	18,979
TX	Odessa-Midland	469	230	316	158	241	217	54	1,684	20,210
TX	San Angelo	437	230	316	158	241	207	25	1,613	19,352
TX	San Antonio	554	230	316	170	241	243	136	1,890	22,677
TX	Sherman-Denison	466	230	316	158	241	216	52	1,678	20,133
TX	Texarkana (Texas portion)	458	230	316	158	241	213	42	1,658	19,890
TX	Tyler	476	230	316	158	241	219	60	1,699	20,390
TX	Victoria	446	230	316	158	241	209	32	1,632	19,581
TX	Waco	495	230	316	158	241	225	76	1,740	20,877

TABLE A4.1 Basic family budgets for one parent, one child, 1999

State	Area name	Monthly expenses								Annual total
		Housing	Food	Child care	Trans.	Health care	Other necess.	Taxes	Total	
TX	Wichita Falls	456	230	316	158	241	213	40	1,653	19,837
TX	Rural	396	230	316	197	241	194	18	1,592	19,100
UT	[HUD FMR] Kane County	470	230	358	158	229	217	151	1,812	21,749
UT	Provo-Orem	553	230	358	148	229	243	236	1,997	23,961
UT	Salt Lake City-Ogden	635	230	358	170	229	268	350	2,240	26,880
UT	Flagstaff (Utah portion)	594	230	358	158	229	255	291	2,115	25,384
UT	Rural	503	230	358	197	229	227	222	1,966	23,586
VA	Charlottesville	645	230	433	158	220	271	362	2,319	27,825
VA	Danville	431	230	433	158	220	205	154	1,830	21,958
VA	Lynchburg	440	230	433	158	220	208	166	1,854	22,251
VA	Norfolk-Va Beach-Newpt News (Va. portion)	576	230	433	170	220	250	322	2,201	26,406
VA	Richmond-Petersburg	620	230	433	161	220	263	351	2,278	27,331
VA	Roanoke	475	230	433	158	220	218	202	1,936	23,228
VA	Washington (Va. portion)	820	230	433	157	220	325	456	2,641	31,688
VA	Johnson City-Kingsport-Bristol (Va. portion)	447	230	433	148	220	210	166	1,854	22,243
VA	Rural	446	230	433	197	220	209	202	1,937	23,242
VT	Burlington	692	230	363	158	429	286	397	2,554	30,646
VT	Rural	601	230	363	197	429	257	369	2,445	29,337
WA	Bellingham	682	230	451	158	243	283	302	2,348	28,175
WA	Bremerton	620	230	451	158	243	263	275	2,240	26,874
WA	Olympia	655	230	451	158	243	274	289	2,300	27,596
WA	Richland-Kennewick-Pasco	675	230	451	158	243	280	297	2,334	28,003
WA	Seattle-Bellevue-Everett	736	230	451	170	243	299	327	2,456	29,473
WA	Spokane	519	230	451	148	243	232	180	2,003	24,038
WA	Tacoma	586	230	451	161	243	253	247	2,170	26,045
WA	Yakima	543	230	451	158	243	240	208	2,072	24,861
WA	Portland-Vancouver (Wash. portion)	645	230	451	158	243	271	285	2,283	27,394
WA	Rural	518	230	451	197	243	232	212	2,083	24,993
WI	Appleton-Oshkosh-Neenah	495	230	423	148	185	225	243	1,949	23,389
WI	Eau Claire	488	230	423	158	185	222	244	1,950	23,397
WI	Green Bay	530	230	423	158	185	235	296	2,058	24,690
WI	Janesville-Beloit	545	230	423	158	185	240	314	2,095	25,136
WI	Kenosha	577	230	423	158	185	250	355	2,178	26,133
WI	La Crosse (Wis. portion)	461	230	423	158	185	214	212	1,883	22,594
WI	Madison	658	230	423	148	185	275	413	2,333	27,992
WI	Milwaukee-Waukesha	605	230	423	170	185	259	393	2,265	27,179
WI	Racine	535	230	423	158	185	237	302	2,070	24,838
WI	Sheboygan	475	230	423	158	185	218	228	1,918	23,010
WI	Wausau	480	230	423	158	185	220	234	1,930	23,159
WI	Duluth-Superior (Wis. portion)	459	230	423	158	185	213	210	1,878	22,535
WI	Minneapolis-St. Paul (Wis. portion)	666	230	423	170	185	278	431	2,383	28,594
WI	Rural	430	230	423	197	185	205	211	1,881	22,575
WV	[HUD FMR] Berkeley County	504	230	316	158	211	227	146	1,792	21,508
WV	Charleston	490	230	316	148	211	223	125	1,744	20,926
WV	Huntington-Ashland (W.Va. portion)	437	230	316	148	211	207	70	1,619	19,433
WV	[HUD FMR] Jefferson County	556	230	316	158	211	244	200	1,915	22,977
WV	Parkersburg-Marietta (W.Va. portion)	417	230	316	158	211	200	60	1,592	19,104
WV	Wheeling (W.Va. portion)	419	230	316	158	211	201	61	1,596	19,149
WV	Washington (W.Va. portion)	820	230	316	157	211	325	406	2,466	29,586
WV	Cumberland (W.Va. portion)	497	230	316	158	211	225	139	1,776	21,317
WV	Steubenville-Weirton (W.Va. portion)	419	230	316	158	211	201	61	1,596	19,149
WV	Rural	375	230	316	197	211	187	54	1,570	18,840
WY	Casper	468	230	364	158	242	216	84	1,762	21,141
WY	Cheyenne	598	230	364	158	242	257	198	2,046	24,549
WY	Rural	445	230	364	197	242	209	90	1,776	21,317

Source: Authors' calculations (see Appendix A)

TABLE A4.2 Basic family budgets for one parent, two children, 1999

State	Area name	Housing	Food	Child care	Trans.	Health care	Other necess.	Taxes	Total	Annual total
									Monthly expenses	
AK	Anchorage	$ 773	$ 351	$ 989	$ 148	$ 251	$ 348	$ 391	$ 3,251	$39,011
AK	Rural	783	351	989	197	251	352	409	3,332	39,981
AL	Anniston	381	351	552	158	301	227	151	2,121	25,451
AL	Birmingham	481	351	552	161	301	258	219	2,323	27,871
AL	Decatur	436	351	552	158	301	244	188	2,229	26,749
AL	Dothan	394	351	552	158	301	231	160	2,147	25,759
AL	Florence	429	351	552	158	301	242	183	2,215	26,585
AL	Gadsden	364	351	552	158	301	222	140	2,087	25,046
AL	Huntsville	518	351	552	148	301	269	256	2,395	28,744
AL	Mobile	482	351	552	161	301	258	219	2,325	27,895
AL	Montgomery	496	351	552	148	301	263	222	2,333	27,997
AL	Tuscaloosa	482	351	552	158	301	258	218	2,320	27,834
AL	Columbus (Ala. portion)	464	351	552	148	301	253	201	2,270	27,240
AL	Rural	360	351	552	197	301	220	157	2,139	25,668
AR	Fayetteville-Springdale-Rogers	506	351	525	148	216	266	138	2,149	25,790
AR	Fort Smith (Ark. portion)	404	351	525	158	216	234	71	1,958	23,499
AR	Jonesboro	397	351	525	158	216	232	66	1,944	23,330
AR	Little Rock-North Little Rock	497	351	525	161	216	263	139	2,151	25,809
AR	Pine Bluff	450	351	525	158	216	248	104	2,052	24,619
AR	Memphis (Ark. portion)	530	351	525	170	216	273	168	2,232	26,789
AR	Texarkana (Ark. portion)	458	351	525	158	216	251	110	2,068	24,811
AR	Rural	368	351	525	197	216	223	67	1,946	23,356
AZ	Flagstaff	594	351	555	158	216	293	159	2,325	27,894
AZ	Phoenix-Mesa	634	351	555	170	216	305	221	2,452	29,420
AZ	Tucson	603	351	555	161	216	296	177	2,358	28,292
AZ	Yuma	563	351	555	158	216	283	140	2,265	27,180
AZ	Las Vegas (Ariz. portion)	693	351	555	170	216	324	275	2,583	30,998
AZ	Rural	495	351	555	197	216	262	117	2,193	26,317
CA	Bakersfield	508	351	786	161	203	266	199	2,475	29,697
CA	Chico-Paradise	564	351	786	158	203	284	240	2,586	31,029
CA	Fresno	500	351	786	161	203	264	191	2,456	29,473
CA	Los Angeles-Long Beach	749	351	786	157	203	341	316	2,903	34,839
CA	Merced	538	351	786	158	203	276	227	2,539	30,465
CA	Modesto	572	351	786	148	203	286	240	2,587	31,043
CA	Oakland	861	351	786	170	203	376	374	3,122	37,459
CA	Orange County	871	351	786	170	203	379	379	3,140	37,674
CA	Redding	519	351	786	158	203	270	208	2,494	29,933
CA	Riverside-San Bernardino	597	351	786	157	203	294	252	2,641	31,689
CA	Sacramento	613	351	786	170	203	299	262	2,685	32,222
CA	Salinas	746	351	786	148	203	340	311	2,886	34,628
CA	San Diego	729	351	786	170	203	335	311	2,886	34,629
CA	San Francisco	1,167	351	786	170	203	471	534	3,683	44,196
CA	San Jose	1,139	351	786	170	203	462	520	3,632	43,580
CA	San Luis Obispo-Atascadero-Paso Robles	727	351	786	158	203	334	305	2,865	34,378
CA	Santa Barbara-Santa Maria-Lompoc	867	351	786	148	203	378	369	3,102	37,223
CA	Santa Cruz-Watsonville	954	351	786	158	203	405	417	3,274	39,289
CA	Santa Rosa	829	351	786	148	203	366	350	3,034	36,407
CA	Stockton-Lodi	592	351	786	161	203	292	252	2,637	31,648
CA	Vallejo-Fairfield-Napa	753	351	786	148	203	342	314	2,898	34,779
CA	Ventura	793	351	786	161	203	355	338	2,987	35,846
CA	Visalia-Tulare-Porterville	506	351	786	148	203	266	187	2,447	29,369
CA	Yolo	664	351	786	158	203	315	278	2,755	33,061
CA	Yuba City	488	351	786	158	203	260	176	2,422	29,069
CA	Rural	564	351	786	197	203	283	251	2,636	31,631
CO	Boulder-Longmont	766	351	819	148	240	346	452	3,122	37,464
CO	Colorado Springs	623	351	819	148	240	302	381	2,864	34,367
CO	Denver	664	351	819	170	240	315	410	2,969	35,625
CO	Fort Collins-Loveland	656	351	819	158	240	312	401	2,937	35,240
CO	Grand Junction	515	351	819	158	240	268	331	2,682	32,186
CO	Greeley	582	351	819	158	240	289	364	2,803	33,637
CO	Pueblo	540	351	819	158	240	276	344	2,727	32,728
CO	Rural	567	351	819	197	240	285	372	2,831	33,973
CT	Bridgeport	703	351	968	148	217	327	402	3,115	37,377

TABLE A4.2 Basic family budgets for one parent, two children, 1999

State	Area name	Housing	Food	Child care	Trans.	Health care	Other necess.	Taxes	Total	Annual total
CT	Danbury	905	351	968	158	217	389	523	3,510	42,118
CT	Hartford	692	351	968	170	217	323	405	3,126	37,506
CT	New Haven-Meriden	785	351	968	161	217	352	454	3,287	39,446
CT	New London-Norwich (Conn. portion)	723	351	968	148	217	333	411	3,150	37,805
CT	Stamford-Norwalk	1,106	351	968	148	217	452	636	3,877	46,528
CT	Waterbury	735	351	968	158	217	337	425	3,189	38,270
CT	Worcester (Conn. portion)	632	351	968	148	217	305	368	2,988	35,858
CT	Rural	705	351	968	197	217	327	425	3,189	38,273
DC	Washington (D.C. portion)	820	351	1,042	157	323	363	752	3,808	45,696
DE	Dover	613	351	645	158	285	299	297	2,648	31,774
DE	Wilmington-Newark (Del. portion)	671	351	645	161	285	317	329	2,759	33,107
DE	Rural	579	351	645	197	285	288	295	2,641	31,686
FL	Daytona Beach	580	351	501	148	267	289	107	2,243	26,915
FL	Fort Lauderdale	698	351	501	170	267	325	228	2,541	30,488
FL	Fort Myers-Cape Coral	578	351	501	148	267	288	106	2,239	26,871
FL	Fort Pierce-Port St. Lucie	657	351	501	148	267	312	169	2,406	28,866
FL	Fort Walton Beach	500	351	501	158	267	264	69	2,109	25,311
FL	Gainesville	536	351	501	158	267	275	88	2,175	26,105
FL	Jacksonville	569	351	501	170	267	285	110	2,254	27,049
FL	Lakeland-Winter Haven	479	351	501	148	267	257	54	2,057	24,689
FL	Melbourne-Titusville-Palm Bay	566	351	501	148	267	284	100	2,217	26,606
FL	Miami	702	351	501	170	267	326	232	2,550	30,597
FL	Naples	732	351	501	158	267	336	239	2,584	31,009
FL	Ocala	500	351	501	158	267	264	69	2,109	25,311
FL	Orlando	678	351	501	170	267	319	207	2,494	29,927
FL	Panama City	500	351	501	158	267	264	69	2,109	25,311
FL	Pensacola	500	351	501	148	267	264	65	2,096	25,151
FL	Punta Gorda	616	351	501	158	267	300	130	2,323	27,870
FL	Sarasota-Bradenton	654	351	501	161	267	312	176	2,421	29,056
FL	Tallahassee	603	351	501	148	267	296	119	2,285	27,423
FL	Tampa-St. Petersburg-Clearwater	584	351	501	170	267	290	118	2,282	27,380
FL	West Palm Beach-Boca Raton	715	351	501	170	267	330	237	2,572	30,862
FL	Rural	514	351	501	197	267	268	92	2,191	26,290
GA	Albany	431	351	661	158	247	242	176	2,266	27,192
GA	Athens	517	351	661	158	247	269	275	2,478	29,738
GA	Atlanta	688	351	661	157	247	322	386	2,812	33,748
GA	Augusta-Aiken (Ga. portion)	503	351	661	148	247	265	248	2,423	29,072
GA	Columbus (Ga. portion)	464	351	661	148	247	253	194	2,318	27,810
GA	Macon	504	351	661	148	247	265	249	2,425	29,104
GA	Savannah	524	351	661	148	247	271	275	2,478	29,730
GA	Chattanooga (Ga. portion)	510	351	661	148	247	267	257	2,441	29,293
GA	Rural	429	351	661	197	247	242	195	2,322	27,861
HI	Honolulu	863	351	668	161	207	376	462	3,088	37,060
HI	Rural	955	351	668	197	207	405	537	3,321	39,853
IA	Cedar Rapids	494	351	651	158	220	262	169	2,305	27,658
IA	Davenport-Moline-Rock Island (Iowa portion)	477	351	651	148	220	257	150	2,254	27,051
IA	Des Moines	551	351	651	148	220	280	243	2,444	29,328
IA	Dubuque	455	351	651	158	220	250	139	2,224	26,687
IA	Iowa City	567	351	651	158	220	285	273	2,504	30,053
IA	Sioux City (Iowa portion)	509	351	651	158	220	267	193	2,348	28,179
IA	Waterloo-Cedar Falls	430	351	651	158	220	242	119	2,171	26,046
IA	Omaha (Iowa portion)	578	351	651	161	220	288	291	2,540	30,477
IA	Rural	419	351	651	197	220	239	134	2,211	26,530
ID	Boise City	540	351	693	148	264	276	290	2,563	30,751
ID	Pocatello	417	351	693	158	264	238	147	2,268	27,210
ID	Rural	450	351	693	197	264	248	223	2,426	29,109
IL	Bloomington-Normal	551	351	722	158	242	280	313	2,616	31,386
IL	Champaign-Urbana	589	351	722	158	242	291	330	2,683	32,190
IL	Chicago	737	351	722	157	242	337	397	2,942	35,307
IL	Decatur	447	351	722	158	242	247	219	2,386	28,629
IL	Kankakee	546	351	722	158	242	278	310	2,607	31,280
IL	Peoria-Pekin	553	351	722	148	242	280	310	2,606	31,273
IL	Rockford	559	351	722	148	242	282	313	2,617	31,401

TABLE A4.2 Basic family budgets for one parent, two children, 1999

State	Area name	Housing	Food	Child care	Trans.	Health care	Other necess.	Taxes	Total	Annual total
IL	Davenport-Moline-Rock Island (Ill. portion)	477	351	722	148	242	257	245	2,442	29,301
IL	St. Louis (Ill. portion)	501	351	722	170	242	264	293	2,543	30,511
IL	Springfield	510	351	722	158	242	267	292	2,541	30,489
IL	Rural	392	351	722	197	242	230	186	2,320	27,842
IN	Bloomington	631	351	637	158	207	304	327	2,615	31,380
IN	Elkhart-Goshen	533	351	637	158	207	274	239	2,398	28,780
IN	Evansville-Henderson (Ind. portion)	489	351	637	148	207	260	186	2,279	27,347
IN	Fort Wayne	501	351	637	148	207	264	194	2,302	27,623
IN	Gary	620	351	637	161	207	301	323	2,600	31,200
IN	Indianapolis	545	351	637	170	207	278	264	2,452	29,427
IN	Kokomo	525	351	637	158	207	272	229	2,378	28,539
IN	Lafayette	583	351	637	158	207	290	297	2,522	30,265
IN	Muncie	434	351	637	158	207	243	157	2,187	26,241
IN	South Bend	556	351	637	148	207	281	257	2,437	29,246
IN	Terre Haute	427	351	637	158	207	241	152	2,173	26,079
IN	Louisville (Ind. portion)	498	351	637	161	207	263	198	2,315	27,780
IN	Cincinnati (Ind. portion)	531	351	637	170	207	273	248	2,418	29,010
IN	Rural	420	351	637	197	207	239	167	2,218	26,618
KS	Lawrence	541	351	693	158	255	276	256	2,530	30,355
KS	Topeka	494	351	693	158	255	262	189	2,401	28,813
KS	Wichita	521	351	693	161	255	270	231	2,482	29,778
KS	Kansas City (Kan. portion)	534	351	693	170	255	274	260	2,537	30,445
KS	Rural	408	351	693	197	255	235	126	2,266	27,186
KY	[HUD FMR] Gallatin County	429	351	567	158	252	242	168	2,167	25,999
KY	[HUD FMR] Grant County	404	351	567	158	252	234	151	2,116	25,396
KY	Lexington	521	351	567	148	252	270	238	2,347	28,169
KY	Louisville (Ky. portion)	498	351	567	161	252	263	219	2,311	27,734
KY	Owensboro	406	351	567	158	252	235	152	2,120	25,444
KY	[HUD FMR] Pendleton County	399	351	567	158	252	232	147	2,106	25,275
KY	Evansville-Henderson (Ky. portion)	489	351	567	148	252	260	206	2,274	27,282
KY	Cincinnati (Ky. portion)	531	351	567	170	252	273	275	2,419	29,033
KY	Clarksville-Hopkinsville (Ky. portion)	443	351	567	158	252	246	179	2,196	26,349
KY	Huntington-Ashland (Ky. portion)	437	351	567	148	252	244	169	2,168	26,018
KY	Rural	374	351	567	197	252	225	151	2,116	25,386
LA	Alexandria	438	351	558	158	253	245	90	2,092	25,106
LA	Baton Rouge	467	351	558	161	253	254	110	2,154	25,844
LA	Houma	413	351	558	158	253	237	74	2,044	24,523
LA	Lafayette	400	351	558	148	253	233	61	2,004	24,051
LA	Lake Charles	553	351	558	158	253	280	163	2,316	27,794
LA	Monroe	451	351	558	158	253	249	98	2,118	25,410
LA	New Orleans	520	351	558	170	253	270	149	2,271	27,252
LA	[HUD FMR] St James Parish	414	351	558	158	253	237	75	2,046	24,547
LA	Shreveport-Bossier City	486	351	558	148	253	259	116	2,172	26,059
LA	Rural	370	351	558	197	253	223	66	2,018	24,218
MA	Barnstable-Yarmouth	831	351	984	158	308	366	583	3,054	36,649
MA	Boston (Mass. portion)	906	351	984	157	308	390	622	3,191	38,290
MA	Brockton	695	351	984	148	308	324	508	2,791	33,494
MA	Fitchburg-Leominster	614	351	984	158	308	299	469	2,656	31,871
MA	Lawrence (Mass. portion)	708	351	984	148	308	328	515	2,815	33,781
MA	Lowell (Mass. portion)	737	351	984	148	308	337	530	2,868	34,419
MA	New Bedford	628	351	984	158	308	303	477	2,682	32,180
MA	Pittsfield	560	351	984	158	308	282	441	2,557	30,682
MA	Springfield	649	351	984	161	308	310	489	2,725	32,698
MA	Worcester (Mass. portion)	632	351	984	148	308	305	475	2,676	32,107
MA	Providence-Fall River-Warwick (Mass. portion)	662	351	984	170	308	314	500	2,762	33,144
MA	Rural	697	351	984	197	308	325	529	2,864	34,370
MD	Baltimore	628	351	794	170	220	303	436	2,903	34,836
MD	[HUD FMR] Columbia	885	351	794	158	220	383	577	3,367	40,408
MD	Cumberland (Md. portion)	497	351	794	158	220	263	357	2,639	31,667
MD	Hagerstown	495	351	794	158	220	262	355	2,635	31,621
MD	Washington (Md. portion)	820	351	794	157	220	363	539	3,244	38,931
MD	Wilmington-Newark (Md. portion)	671	351	794	161	220	317	457	2,970	35,642
MD	Rural	565	351	794	197	220	284	412	2,823	33,872

TABLE A4.2 Basic family budgets for one parent, two children, 1999

State	Area name	Housing	Food	Child care	Trans.	Health care	Other necess.	Taxes	Total	Annual total
ME	Bangor	543	351	625	158	359	277	278	2,591	31,086
ME	Lewiston-Auburn	495	351	625	158	359	262	231	2,480	29,763
ME	Portland	641	351	625	158	359	307	332	2,773	33,275
ME	Portsmouth-Rochester (Maine portion)	710	351	625	158	359	329	371	2,902	34,818
ME	Rural	543	351	625	197	359	277	295	2,646	31,757
MI	Ann Arbor	698	351	687	161	196	325	368	2,786	33,428
MI	Benton Harbor	497	351	687	158	196	263	218	2,369	28,422
MI	Detroit	634	351	687	157	196	305	336	2,666	31,986
MI	Flint	521	351	687	148	196	270	238	2,411	28,928
MI	Grand Rapids-Muskegon-Holland	559	351	687	170	196	282	305	2,549	30,591
MI	Jackson	502	351	687	158	196	264	224	2,381	28,573
MI	Kalamazoo-Battle Creek	530	351	687	148	196	273	249	2,434	29,202
MI	Lansing-East Lansing	597	351	687	148	196	294	315	2,587	31,045
MI	Saginaw-Bay City-Midland	502	351	687	148	196	264	215	2,363	28,353
MI	Rural	433	351	687	197	196	243	182	2,287	27,448
MN	Duluth-Superior (Minn. portion)	459	351	1,066	158	251	251	327	2,863	34,352
MN	Minneapolis-St. Paul (Minn. portion)	666	351	1,066	170	251	315	445	3,265	39,175
MN	Rochester	569	351	1,066	158	251	285	386	3,065	36,781
MN	St. Cloud	491	351	1,066	158	251	261	344	2,921	35,051
MN	Fargo-Moorhead (Minn. portion)	550	351	1,066	158	251	279	375	3,030	36,355
MN	Grand Forks (Minn. portion)	536	351	1,066	158	251	275	367	3,003	36,041
MN	La Crosse (Minn. portion)	461	351	1,066	158	251	252	328	2,866	34,395
MN	Rural	444	351	1,066	197	251	246	335	2,890	34,678
MO	Columbia	475	351	605	158	203	256	143	2,191	26,289
MO	Joplin	388	351	605	158	203	229	83	2,016	24,195
MO	Kansas City (Mo. portion)	534	351	605	170	203	274	192	2,329	27,947
MO	St. Joseph	393	351	605	158	203	231	86	2,026	24,315
MO	St. Louis (Mo. portion)	501	351	605	170	203	264	168	2,263	27,151
MO	Springfield	435	351	605	148	203	244	111	2,096	25,151
MO	Rural	368	351	605	197	203	223	90	2,036	24,426
MS	Biloxi-Gulfport-Pascagoula	479	351	459	148	229	257	52	1,976	23,710
MS	Hattiesburg	398	351	459	158	229	232	5	1,832	21,989
MS	Jackson	504	351	459	148	229	265	68	2,025	24,296
MS	Memphis (Miss. portion)	530	351	459	170	229	273	95	2,108	25,299
MS	Rural	375	351	459	197	229	225	10	1,846	22,154
MT	Billings	501	351	619	158	288	264	255	2,435	29,221
MT	Great Falls	491	351	619	158	288	261	242	2,409	28,910
MT	Missoula	504	351	619	158	288	265	259	2,443	29,315
MT	Rural	470	351	619	197	288	255	254	2,434	29,203
NC	Asheville	538	351	498	158	241	276	96	2,158	25,891
NC	Charlotte-Gastonia-Rock Hill (N.C. portion)	551	351	498	170	241	280	111	2,203	26,437
NC	Fayetteville	476	351	498	148	241	256	47	2,019	24,223
NC	Goldsboro	429	351	498	158	241	242	20	1,939	23,266
NC	Greensboro--Winston-Salem--High Point	550	351	498	170	241	279	111	2,201	26,415
NC	Greenville	525	351	498	158	241	272	87	2,132	25,578
NC	Hickory-Morganton	488	351	498	148	241	260	56	2,043	24,511
NC	Jacksonville	460	351	498	158	241	251	41	2,001	24,014
NC	Raleigh-Durham-Chapel Hill	645	351	498	170	241	309	203	2,418	29,011
NC	Rocky Mount	429	351	498	158	241	242	20	1,939	23,266
NC	Wilmington	602	351	498	158	241	295	140	2,286	27,433
NC	Norfolk-Va Beach-Newpt News (N.C. portion)	576	351	498	170	241	287	129	2,253	27,040
NC	Rural	428	351	498	197	241	241	40	1,997	23,962
ND	Bismarck	503	351	680	158	204	265	229	2,389	28,671
ND	Fargo-Moorhead (N.D. portion)	550	351	680	158	204	279	294	2,516	30,187
ND	Grand Forks (N.D. portion)	536	351	680	158	204	275	275	2,478	29,741
ND	Rural	274	351	680	197	204	194	36	1,936	23,227
NE	Lincoln	525	351	539	161	212	272	31	2,090	25,082
NE	Omaha (Neb. portion)	578	351	539	161	212	288	86	2,216	26,586
NE	Sioux City (Neb. portion)	509	351	539	158	212	267	19	2,055	24,655
NE	Rural	405	351	539	197	212	234	(52)	1,886	22,634
NH	Manchester	677	351	840	158	320	319	333	2,998	35,971
NH	Nashua	774	351	840	158	320	349	370	3,162	37,942
NH	Portsmouth-Rochester (N.H. portion)	710	351	840	158	320	329	346	3,053	36,641

TABLE A4.2 Basic family budgets for one parent, two children, 1999

		Monthly expenses							Annual
State	Area name	Housing	Food	Child care	Trans.	Health care	Other necess.	Taxes	Total	total
NH	Boston (N.H. portion)	906	351	840	157	320	390	421	3,385	40,615
NH	Lawrence (N.H. portion)	708	351	840	148	320	328	342	3,038	36,453
NH	Lowell (N.H. portion)	737	351	840	148	320	337	353	3,087	37,042
NH	Rural	683	351	840	197	320	320	347	3,059	36,702
NJ	Atlantic-Cape May	739	351	641	148	223	338	315	2,755	33,056
NJ	Bergen-Passaic	878	351	641	170	223	381	381	3,025	36,300
NJ	Jersey City	776	351	641	161	223	349	334	2,836	34,028
NJ	Middlesex-Somerset-Hunterdon	960	351	641	170	223	406	415	3,167	38,005
NJ	Monmouth-Ocean	879	351	641	170	223	381	381	3,027	36,319
NJ	Newark	820	351	641	170	223	363	356	2,925	35,094
NJ	Trenton	810	351	641	148	223	360	345	2,878	34,533
NJ	Vineland-Millville-Bridgeton	692	351	641	158	223	323	298	2,686	32,229
NJ	Philadelphia (N.J. portion)	722	351	641	157	223	333	310	2,737	32,842
NM	Albuquerque	584	351	650	161	255	290	271	2,561	30,733
NM	Las Cruces	436	351	650	158	255	244	122	2,215	26,577
NM	Santa Fe	740	351	650	158	255	338	347	2,838	34,055
NM	Rural	427	351	650	197	255	241	135	2,256	27,071
NV	Las Vegas (Nev. portion)	693	351	605	170	249	324	253	2,645	31,744
NV	Reno	708	351	605	148	249	328	253	2,642	31,702
NV	Rural	623	351	605	197	249	302	234	2,561	30,734
NY	Albany-Schenectady-Troy	601	351	975	161	267	295	345	2,995	35,937
NY	Binghamton	498	351	975	158	267	263	289	2,801	33,616
NY	Buffalo-Niagara Falls	507	351	975	170	267	266	299	2,836	34,028
NY	Dutchess County	877	351	975	148	267	381	596	3,595	43,138
NY	Elmira	490	351	975	158	267	261	285	2,787	33,439
NY	Glens Falls	565	351	975	158	267	284	324	2,924	35,088
NY	Jamestown	480	351	975	158	267	258	280	2,768	33,219
NY	Nassau-Suffolk	1,105	351	975	170	267	451	731	4,051	48,606
NY	New York	891	351	975	157	267	385	607	3,634	43,602
NY	Newburgh (N.Y. portion)	712	351	975	148	267	329	397	3,180	38,162
NY	Rochester	606	351	975	170	267	297	351	3,017	36,206
NY	Syracuse	569	351	975	161	267	285	328	2,936	35,232
NY	Utica-Rome	489	351	975	148	267	260	281	2,771	33,257
NY	Rural	541	351	975	197	267	277	328	2,936	35,228
OH	Akron	554	351	692	161	189	281	221	2,448	29,380
OH	Canton-Massillon	472	351	692	148	189	255	128	2,235	26,823
OH	Cincinnati (Ohio portion)	531	351	692	170	189	273	201	2,409	28,903
OH	Cleveland-Lorain-Elyria	594	351	692	170	189	293	273	2,562	30,746
OH	Columbus	553	351	692	170	189	280	228	2,464	29,567
OH	Dayton-Springfield	542	351	692	161	189	277	206	2,418	29,017
OH	Hamilton-Middletown	566	351	692	148	189	284	223	2,454	29,447
OH	Lima	448	351	692	158	189	248	117	2,203	26,430
OH	Mansfield	433	351	692	158	189	243	107	2,173	26,075
OH	Steubenville-Weirton (Ohio portion)	419	351	692	158	189	239	97	2,144	25,733
OH	Toledo	528	351	692	161	189	272	189	2,383	28,592
OH	Youngstown-Warren	439	351	692	161	189	245	113	2,190	26,279
OH	Huntington-Ashland (Ohio portion)	437	351	692	148	189	244	104	2,165	25,985
OH	Parkersburg-Marietta (Ohio portion)	417	351	692	158	189	238	95	2,141	25,686
OH	Wheeling (Ohio portion)	419	351	692	158	189	239	97	2,144	25,733
OH	Rural	428	351	692	197	189	242	124	2,223	26,676
OK	Enid	398	351	570	158	224	232	75	2,008	24,092
OK	Lawton	469	351	570	158	224	254	125	2,150	25,803
OK	Oklahoma City	468	351	570	170	224	254	131	2,168	26,016
OK	Tulsa	520	351	570	161	224	270	164	2,260	27,119
OK	Fort Smith (Okla. portion)	404	351	570	158	224	234	79	2,020	24,237
OK	Rural	364	351	570	197	224	221	71	1,998	23,971
OR	Eugene-Springfield	597	351	610	148	245	294	263	2,508	30,091
OR	Medford-Ashland	601	351	610	158	245	295	334	2,594	31,126
OR	Portland-Vancouver (Ore. portion)	645	351	610	158	245	309	360	2,677	32,118
OR	Salem	568	351	610	148	245	285	221	2,428	29,134
OR	Rural	522	351	610	197	245	271	209	2,404	28,845
PA	Allentown-Bethlehem-Easton	669	351	791	161	191	316	382	2,861	34,332
PA	Altoona	431	351	791	158	191	242	231	2,395	28,736

TABLE A4.2 Basic family budgets for one parent, two children, 1999

State	Area name	Housing	Food	Child care	Trans.	Health care	Other necess.	Taxes	Total	Annual total
PA	Erie	441	351	791	148	191	245	234	2,401	28,815
PA	Harrisburg-Lebanon-Carlisle	559	351	791	161	191	282	333	2,668	32,013
PA	Johnstown	439	351	791	158	191	245	240	2,414	28,971
PA	Lancaster	576	351	791	148	191	287	336	2,681	32,166
PA	Philadelphia (Pa. portion)	722	351	791	157	191	333	405	2,949	35,387
PA	Pittsburgh	495	351	791	170	191	262	308	2,568	30,815
PA	Reading	544	351	791	148	191	277	322	2,624	31,491
PA	Scranton--Wilkes-Barre--Hazelton	480	351	791	161	191	258	290	2,521	30,249
PA	Sharon	439	351	791	158	191	245	240	2,414	28,971
PA	State College	624	351	791	158	191	302	361	2,778	33,331
PA	Williamsport	441	351	791	158	191	245	242	2,419	29,029
PA	York	544	351	791	148	191	277	322	2,624	31,491
PA	Newburgh (Pa. portion)	712	351	791	148	191	329	397	2,919	35,033
PA	Rural	458	351	791	197	191	251	296	2,534	30,408
RI	Providence-Fall River-Warwick (R.I. portion)	662	351	878	170	311	314	409	3,096	37,153
RI	New London-Norwich (R.I. portion)	723	351	878	148	311	333	430	3,175	38,095
RI	Rural	828	351	878	197	311	366	498	3,429	41,152
SC	Charleston-North Charleston	534	351	612	161	212	274	113	2,257	27,085
SC	Columbia	544	351	612	161	212	277	120	2,277	27,325
SC	Florence	470	351	612	158	212	254	75	2,132	25,582
SC	Greenville-Spartanburg-Anderson	483	351	612	161	212	259	83	2,160	25,923
SC	Myrtle Beach	549	351	612	158	212	279	122	2,282	27,385
SC	Sumter	433	351	612	158	212	243	56	2,064	24,766
SC	Augusta-Aiken (S.C. portion)	503	351	612	148	212	265	89	2,179	26,148
SC	Charlotte-Gastonia-Rock Hill (S.C. portion)	551	351	612	170	212	280	130	2,306	27,668
SC	Rural	425	351	612	197	212	240	67	2,104	25,242
SD	Rapid City	553	351	538	158	240	280	101	2,221	26,653
SD	Sioux Falls	591	351	538	158	240	292	121	2,291	27,492
SD	Rural	435	351	538	197	240	244	54	2,059	24,709
TN	Chattanooga (Tenn. portion)	510	351	607	148	218	267	93	2,194	26,329
TN	Clarksville-Hopkinsville (Tenn. portion)	443	351	607	158	218	246	61	2,084	25,012
TN	Jackson	462	351	607	158	218	252	71	2,119	25,430
TN	Johnson City-Kingsport-Bristol (Tenn. portion)	447	351	607	148	218	247	60	2,078	24,939
TN	Knoxville	468	351	607	161	218	254	76	2,135	25,619
TN	Memphis (Tenn. portion)	530	351	607	170	218	273	113	2,262	27,147
TN	Nashville	626	351	607	170	218	303	199	2,474	29,688
TN	Rural	365	351	607	197	218	222	36	1,996	23,951
TX	Abilene	479	351	556	158	256	257	75	2,133	25,591
TX	Amarillo	443	351	556	158	256	246	56	2,066	24,796
TX	Austin-San Marcos	699	351	556	170	256	325	243	2,602	31,220
TX	Beaumont-Port Arthur	474	351	556	148	256	256	69	2,110	25,319
TX	Brazoria	619	351	556	158	256	301	172	2,412	28,947
TX	Brownsville-Harlingen-San Benito	532	351	556	148	256	274	99	2,217	26,599
TX	Bryan-College Station	553	351	556	158	256	280	114	2,269	27,222
TX	Corpus Christi	552	351	556	148	256	280	110	2,253	27,039
TX	Dallas	718	351	556	157	256	331	247	2,617	31,398
TX	El Paso	527	351	556	161	256	272	102	2,225	26,704
TX	Fort Worth-Arlington	588	351	556	170	256	291	150	2,363	28,353
TX	Galveston-Texas City	562	351	556	158	256	283	119	2,285	27,421
TX	Houston	601	351	556	157	256	295	153	2,369	28,430
TX	Killeen-Temple	522	351	556	148	256	271	94	2,198	26,377
TX	Laredo	485	351	556	158	256	259	79	2,144	25,723
TX	Longview-Marshall	439	351	556	158	256	245	54	2,059	24,708
TX	Lubbock	499	351	556	158	256	263	86	2,169	26,030
TX	McAllen-Edinburg-Mission	418	351	556	161	256	238	44	2,025	24,300
TX	Odessa-Midland	469	351	556	158	256	254	70	2,114	25,370
TX	San Angelo	437	351	556	158	256	244	53	2,055	24,665
TX	San Antonio	554	351	556	170	256	281	120	2,288	27,459
TX	Sherman-Denison	466	351	556	158	256	253	68	2,109	25,302
TX	Texarkana (Texas portion)	458	351	556	158	256	251	64	2,094	25,127
TX	Tyler	476	351	556	158	256	256	74	2,127	25,525
TX	Victoria	446	351	556	158	256	247	58	2,072	24,862
TX	Waco	495	351	556	158	256	262	84	2,162	25,943

TABLE A4.2 Basic family budgets for one parent, two children, 1999

State	Area name	Housing	Food	Child care	Trans.	Health care	Other necess.	Taxes	Total	Annual total
TX	Wichita Falls	456	351	556	158	256	250	63	2,090	25,082
TX	Rural	396	351	556	197	256	232	48	2,036	24,429
UT	[HUD FMR] Kane County	470	351	560	158	259	254	163	2,215	26,581
UT	Provo-Orem	553	351	560	148	259	280	237	2,388	28,657
UT	Salt Lake City-Ogden	635	351	560	170	259	306	338	2,619	31,429
UT	Flagstaff (Utah portion)	594	351	560	158	259	293	301	2,515	30,178
UT	Rural	503	351	560	197	259	265	220	2,354	28,245
VA	Charlottesville	645	351	681	158	230	309	347	2,719	32,633
VA	Danville	431	351	681	158	230	242	161	2,254	27,042
VA	Lynchburg	440	351	681	158	230	245	167	2,271	27,256
VA	Norfolk-Va Beach-Newpt News (Va. portion)	576	351	681	170	230	287	316	2,611	31,332
VA	Richmond-Petersburg	620	351	681	161	230	301	335	2,678	32,139
VA	Roanoke	475	351	681	158	230	256	200	2,351	28,206
VA	Washington (Va. portion)	820	351	681	157	230	363	437	3,039	36,464
VA	Johnson City-Kingsport-Bristol (Va. portion)	447	351	681	148	230	247	167	2,271	27,249
VA	Rural	446	351	681	197	230	247	201	2,352	28,224
VT	Burlington	692	351	592	158	429	323	354	2,898	34,777
VT	Rural	601	351	592	197	429	295	325	2,789	33,466
WA	Bellingham	682	351	734	158	243	320	282	2,770	33,239
WA	Bremerton	620	351	734	158	243	301	258	2,665	31,978
WA	Olympia	655	351	734	158	243	312	271	2,724	32,691
WA	Richland-Kennewick-Pasco	675	351	734	158	243	318	279	2,758	33,096
WA	Seattle-Bellevue-Everett	736	351	734	170	243	337	306	2,878	34,534
WA	Spokane	519	351	734	148	243	270	191	2,456	29,472
WA	Tacoma	586	351	734	161	243	290	246	2,612	31,338
WA	Yakima	543	351	734	158	243	277	223	2,529	30,346
WA	Portland-Vancouver (Wash. portion)	645	351	734	158	243	309	267	2,707	32,486
WA	Rural	518	351	734	197	243	269	228	2,541	30,488
WI	Appleton-Oshkosh-Neenah	495	351	710	148	197	262	331	2,494	29,925
WI	Eau Claire	488	351	710	158	197	260	331	2,495	29,934
WI	Green Bay	530	351	710	158	197	273	375	2,593	31,114
WI	Janesville-Beloit	545	351	710	158	197	278	383	2,621	31,452
WI	Kenosha	577	351	710	158	197	288	402	2,681	32,175
WI	La Crosse (Wis. portion)	461	351	710	158	197	252	289	2,417	29,001
WI	Madison	658	351	710	148	197	313	444	2,820	33,845
WI	Milwaukee-Waukesha	605	351	710	170	197	296	423	2,753	33,031
WI	Racine	535	351	710	158	197	275	378	2,602	31,227
WI	Sheboygan	475	351	710	158	197	256	311	2,457	29,486
WI	Wausau	480	351	710	158	197	258	319	2,472	29,658
WI	Duluth-Superior (Wis. portion)	459	351	710	158	197	251	286	2,411	28,933
WI	Minneapolis-St. Paul (Wis. portion)	666	351	710	170	197	315	459	2,868	34,413
WI	Rural	430	351	710	197	197	242	288	2,415	28,981
WV	[HUD FMR] Berkeley County	504	351	602	158	225	265	183	2,288	27,456
WV	Charleston	490	351	602	148	225	261	169	2,246	26,957
WV	Huntington-Ashland (W.Va. portion)	437	351	602	148	225	244	136	2,143	25,721
WV	[HUD FMR] Jefferson County	556	351	602	158	225	281	240	2,413	28,958
WV	Parkersburg-Marietta (W.Va. portion)	417	351	602	158	225	238	128	2,119	25,423
WV	Wheeling (W.Va. portion)	419	351	602	158	225	239	129	2,122	25,469
WV	Washington (W.Va. portion)	820	351	602	157	225	363	407	2,925	35,104
WV	Cumberland (W.Va. portion)	497	351	602	158	225	263	179	2,275	27,294
WV	Steubenville-Weirton (W.Va. portion)	419	351	602	158	225	239	129	2,122	25,469
WV	Rural	375	351	602	197	225	225	120	2,095	25,140
WY	Casper	468	351	528	158	266	254	62	2,086	25,036
WY	Cheyenne	598	351	528	158	266	294	131	2,325	27,904
WY	Rural	445	351	528	197	266	247	66	2,099	25,187

Source: Author's calculations (see Appendix A)

TABLE A4.3 Basic family budgets for one parent, three children, 1999

State	Area name	Housing	Food	Child care	Trans.	Health care	Other necess.	Taxes	Total	Annual total
AK	Anchorage	$ 1,075	$ 489	$ 1,363	$ 148	$ 271	$ 391	$ 549	$ 4,285	$51,422
AK	Rural	1,053	489	1,363	197	271	394	557	4,323	51,882
AL	Anniston	532	489	809	158	334	270	363	2,954	35,448
AL	Birmingham	653	489	809	161	334	301	419	3,165	37,984
AL	Decatur	564	489	809	158	334	287	381	3,021	36,248
AL	Dothan	542	489	809	158	334	274	368	2,973	35,677
AL	Florence	535	489	809	158	334	284	370	2,978	35,740
AL	Gadsden	472	489	809	158	334	264	339	2,865	34,381
AL	Huntsville	690	489	809	148	334	312	432	3,214	38,566
AL	Mobile	649	489	809	161	334	301	418	3,160	37,924
AL	Montgomery	675	489	809	148	334	305	424	3,184	38,208
AL	Tuscaloosa	663	489	809	158	334	301	422	3,175	38,099
AL	Columbus (Ala. portion)	607	489	809	148	334	295	396	3,078	36,936
AL	Rural	471	489	809	197	334	263	353	2,915	34,982
AR	Fayetteville-Springdale-Rogers	684	489	724	148	230	308	354	2,938	35,258
AR	Fort Smith (Ark. portion)	540	489	724	158	230	277	285	2,702	32,429
AR	Jonesboro	547	489	724	158	230	275	287	2,709	32,512
AR	Little Rock-North Little Rock	688	489	724	161	230	306	360	2,958	35,499
AR	Pine Bluff	568	489	724	158	230	291	302	2,762	33,148
AR	Memphis (Ark. portion)	736	489	724	170	230	316	389	3,054	36,652
AR	Texarkana (Ark. portion)	604	489	724	158	230	293	319	2,817	33,805
AR	Rural	491	489	724	197	230	266	276	2,673	32,081
AZ	Flagstaff	797	489	757	158	227	336	322	3,084	37,012
AZ	Phoenix-Mesa	882	489	757	170	227	348	359	3,232	38,789
AZ	Tucson	839	489	757	161	227	338	338	3,149	37,787
AZ	Yuma	782	489	757	158	227	326	313	3,051	36,614
AZ	Las Vegas (Ariz. portion)	965	489	757	170	227	366	395	3,369	40,428
AZ	Rural	495	489	757	197	227	305	221	2,691	32,293
CA	Bakersfield	706	489	1,097	161	203	309	328	3,293	39,514
CA	Chico-Paradise	773	489	1,097	158	203	326	360	3,406	40,878
CA	Fresno	695	489	1,097	161	203	306	322	3,274	39,286
CA	Los Angeles-Long Beach	1,011	489	1,097	157	203	384	480	3,821	45,851
CA	Merced	743	489	1,097	158	203	318	345	3,353	40,237
CA	Modesto	797	489	1,097	148	203	329	367	3,430	41,162
CA	Oakland	1,180	489	1,097	170	203	418	576	4,134	49,608
CA	Orange County	1,212	489	1,097	170	203	422	591	4,185	50,214
CA	Redding	722	489	1,097	158	203	312	334	3,315	39,786
CA	Riverside-San Bernardino	829	489	1,097	157	203	337	387	3,498	41,980
CA	Sacramento	850	489	1,097	170	203	342	402	3,554	42,643
CA	Salinas	1,038	489	1,097	148	203	383	488	3,846	46,148
CA	San Diego	1,014	489	1,097	170	203	377	485	3,836	46,027
CA	San Francisco	1,601	489	1,097	170	203	513	947	5,020	60,246
CA	San Jose	1,561	489	1,097	170	203	505	907	4,932	59,184
CA	San Luis Obispo-Atascadero-Paso Robles	1,009	489	1,097	158	203	377	476	3,809	45,709
CA	Santa Barbara-Santa Maria-Lompoc	1,207	489	1,097	148	203	420	579	4,143	49,722
CA	Santa Cruz-Watsonville	1,326	489	1,097	158	203	447	658	4,378	52,533
CA	Santa Rosa	1,153	489	1,097	148	203	408	550	4,049	48,583
CA	Stockton-Lodi	823	489	1,097	161	203	335	385	3,493	41,920
CA	Vallejo-Fairfield-Napa	1,045	489	1,097	148	203	385	492	3,859	46,307
CA	Ventura	1,055	489	1,097	161	203	397	507	3,910	46,915
CA	Visalia-Tulare-Porterville	706	489	1,097	148	203	308	322	3,274	39,288
CA	Yolo	920	489	1,097	158	203	357	432	3,656	43,871
CA	Yuba City	680	489	1,097	158	203	303	313	3,243	38,916
CA	Rural	779	489	1,097	197	203	326	378	3,470	41,638
CO	Boulder-Longmont	1,067	489	1,187	148	256	389	659	4,196	50,347
CO	Colorado Springs	868	489	1,187	148	256	345	567	3,860	46,325
CO	Denver	922	489	1,187	170	256	357	601	3,983	47,797
CO	Fort Collins-Loveland	911	489	1,187	158	256	355	591	3,947	47,361
CO	Grand Junction	693	489	1,187	158	256	311	492	3,586	43,036
CO	Greeley	807	489	1,187	158	256	332	543	3,772	45,265
CO	Pueblo	727	489	1,187	158	256	319	508	3,644	43,727
CO	Rural	765	489	1,187	197	256	327	540	3,762	45,141
CT	Bridgeport	878	489	1,367	148	230	369	634	4,115	49,374

TABLE A4.3 Basic family budgets for one parent, three children, 1999

State	Area name	Monthly expenses								Annual total
		Housing	Food	Child care	Trans.	Health care	Other necess.	Taxes	Total	
CT	Danbury	1,194	489	1,367	158	230	432	882	4,751	57,011
CT	Hartford	868	489	1,367	170	230	366	637	4,127	49,520
CT	New Haven-Meriden	1,005	489	1,367	161	230	395	714	4,360	52,315
CT	New London-Norwich (Conn. portion)	905	489	1,367	148	230	376	646	4,160	49,919
CT	Stamford-Norwalk	1,482	489	1,367	148	230	494	1,106	5,316	63,792
CT	Waterbury	917	489	1,367	158	230	379	660	4,199	50,386
CT	Worcester (Conn. portion)	789	489	1,367	148	230	347	584	3,954	47,448
CT	Rural	952	489	1,367	197	230	370	688	4,292	51,499
DC	Washington (D.C. portion)	1,118	489	1,434	157	323	406	1,188	5,114	61,368
DE	Dover	795	489	877	158	314	342	429	3,403	40,833
DE	Wilmington-Newark (Del. portion)	911	489	877	161	314	360	484	3,595	43,139
DE	Rural	761	489	877	197	314	331	427	3,395	40,746
FL	Daytona Beach	770	489	663	148	290	331	243	2,933	35,199
FL	Fort Lauderdale	971	489	663	170	290	368	319	3,269	39,231
FL	Fort Myers-Cape Coral	807	489	663	148	290	331	253	2,980	35,762
FL	Fort Pierce-Port St. Lucie	854	489	663	148	290	355	274	3,073	36,872
FL	Fort Walton Beach	678	489	663	158	290	306	211	2,794	33,533
FL	Gainesville	734	489	663	158	290	318	231	2,881	34,576
FL	Jacksonville	752	489	663	170	290	328	243	2,934	35,213
FL	Lakeland-Winter Haven	594	489	663	148	290	300	182	2,665	31,981
FL	Melbourne-Titusville-Palm Bay	758	489	663	148	290	327	238	2,912	34,945
FL	Miami	965	489	663	170	290	369	317	3,263	39,158
FL	Naples	1,018	489	663	158	290	378	332	3,327	39,925
FL	Ocala	657	489	663	158	290	306	205	2,767	33,207
FL	Orlando	891	489	663	170	290	362	293	3,158	37,893
FL	Panama City	638	489	663	158	290	306	199	2,743	32,913
FL	Pensacola	669	489	663	148	290	306	206	2,770	33,245
FL	Punta Gorda	855	489	663	158	290	342	274	3,070	36,838
FL	Sarasota-Bradenton	841	489	663	161	290	354	274	3,071	36,854
FL	Tallahassee	788	489	663	148	290	338	250	2,966	35,587
FL	Tampa-St. Petersburg-Clearwater	776	489	663	170	290	333	251	2,971	35,658
FL	West Palm Beach-Boca Raton	950	489	663	170	290	373	314	3,249	38,986
FL	Rural	648	489	663	197	290	311	215	2,813	33,754
GA	Albany	588	489	943	158	257	285	379	3,099	37,185
GA	Athens	706	489	943	158	257	312	437	3,301	39,618
GA	Atlanta	916	489	943	157	257	365	542	3,669	44,029
GA	Augusta-Aiken (Ga. portion)	683	489	943	148	257	307	422	3,250	38,996
GA	Columbus (Ga. portion)	607	489	943	148	257	295	387	3,126	37,515
GA	Macon	695	489	943	148	257	308	427	3,267	39,204
GA	Savannah	707	489	943	148	257	314	434	3,293	39,512
GA	Chattanooga (Ga. portion)	659	489	943	148	257	310	413	3,219	38,631
GA	Rural	559	489	943	197	257	284	383	3,112	37,340
HI	Honolulu	1,167	489	917	161	207	419	680	4,040	48,480
HI	Rural	1,252	489	917	197	207	448	747	4,256	51,075
IA	Cedar Rapids	688	489	843	158	230	305	385	3,096	37,149
IA	Davenport-Moline-Rock Island (Iowa portion)	617	489	843	148	230	299	351	2,976	35,712
IA	Des Moines	715	489	843	148	230	322	399	3,145	37,739
IA	Dubuque	581	489	843	158	230	293	326	2,918	35,019
IA	Iowa City	787	489	843	158	230	327	433	3,266	39,195
IA	Sioux City (Iowa portion)	635	489	843	158	230	309	365	3,028	36,339
IA	Waterloo-Cedar Falls	573	489	843	158	230	285	320	2,896	34,754
IA	Omaha (Iowa portion)	758	489	843	161	223	331	422	3,226	38,709
IA	Rural	534	489	843	197	230	281	319	2,892	34,700
ID	Boise City	750	489	1,075	148	264	319	492	3,536	42,428
ID	Pocatello	568	489	1,075	158	264	281	399	3,233	38,793
ID	Rural	604	489	1,075	197	264	291	437	3,356	40,275
IL	Bloomington-Normal	765	489	1,010	158	257	322	446	3,446	41,355
IL	Champaign-Urbana	808	489	1,010	158	257	334	465	3,520	42,238
IL	Chicago	922	489	1,010	157	257	380	519	3,734	44,808
IL	Decatur	604	489	1,010	158	257	290	379	3,186	38,235
IL	Kankakee	697	489	1,010	158	257	321	422	3,353	40,232
IL	Peoria-Pekin	735	489	1,010	148	257	323	432	3,394	40,727
IL	Rockford	703	489	1,010	148	257	325	422	3,353	40,239

TABLE A4.3 Basic family budgets for one parent, three children, 1999

State	Area name	Monthly expenses								Annual total
		Housing	Food	Child care	Trans.	Health care	Other necess.	Taxes	Total	
IL	Davenport-Moline-Rock Island (Ill. portion)	679	489	1,010	158	257	299	387	3,278	39,340
IL	St. Louis (Ill. portion)	617	489	1,010	148	257	307	398	3,226	38,707
IL	Springfield	652	489	1,010	170	257	310	416	3,304	39,644
IL	Rural	515	489	1,010	197	257	273	356	3,096	37,157
IN	Bloomington	876	489	880	158	220	347	460	3,430	41,154
IN	Elkhart-Goshen	682	489	880	158	220	317	381	3,126	37,514
IN	Evansville-Henderson (Ind. portion)	612	489	880	148	220	303	348	3,000	36,002
IN	Fort Wayne	646	489	880	148	220	307	362	3,051	36,614
IN	Gary	778	489	880	161	220	344	426	3,297	39,563
IN	Indianapolis	682	489	880	170	220	320	387	3,148	37,781
IN	Kokomo	675	489	880	158	220	314	378	3,113	37,360
IN	Lafayette	811	489	880	158	220	332	432	3,322	39,859
IN	Muncie	588	489	880	158	220	286	337	2,958	35,491
IN	South Bend	694	489	880	148	220	324	385	3,139	37,671
IN	Terre Haute	533	489	880	158	220	284	317	2,880	34,562
IN	Louisville (Ind. portion)	687	489	880	161	220	306	380	3,123	37,473
IN	Cincinnati (Ind. portion)	712	489	880	170	220	316	396	3,183	38,199
IN	Rural	541	489	880	197	220	282	333	2,942	35,300
KS	Lawrence	752	489	917	158	278	319	399	3,312	39,747
KS	Topeka	668	489	917	158	278	305	359	3,174	38,082
KS	Wichita	704	489	917	161	278	313	378	3,241	38,887
KS	Kansas City (Kan. portion)	739	489	917	170	278	317	398	3,309	39,708
KS	Rural	528	489	917	197	278	278	307	2,995	35,934
KY	[HUD FMR] Gallatin County	538	489	831	158	252	284	368	2,919	35,031
KY	[HUD FMR] Grant County	564	489	831	158	252	277	375	2,945	35,337
KY	Lexington	711	489	831	148	252	313	445	3,188	38,260
KY	Louisville (Ky. portion)	687	489	831	161	252	306	437	3,163	37,951
KY	Owensboro	545	489	831	158	252	277	368	2,919	35,029
KY	[HUD FMR] Pendleton County	501	489	831	158	252	275	349	2,854	34,251
KY	Evansville-Henderson (Ky. portion)	612	489	831	148	252	303	401	3,036	36,428
KY	Cincinnati (Ky. portion)	712	489	831	170	252	316	455	3,225	38,704
KY	Clarksville-Hopkinsville (Ky. portion)	605	489	831	158	252	289	396	3,019	36,230
KY	Huntington-Ashland (Ky. portion)	557	489	831	148	252	287	373	2,936	35,232
KY	Rural	484	489	831	197	252	267	355	2,874	34,487
LA	Alexandria	607	489	790	158	272	287	287	2,890	34,681
LA	Baton Rouge	648	489	790	161	272	296	306	2,962	35,546
LA	Houma	574	489	790	158	272	280	273	2,835	34,021
LA	Lafayette	551	489	790	148	272	275	260	2,785	33,423
LA	Lake Charles	725	489	790	158	272	323	341	3,098	37,175
LA	Monroe	608	489	790	158	272	291	289	2,897	34,764
LA	New Orleans	708	489	790	170	272	313	336	3,078	36,940
LA	[HUD FMR] St James Parish	516	489	790	158	272	280	252	2,756	33,077
LA	Shreveport-Bossier City	650	489	790	148	272	302	304	2,956	35,466
LA	Rural	486	489	790	197	272	266	250	2,750	33,005
MA	Barnstable-Yarmouth	1,040	489	1,353	158	308	409	850	4,606	55,276
MA	Boston (Mass. portion)	1,132	489	1,353	157	308	432	932	4,803	57,632
MA	Brockton	865	489	1,353	148	308	367	708	4,238	50,851
MA	Fitchburg-Leominster	790	489	1,353	158	308	342	672	4,111	49,329
MA	Lawrence (Mass. portion)	885	489	1,353	148	308	371	717	4,271	51,255
MA	Lowell (Mass. portion)	924	489	1,353	148	308	380	740	4,341	52,096
MA	New Bedford	785	489	1,353	158	308	346	671	4,110	49,318
MA	Pittsfield	702	489	1,353	158	308	325	630	3,964	47,568
MA	Springfield	811	489	1,353	161	308	353	686	4,160	49,919
MA	Worcester (Mass. portion)	789	489	1,353	148	308	347	670	4,104	49,246
MA	Providence-Fall River-Warwick (Mass. portion)	831	489	1,353	170	308	357	699	4,207	50,482
MA	Rural	892	489	1,353	197	308	368	743	4,350	52,200
MD	Baltimore	831	489	1,148	170	233	346	636	3,853	46,241
MD	[HUD FMR] Columbia	1,170	489	1,148	158	233	426	837	4,460	53,524
MD	Cumberland (Md. portion)	657	489	1,148	158	233	306	537	3,527	42,330
MD	Hagerstown	649	489	1,148	158	233	305	534	3,515	42,182
MD	Washington (Md. portion)	1,118	489	1,148	157	233	406	782	4,332	51,986
MD	Wilmington-Newark (Md. portion)	911	489	1,148	161	233	360	672	3,974	47,683
MD	Rural	751	489	1,148	197	233	327	604	3,748	44,976

TABLE A4.3 Basic family budgets for one parent, three children, 1999

State	Area name	Housing	Food	Child care	Trans.	Health care	Other necess.	Taxes	Total	Annual total
ME	Bangor	709	489	841	158	359	320	385	3,260	39,119
ME	Lewiston-Auburn	620	489	841	158	359	305	341	3,112	37,347
ME	Portland	802	489	841	158	359	350	437	3,435	41,225
ME	Portsmouth-Rochester (Maine portion)	910	489	841	158	359	372	494	3,622	43,459
ME	Rural	702	489	841	197	359	320	399	3,306	39,674
MI	Ann Arbor	915	489	903	161	210	368	479	3,525	42,298
MI	Benton Harbor	622	489	903	158	210	306	347	3,034	36,407
MI	Detroit	793	489	903	157	210	348	425	3,325	39,903
MI	Flint	666	489	903	148	210	313	362	3,091	37,096
MI	Grand Rapids-Muskegon-Holland	701	489	903	170	210	325	388	3,186	38,231
MI	Jackson	628	489	903	158	210	307	350	3,044	36,531
MI	Kalamazoo-Battle Creek	664	489	903	148	210	316	363	3,092	37,108
MI	Lansing-East Lansing	780	489	903	148	210	337	413	3,280	39,355
MI	Saginaw-Bay City-Midland	628	489	903	148	210	307	346	3,031	36,375
MI	Rural	564	489	903	197	210	286	333	2,982	35,780
MN	Duluth-Superior (Minn. portion)	613	489	1,544	158	277	294	536	3,911	46,932
MN	Minneapolis-St. Paul (Minn. portion)	901	489	1,544	170	277	358	702	4,442	53,299
MN	Rochester	788	489	1,544	158	277	328	614	4,197	50,369
MN	St. Cloud	621	489	1,544	158	277	304	544	3,937	47,239
MN	Fargo-Moorhead (Minn. portion)	763	489	1,544	158	277	322	612	4,165	49,983
MN	Grand Forks (Minn. portion)	739	489	1,544	158	277	318	600	4,125	49,499
MN	La Crosse (Minn. portion)	617	489	1,544	158	277	294	538	3,918	47,012
MN	Rural	560	489	1,544	197	277	289	529	3,886	46,626
MO	Columbia	660	489	866	158	214	299	364	3,049	36,587
MO	Joplin	511	489	866	158	214	272	296	2,805	33,664
MO	Kansas City (Mo. portion)	739	489	866	170	214	317	406	3,201	38,416
MO	St. Joseph	496	489	866	158	214	273	290	2,786	33,436
MO	St. Louis (Mo. portion)	652	489	866	170	214	307	369	3,067	36,802
MO	Springfield	601	489	866	148	214	286	333	2,937	35,244
MO	Rural	480	489	866	197	214	265	297	2,808	33,694
MS	Biloxi-Gulfport-Pascagoula	668	489	637	148	242	300	249	2,732	32,786
MS	Hattiesburg	534	489	637	158	242	275	181	2,516	30,186
MS	Jackson	670	489	637	148	242	308	252	2,746	32,948
MS	Memphis (Miss. portion)	736	489	637	170	242	316	289	2,879	34,548
MS	Rural	483	489	637	197	242	268	164	2,479	29,749
MT	Billings	673	489	877	158	317	307	443	3,263	39,161
MT	Great Falls	639	489	877	158	317	304	427	3,210	38,520
MT	Missoula	649	489	877	158	317	308	433	3,230	38,761
MT	Rural	620	489	877	197	317	297	433	3,230	38,764
NC	Asheville	701	489	672	158	257	318	275	2,869	34,429
NC	Charlotte-Gastonia-Rock Hill (N.C. portion)	726	489	672	170	257	322	292	2,928	35,142
NC	Fayetteville	659	489	672	148	257	299	245	2,768	33,220
NC	Goldsboro	552	489	672	158	257	284	189	2,601	31,215
NC	Greensboro--Winston-Salem--High Point	758	489	672	170	257	322	306	2,974	35,683
NC	Greenville	708	489	672	158	257	314	276	2,873	34,481
NC	Hickory-Morganton	615	489	672	148	257	303	228	2,711	32,534
NC	Jacksonville	638	489	672	158	257	294	238	2,745	32,941
NC	Raleigh-Durham-Chapel Hill	866	489	672	170	257	351	363	3,169	38,028
NC	Rocky Mount	568	489	672	158	257	284	196	2,623	31,482
NC	Wilmington	823	489	672	158	257	338	334	3,071	36,848
NC	Norfolk-Va Beach-Newpt News (N.C. portion)	803	489	672	170	257	330	328	3,049	36,588
NC	Rural	559	489	672	197	257	284	208	2,666	31,998
ND	Bismarck	700	489	983	158	211	307	447	3,295	39,544
ND	Fargo-Moorhead (N.D. portion)	763	489	983	158	211	322	483	3,409	40,907
ND	Grand Forks (N.D. portion)	739	489	983	158	211	318	470	3,367	40,409
ND	Rural	498	489	983	197	211	236	341	2,955	35,461
NE	Lincoln	697	489	764	161	223	314	278	2,927	35,119
NE	Omaha (Neb. portion)	758	489	764	161	223	331	308	3,034	36,402
NE	Sioux City (Neb. portion)	635	489	764	158	223	309	251	2,829	33,953
NE	Rural	519	489	764	197	223	277	209	2,679	32,144
NH	Manchester	846	489	1,199	158	367	361	456	3,876	46,515
NH	Nashua	1,053	489	1,199	158	367	391	526	4,183	50,194
NH	Portsmouth-Rochester (N.H. portion)	910	489	1,199	158	367	372	478	3,972	47,668

TABLE A4.3 Basic family budgets for one parent, three children, 1999

State	Area name	Housing	Food	Child care	Trans.	Health care	Other necess.	Taxes	Total	Annual total
NH	Boston (N.H. portion)	1,132	489	1,199	157	367	432	563	4,339	52,073
NH	Lawrence (N.H. portion)	885	489	1,199	148	367	371	468	3,927	47,122
NH	Lowell (N.H. portion)	924	489	1,199	148	367	380	482	3,989	47,867
NH	Rural	903	489	1,199	197	367	363	485	4,003	48,040
NJ	Atlantic-Cape May	926	489	845	148	230	381	398	3,417	41,001
NJ	Bergen-Passaic	1,170	489	845	170	230	424	498	3,826	45,912
NJ	Jersey City	986	489	845	161	230	392	425	3,528	42,339
NJ	Middlesex-Somerset-Hunterdon	1,304	489	845	170	230	449	549	4,037	48,443
NJ	Monmouth-Ocean	1,168	489	845	170	230	424	497	3,824	45,885
NJ	Newark	1,033	489	845	170	230	406	448	3,621	43,452
NJ	Trenton	1,097	489	845	148	230	403	460	3,672	44,065
NJ	Vineland-Millville-Bridgeton	862	489	845	158	230	366	376	3,325	39,905
NJ	Philadelphia (N.J. portion)	903	489	845	157	230	375	392	3,391	40,693
NM	Albuquerque	805	489	958	161	276	333	433	3,455	41,458
NM	Las Cruces	598	489	958	158	276	287	331	3,096	37,153
NM	Santa Fe	993	489	958	158	276	381	527	3,781	45,378
NM	Rural	567	489	958	197	276	284	333	3,103	37,240
NV	Las Vegas (Nev. portion)	965	489	805	170	269	366	352	3,416	40,993
NV	Reno	986	489	805	148	269	371	353	3,420	41,045
NV	Rural	845	489	805	197	269	345	318	3,267	39,208
NY	Albany-Schenectady-Troy	754	489	1,296	161	267	338	608	3,913	46,952
NY	Binghamton	634	489	1,296	158	267	306	543	3,692	44,309
NY	Buffalo-Niagara Falls	634	489	1,296	170	267	309	550	3,714	44,574
NY	Dutchess County	1,140	489	1,296	148	267	423	854	4,617	55,409
NY	Elmira	621	489	1,296	158	267	303	536	3,670	44,042
NY	Glens Falls	707	489	1,296	158	267	327	582	3,825	45,905
NY	Jamestown	621	489	1,296	158	267	300	535	3,666	43,990
NY	Nassau-Suffolk	1,537	489	1,296	170	267	494	1,216	5,470	65,635
NY	New York	1,114	489	1,296	157	267	428	845	4,595	55,144
NY	Newburgh (N.Y. portion)	903	489	1,296	148	267	372	680	4,155	49,857
NY	Rochester	777	489	1,296	170	267	339	622	3,961	47,531
NY	Syracuse	726	489	1,296	161	267	328	592	3,859	46,305
NY	Utica-Rome	621	489	1,296	148	267	303	532	3,656	43,876
NY	Rural	705	489	1,296	197	267	319	595	3,868	46,419
OH	Akron	693	489	1,027	161	199	323	383	3,274	39,293
OH	Canton-Massillon	590	489	1,027	148	199	298	331	3,081	36,972
OH	Cincinnati (Ohio portion)	712	489	1,027	170	199	316	391	3,304	39,643
OH	Cleveland-Lorain-Elyria	755	489	1,027	170	199	336	441	3,417	40,999
OH	Columbus	702	489	1,027	170	199	323	390	3,299	39,592
OH	Dayton-Springfield	700	489	1,027	161	199	320	384	3,279	39,346
OH	Hamilton-Middletown	708	489	1,027	148	199	327	385	3,282	39,389
OH	Lima	571	489	1,027	158	199	290	325	3,058	36,694
OH	Mansfield	541	489	1,027	158	199	286	312	3,011	36,126
OH	Steubenville-Weirton (Ohio portion)	535	489	1,027	158	199	281	308	2,996	35,955
OH	Toledo	680	489	1,027	161	199	315	375	3,246	38,946
OH	Youngstown-Warren	552	489	1,027	161	199	288	318	3,033	36,392
OH	Huntington-Ashland (Ohio portion)	557	489	1,027	148	199	287	315	3,021	36,252
OH	Parkersburg-Marietta (Ohio portion)	541	489	1,027	158	199	281	310	3,004	36,044
OH	Wheeling (Ohio portion)	535	489	1,027	158	199	281	308	2,996	35,955
OH	Rural	550	489	1,027	197	199	284	329	3,075	36,898
OK	Enid	554	489	827	158	237	275	311	2,851	34,212
OK	Lawton	651	489	827	158	237	297	361	3,019	36,234
OK	Oklahoma City	651	489	827	170	237	297	366	3,037	36,447
OK	Tulsa	724	489	827	161	237	313	399	3,150	37,800
OK	Fort Smith (Okla. portion)	540	489	827	158	237	277	306	2,834	34,005
OK	Rural	487	489	827	197	237	264	295	2,797	33,560
OR	Eugene-Springfield	833	489	809	148	245	337	532	3,393	40,718
OR	Medford-Ashland	835	489	809	158	245	338	538	3,411	40,938
OR	Portland-Vancouver (Ore. portion)	897	489	809	158	245	351	571	3,520	42,239
OR	Salem	782	489	809	148	245	328	506	3,307	39,685
OR	Rural	723	489	809	197	245	313	496	3,272	39,269
PA	Allentown-Bethlehem-Easton	871	489	1,068	161	203	359	510	3,661	43,929
PA	Altoona	562	489	1,068	158	203	285	378	3,143	37,714

TABLE A4.3 Basic family budgets for one parent, three children, 1999

State	Area name	Monthly expenses								Annual total
		Housing	Food	Child care	Trans.	Health care	Other necess.	Taxes	Total	
PA	Erie	569	489	1,068	148	203	288	378	3,144	37,724
PA	Harrisburg-Lebanon-Carlisle	704	489	1,068	161	203	325	441	3,391	40,693
PA	Johnstown	569	489	1,068	158	203	288	381	3,156	37,867
PA	Lancaster	752	489	1,068	148	203	330	455	3,445	41,342
PA	Philadelphia (Pa. portion)	903	489	1,068	157	203	375	525	3,720	44,645
PA	Pittsburgh	620	489	1,068	170	203	305	409	3,264	39,174
PA	Reading	679	489	1,068	148	203	320	427	3,334	40,008
PA	Scranton--Wilkes-Barre--Hazelton	599	489	1,068	161	203	300	397	3,217	38,608
PA	Sharon	569	489	1,068	158	203	288	381	3,156	37,867
PA	State College	818	489	1,068	158	203	345	486	3,567	42,798
PA	Williamsport	569	489	1,068	158	203	288	381	3,156	37,876
PA	York	678	489	1,068	148	203	320	426	3,333	39,992
PA	Newburgh (Pa. portion)	903	489	1,068	148	203	372	521	3,704	44,453
PA	Rural	600	489	1,068	197	203	293	407	3,258	39,100
RI	Providence-Fall River-Warwick (R.I. portion)	831	489	1,226	170	348	357	560	3,981	47,775
RI	New London-Norwich (R.I. portion)	905	489	1,226	148	348	376	585	4,077	48,929
RI	Rural	1,056	489	1,226	197	348	408	690	4,415	52,983
SC	Charleston-North Charleston	710	489	911	161	223	317	316	3,127	37,519
SC	Columbia	719	489	911	161	223	320	321	3,144	37,726
SC	Florence	587	489	911	158	223	297	254	2,919	35,027
SC	Greenville-Spartanburg-Anderson	609	489	911	161	223	301	266	2,961	35,527
SC	Myrtle Beach	686	489	911	158	223	322	306	3,094	37,133
SC	Sumter	592	489	911	158	223	286	251	2,910	34,917
SC	Augusta-Aiken (S.C. portion)	683	489	911	148	223	307	295	3,056	36,676
SC	Charlotte-Gastonia-Rock Hill (S.C. portion)	726	489	911	170	223	322	329	3,170	38,044
SC	Rural	543	489	911	197	223	283	246	2,892	34,706
SD	Rapid City	752	489	735	158	257	323	249	2,963	35,552
SD	Sioux Falls	748	489	735	158	257	335	252	2,973	35,672
SD	Rural	577	489	735	197	257	286	199	2,740	32,874
TN	Chattanooga (Tenn. portion)	659	489	874	148	230	310	248	2,958	35,498
TN	Clarksville-Hopkinsville (Tenn. portion)	605	489	874	158	230	289	229	2,874	34,485
TN	Jackson	639	489	874	158	230	295	241	2,925	35,104
TN	Johnson City-Kingsport-Bristol (Tenn. portion)	581	489	874	148	230	290	220	2,832	33,985
TN	Knoxville	624	489	874	161	230	297	238	2,913	34,952
TN	Memphis (Tenn. portion)	736	489	874	170	230	316	279	3,095	37,135
TN	Nashville	853	489	874	170	230	346	322	3,284	39,412
TN	Rural	480	489	874	197	230	265	197	2,732	32,782
TX	Abilene	646	489	796	158	272	300	234	2,893	34,722
TX	Amarillo	618	489	796	158	272	289	222	2,843	34,115
TX	Austin-San Marcos	970	489	796	170	272	368	352	3,417	41,006
TX	Beaumont-Port Arthur	628	489	796	148	272	298	225	2,856	34,272
TX	Brazoria	862	489	796	158	272	343	310	3,229	38,747
TX	Brownsville-Harlingen-San Benito	666	489	796	148	272	316	241	2,928	35,140
TX	Bryan-College Station	771	489	796	158	272	323	277	3,085	37,018
TX	Corpus Christi	752	489	796	148	272	323	269	3,048	36,571
TX	Dallas	994	489	796	157	272	374	357	3,438	41,260
TX	El Paso	730	489	796	161	272	315	264	3,026	36,308
TX	Fort Worth-Arlington	820	489	796	170	272	334	298	3,179	38,145
TX	Galveston-Texas City	780	489	796	158	272	326	280	3,100	37,201
TX	Houston	837	489	796	157	272	338	300	3,189	38,262
TX	Killeen-Temple	726	489	796	148	272	313	258	3,002	36,023
TX	Laredo	606	489	796	158	272	302	222	2,844	34,131
TX	Longview-Marshall	599	489	796	158	272	288	216	2,817	33,801
TX	Lubbock	695	489	796	158	272	306	250	2,965	35,579
TX	McAllen-Edinburg-Mission	522	489	796	161	272	281	193	2,713	32,554
TX	Odessa-Midland	652	489	796	158	272	297	234	2,897	34,768
TX	San Angelo	600	489	796	158	272	287	216	2,817	33,807
TX	San Antonio	771	489	796	170	272	323	281	3,102	37,220
TX	Sherman-Denison	595	489	796	158	272	296	217	2,822	33,869
TX	Texarkana (Texas portion)	604	489	796	158	272	293	219	2,831	33,971
TX	Tyler	660	489	796	158	272	299	237	2,910	34,926
TX	Victoria	619	489	796	158	272	290	223	2,845	34,145
TX	Waco	659	489	796	158	272	305	239	2,917	35,002

TABLE A4.3 Basic family budgets for one parent, three children, 1999

State	Area name	Housing	Food	Child care	Trans.	Health care	Other necess.	Taxes	Total	Annual total
TX	Wichita Falls	607	489	796	158	272	293	220	2,834	34,006
TX	Rural	533	489	796	197	272	274	204	2,765	33,174
UT	[HUD FMR] Kane County	630	489	762	158	259	297	347	2,941	35,291
UT	Provo-Orem	766	489	762	148	259	323	409	3,156	37,867
UT	Salt Lake City-Ogden	884	489	762	170	259	348	477	3,389	40,672
UT	Flagstaff (Utah portion)	797	489	762	158	259	336	431	3,231	38,768
UT	Rural	670	489	762	197	259	307	384	3,068	36,813
VA	Charlottesville	857	489	929	158	238	351	492	3,514	42,167
VA	Danville	578	489	929	158	238	285	355	3,032	36,379
VA	Lynchburg	578	489	929	158	238	288	356	3,035	36,424
VA	Norfolk-Va Beach-Newpt News (Va. portion)	803	489	929	170	238	330	467	3,426	41,115
VA	Richmond-Petersburg	863	489	929	161	238	344	493	3,516	42,193
VA	Roanoke	610	489	929	158	238	299	373	3,095	37,142
VA	Washington (Va. portion)	1,118	489	929	157	238	406	617	3,953	47,439
VA	Johnson City-Kingsport-Bristol (Va. portion)	581	489	929	148	238	290	355	3,029	36,352
VA	Rural	600	489	929	197	238	290	381	3,123	37,480
VT	Burlington	943	489	821	158	429	366	476	3,681	44,168
VT	Rural	789	489	821	197	429	338	424	3,486	41,832
WA	Bellingham	942	489	1,018	158	243	363	395	3,608	43,292
WA	Bremerton	838	489	1,018	158	243	344	359	3,448	41,381
WA	Olympia	901	489	1,018	158	243	355	381	3,544	42,526
WA	Richland-Kennewick-Pasco	940	489	1,018	158	243	361	394	3,602	43,227
WA	Seattle-Bellevue-Everett	1,022	489	1,018	170	243	380	427	3,749	44,992
WA	Spokane	705	489	1,018	148	243	312	308	3,224	38,684
WA	Tacoma	815	489	1,018	161	243	333	350	3,409	40,912
WA	Yakima	728	489	1,018	158	243	320	320	3,275	39,303
WA	Portland-Vancouver (Wash. portion)	897	489	1,018	158	243	351	379	3,535	42,416
WA	Rural	685	489	1,018	197	243	312	317	3,260	39,121
WI	Appleton-Oshkosh-Neenah	625	489	996	148	208	305	502	3,274	39,286
WI	Eau Claire	626	489	996	158	208	303	506	3,286	39,430
WI	Green Bay	736	489	996	158	208	316	560	3,463	41,554
WI	Janesville-Beloit	682	489	996	158	208	320	538	3,392	40,702
WI	Kenosha	794	489	996	158	208	330	592	3,567	42,809
WI	La Crosse (Wis. portion)	617	489	996	158	208	294	498	3,261	39,130
WI	Madison	914	489	996	148	208	355	652	3,763	45,151
WI	Milwaukee-Waukesha	758	489	996	170	208	339	586	3,547	42,559
WI	Racine	691	489	996	158	208	317	541	3,400	40,805
WI	Sheboygan	593	489	996	158	208	299	490	3,233	38,792
WI	Wausau	654	489	996	158	208	300	517	3,323	39,871
WI	Duluth-Superior (Wis. portion)	613	489	996	158	208	294	496	3,254	39,051
WI	Minneapolis-St. Paul (Wis. portion)	901	489	996	170	208	358	657	3,779	45,354
WI	Rural	553	489	996	197	208	285	483	3,212	38,544
WV	[HUD FMR] Berkeley County	629	489	888	158	253	308	369	3,093	37,120
WV	Charleston	673	489	888	148	253	303	380	3,135	37,614
WV	Huntington-Ashland (W.Va. portion)	557	489	888	148	253	287	331	2,953	35,434
WV	[HUD FMR] Jefferson County	723	489	888	158	253	324	410	3,244	38,932
WV	Parkersburg-Marietta (W.Va. portion)	541	489	888	158	253	281	326	2,935	35,225
WV	Wheeling (W.Va. portion)	535	489	888	158	253	281	324	2,928	35,137
WV	Washington (W.Va. portion)	1,118	489	888	157	253	406	588	3,898	46,775
WV	Cumberland (W.Va. portion)	657	489	888	158	253	306	379	3,129	37,545
WV	Steubenville-Weirton (W.Va. portion)	535	489	888	158	253	281	324	2,928	35,137
WV	Rural	485	489	888	197	253	268	315	2,894	34,728
WY	Casper	642	489	692	158	290	297	206	2,773	33,275
WY	Cheyenne	764	489	692	158	290	337	254	2,983	35,793
WY	Rural	594	489	692	197	290	289	202	2,752	33,029

Source: Author's calculations (see Appendix A)

TABLE A4.4 Basic family budgets for two parents, one child, 1999

State	Area name	Housing	Food	Child care	Trans.	Health care	Other necess.	Taxes	Total	Annual total
									Monthly expenses	
AK	Anchorage	773	388	616	208	262	360	408	3,015	36,181
AK	Rural	783	388	616	277	262	363	432	3,122	37,460
AL	Anniston	381	388	295	222	331	238	236	2,091	25,095
AL	Birmingham	481	388	295	226	331	269	322	2,313	27,755
AL	Decatur	436	388	295	222	331	256	294	2,221	26,651
AL	Dothan	394	388	295	222	331	242	249	2,121	25,454
AL	Florence	429	388	295	222	331	253	287	2,205	26,457
AL	Gadsden	364	388	295	222	331	233	220	2,052	24,628
AL	Huntsville	518	388	295	208	331	281	336	2,357	28,286
AL	Mobile	482	388	295	226	331	270	323	2,315	27,776
AL	Montgomery	496	388	295	208	331	274	323	2,315	27,781
AL	Tuscaloosa	482	388	295	222	331	270	321	2,308	27,700
AL	Columbus (Ala. portion)	464	388	295	208	331	264	307	2,258	27,094
AL	Rural	360	388	295	277	331	232	257	2,140	25,684
AR	Fayetteville-Springdale-Rogers	506	388	325	208	221	277	231	2,157	25,883
AR	Fort Smith (Ark. portion)	404	388	325	222	221	246	138	1,943	23,319
AR	Jonesboro	397	388	325	222	221	243	131	1,927	23,126
AR	Little Rock-North Little Rock	497	388	325	226	221	274	238	2,169	26,033
AR	Pine Bluff	450	388	325	222	221	260	186	2,052	24,623
AR	Memphis (Ark. portion)	530	388	325	240	221	285	278	2,267	27,198
AR	Texarkana (Ark. portion)	458	388	325	222	221	262	194	2,070	24,841
AR	Rural	368	388	325	277	221	234	144	1,958	23,491
AZ	Flagstaff	594	388	353	222	221	304	294	2,376	28,512
AZ	Phoenix-Mesa	634	388	353	240	221	317	318	2,471	29,647
AZ	Tucson	603	388	353	226	221	307	299	2,398	28,777
AZ	Yuma	563	388	353	222	221	295	277	2,319	27,827
AZ	Las Vegas (Ariz. portion)	693	388	353	240	221	335	344	2,574	30,892
AZ	Rural	495	388	353	277	221	274	266	2,274	27,292
CA	Bakersfield	508	388	476	226	224	278	260	2,359	28,312
CA	Chico-Paradise	564	388	476	222	224	295	280	2,449	29,382
CA	Fresno	500	388	476	226	224	275	257	2,346	28,148
CA	Los Angeles-Long Beach	749	388	476	221	224	353	366	2,775	33,305
CA	Merced	538	388	476	222	224	287	270	2,404	28,849
CA	Modesto	572	388	476	208	224	298	279	2,445	29,335
CA	Oakland	861	388	476	240	224	387	426	3,001	36,014
CA	Orange County	871	388	476	240	224	390	430	3,019	36,227
CA	Redding	519	388	476	222	224	281	262	2,372	28,462
CA	Riverside-San Bernardino	597	388	476	221	224	305	294	2,505	30,054
CA	Sacramento	613	388	476	240	224	310	308	2,558	30,700
CA	Salinas	746	388	476	208	224	352	360	2,753	33,035
CA	San Diego	729	388	476	240	224	346	363	2,765	33,185
CA	San Francisco	1,167	388	476	240	224	482	571	3,548	42,572
CA	San Jose	1,139	388	476	240	224	473	558	3,498	41,972
CA	San Luis Obispo-Atascadero-Paso Robles	727	388	476	222	224	346	355	2,737	32,848
CA	Santa Barbara-Santa Maria-Lompoc	867	388	476	208	224	389	417	2,969	35,629
CA	Santa Cruz-Watsonville	954	388	476	222	224	416	463	3,143	37,712
CA	Santa Rosa	829	388	476	208	224	377	399	2,901	34,815
CA	Stockton-Lodi	592	388	476	226	224	304	294	2,503	30,039
CA	Vallejo-Fairfield-Napa	753	388	476	208	224	354	363	2,766	33,186
CA	Ventura	793	388	476	226	224	366	389	2,862	34,339
CA	Visalia-Tulare-Porterville	506	388	476	208	224	277	251	2,330	27,960
CA	Yolo	664	388	476	222	224	326	326	2,625	31,499
CA	Yuba City	488	388	476	222	224	272	248	2,317	27,802
CA	Rural	564	388	476	277	224	295	298	2,521	30,252
CO	Boulder-Longmont	766	388	451	208	242	358	448	2,862	34,339
CO	Colorado Springs	623	388	451	208	242	313	377	2,604	31,242
CO	Denver	664	388	451	240	242	326	410	2,721	32,649
CO	Fort Collins-Loveland	656	388	451	222	242	324	399	2,682	32,179
CO	Grand Junction	515	388	451	222	242	280	329	2,427	29,125
CO	Greeley	582	388	451	222	242	301	362	2,548	30,576
CO	Pueblo	540	388	451	222	242	288	342	2,472	29,667
CO	Rural	567	388	451	277	242	296	376	2,598	31,175
CT	Bridgeport	703	388	568	208	222	338	376	2,804	33,645

TABLE A4.4 Basic family budgets for two parents, one child, 1999

State	Area name	Housing	Food	Child care	Trans.	Health care	Other necess.	Taxes	Total	Annual total
CT	Danbury	905	388	568	222	222	401	467	3,172	38,068
CT	Hartford	692	388	568	240	222	335	381	2,826	33,913
CT	New Haven-Meriden	785	388	568	226	222	364	417	2,970	35,640
CT	New London-Norwich (Conn. portion)	723	388	568	208	222	344	385	2,838	34,061
CT	Stamford-Norwalk	1,106	388	568	208	222	463	561	3,517	42,199
CT	Waterbury	735	388	568	222	222	348	394	2,877	34,524
CT	Worcester (Conn. portion)	632	388	568	208	222	316	342	2,676	32,116
CT	Rural	705	388	568	277	222	339	399	2,899	34,783
DC	Washington (D.C. portion)	820	388	650	221	329	375	717	3,500	41,998
DE	Dover	613	388	413	222	312	310	370	2,628	31,533
DE	Wilmington-Newark (Del. portion)	671	388	413	226	312	328	399	2,737	32,848
DE	Rural	579	388	413	277	312	300	374	2,642	31,708
FL	Daytona Beach	580	388	340	208	281	300	259	2,357	28,285
FL	Fort Lauderdale	698	388	340	240	281	337	314	2,597	31,168
FL	Fort Myers-Cape Coral	578	388	340	208	281	300	258	2,354	28,243
FL	Fort Pierce-Port St. Lucie	657	388	340	208	281	324	289	2,487	29,848
FL	Fort Walton Beach	500	388	340	222	281	275	228	2,234	26,810
FL	Gainesville	536	388	340	222	281	287	244	2,297	27,567
FL	Jacksonville	569	388	340	240	281	297	264	2,379	28,547
FL	Lakeland-Winter Haven	479	388	340	208	281	269	199	2,164	25,971
FL	Melbourne-Titusville-Palm Bay	566	388	340	208	281	296	251	2,331	27,969
FL	Miami	702	388	340	240	281	338	315	2,604	31,250
FL	Naples	732	388	340	222	281	347	321	2,632	31,581
FL	Ocala	500	388	340	222	281	275	228	2,234	26,810
FL	Orlando	678	388	340	240	281	331	306	2,564	30,762
FL	Panama City	500	388	340	222	281	275	228	2,234	26,810
FL	Pensacola	500	388	340	208	281	275	219	2,212	26,548
FL	Punta Gorda	616	388	340	222	281	311	277	2,435	29,223
FL	Sarasota-Bradenton	654	388	340	226	281	323	293	2,506	30,067
FL	Tallahassee	603	388	340	208	281	307	268	2,396	28,751
FL	Tampa-St. Petersburg-Clearwater	584	388	340	240	281	301	270	2,404	28,852
FL	West Palm Beach-Boca Raton	715	388	340	240	281	342	320	2,626	31,514
FL	Rural	514	388	340	277	281	280	252	2,332	27,985
GA	Albany	431	388	379	222	254	254	267	2,194	26,330
GA	Athens	517	388	379	222	254	281	326	2,366	28,394
GA	Atlanta	688	388	379	221	254	334	416	2,679	32,146
GA	Augusta-Aiken (Ga. portion)	503	388	379	208	254	276	311	2,319	27,827
GA	Columbus (Ga. portion)	464	388	379	208	254	264	290	2,247	26,965
GA	Macon	504	388	379	208	254	277	311	2,321	27,847
GA	Savannah	524	388	379	208	254	283	324	2,360	28,322
GA	Chattanooga (Ga. portion)	510	388	379	208	254	278	314	2,332	27,980
GA	Rural	429	388	379	277	254	253	299	2,279	27,346
HI	Honolulu	863	388	420	226	218	388	539	3,042	36,502
HI	Rural	955	388	420	277	218	416	616	3,291	39,495
IA	Cedar Rapids	494	388	459	222	223	273	309	2,369	28,427
IA	Davenport-Moline-Rock Island (Iowa portion)	477	388	459	208	223	268	293	2,317	27,807
IA	Des Moines	551	388	459	208	223	291	334	2,455	29,458
IA	Dubuque	455	388	459	222	223	261	287	2,296	27,553
IA	Iowa City	567	388	459	222	223	296	347	2,502	30,026
IA	Sioux City (Iowa portion)	509	388	459	222	223	278	316	2,396	28,753
IA	Waterloo-Cedar Falls	430	388	459	222	223	254	275	2,251	27,012
IA	Omaha (Iowa portion)	578	388	459	226	223	300	354	2,529	30,342
IA	Rural	419	388	459	277	223	250	290	2,307	27,679
ID	Boise City	540	388	312	208	280	288	272	2,289	27,462
ID	Pocatello	417	388	312	222	280	250	163	2,031	24,374
ID	Rural	450	388	312	277	280	260	245	2,212	26,539
IL	Bloomington-Normal	551	388	433	222	256	291	353	2,494	29,927
IL	Champaign-Urbana	589	388	433	222	256	303	370	2,561	30,732
IL	Chicago	737	388	433	221	256	349	436	2,820	33,845
IL	Decatur	447	388	433	222	256	259	303	2,308	27,696
IL	Kankakee	546	388	433	222	256	290	350	2,485	29,822
IL	Peoria-Pekin	553	388	433	208	256	292	349	2,480	29,754
IL	Rockford	559	388	433	208	256	294	352	2,490	29,880

TABLE A4.4 Basic family budgets for two parents, one child, 1999

State	Area name	Housing	Food	Child care	Trans.	Health care	Other necess.	Taxes	Total	Annual total
IL	Davenport-Moline-Rock Island (Ill. portion)	477	388	433	208	256	268	315	2,346	28,146
IL	St. Louis (Ill. portion)	501	388	433	240	256	276	336	2,430	29,161
IL	Springfield	510	388	433	222	256	278	334	2,422	29,061
IL	Rural	392	388	433	277	256	242	297	2,286	27,426
IN	Bloomington	631	388	394	222	214	316	380	2,544	30,532
IN	Elkhart-Goshen	533	388	394	222	214	286	334	2,371	28,447
IN	Evansville-Henderson (Ind. portion)	489	388	394	208	214	272	307	2,272	27,263
IN	Fort Wayne	501	388	394	208	214	276	312	2,293	27,518
IN	Gary	620	388	394	226	214	313	376	2,531	30,372
IN	Indianapolis	545	388	394	240	214	289	346	2,416	28,994
IN	Kokomo	525	388	394	222	214	283	331	2,356	28,277
IN	Lafayette	583	388	394	222	214	301	357	2,459	29,511
IN	Muncie	434	388	394	222	214	255	272	2,178	26,140
IN	South Bend	556	388	394	208	214	293	340	2,393	28,720
IN	Terre Haute	427	388	394	222	214	253	262	2,159	25,909
IN	Louisville (Ind. portion)	498	388	394	226	214	275	317	2,312	27,746
IN	Cincinnati (Ind. portion)	531	388	394	240	214	285	340	2,391	28,696
IN	Rural	420	388	394	277	214	251	299	2,243	26,910
KS	Lawrence	541	388	468	222	276	288	337	2,520	30,235
KS	Topeka	494	388	468	222	276	273	315	2,436	29,234
KS	Wichita	521	388	468	226	276	282	329	2,490	29,885
KS	Kansas City (Kan. portion)	534	388	468	240	276	286	340	2,532	30,378
KS	Rural	408	388	468	277	276	247	295	2,359	28,306
KY	[HUD FMR] Gallatin County	429	388	303	222	286	253	255	2,136	25,632
KY	[HUD FMR] Grant County	404	388	303	222	286	246	220	2,068	24,819
KY	Lexington	521	388	303	208	286	282	325	2,313	27,755
KY	Louisville (Ky. portion)	498	388	303	226	286	275	320	2,296	27,553
KY	Owensboro	406	388	303	222	286	246	222	2,073	24,875
KY	[HUD FMR] Pendleton County	399	388	303	222	286	244	215	2,057	24,678
KY	Evansville-Henderson (Ky. portion)	489	388	303	208	286	272	308	2,255	27,054
KY	Cincinnati (Ky. portion)	531	388	303	240	286	285	346	2,378	28,540
KY	Clarksville-Hopkinsville (Ky. portion)	443	388	303	222	286	258	272	2,171	26,054
KY	Huntington-Ashland (Ky. portion)	437	388	303	208	286	256	253	2,131	25,568
KY	Rural	374	388	303	277	286	236	241	2,105	25,259
LA	Alexandria	438	388	325	222	263	256	189	2,081	24,968
LA	Baton Rouge	467	388	325	226	263	265	218	2,152	25,826
LA	Houma	413	388	325	222	263	248	167	2,026	24,312
LA	Lafayette	400	388	325	208	263	244	143	1,972	23,661
LA	Lake Charles	553	388	325	222	263	292	274	2,317	27,805
LA	Monroe	451	388	325	222	263	260	200	2,109	25,310
LA	New Orleans	520	388	325	240	263	282	266	2,284	27,404
LA	[HUD FMR] St James Parish	414	388	325	222	263	249	168	2,028	24,339
LA	Shreveport-Bossier City	486	388	325	208	263	271	222	2,164	25,964
LA	Rural	370	388	325	277	263	235	166	2,024	24,288
MA	Barnstable-Yarmouth	831	388	616	222	387	378	640	3,462	41,545
MA	Boston (Mass. portion)	906	388	616	221	387	401	679	3,598	43,178
MA	Brockton	695	388	616	208	387	336	564	3,194	38,332
MA	Fitchburg-Leominster	614	388	616	222	387	311	527	3,065	36,782
MA	Lawrence (Mass. portion)	708	388	616	208	387	340	571	3,218	38,618
MA	Lowell (Mass. portion)	737	388	616	208	387	349	586	3,271	39,254
MA	New Bedford	628	388	616	222	387	315	535	3,091	37,088
MA	Pittsfield	560	388	616	222	387	294	500	2,967	35,600
MA	Springfield	649	388	616	226	387	322	547	3,136	37,626
MA	Worcester (Mass. portion)	632	388	616	208	387	316	532	3,079	36,953
MA	Providence-Fall River-Warwick (Mass. portion)	662	388	616	240	387	326	559	3,178	38,133
MA	Rural	697	388	616	277	387	337	593	3,295	39,538
MD	Baltimore	628	388	439	240	226	315	449	2,686	32,233
MD	[HUD FMR] Columbia	885	388	439	222	226	395	587	3,143	37,713
MD	Cumberland (Md. portion)	497	388	439	222	226	274	369	2,416	28,993
MD	Hagerstown	495	388	439	222	226	274	368	2,412	28,949
MD	Washington (Md. portion)	820	388	439	221	226	375	550	3,020	36,234
MD	Wilmington-Newark (Md. portion)	671	388	439	226	226	328	468	2,748	32,972
MD	Rural	565	388	439	277	226	295	430	2,621	31,452

TABLE A4.4 Basic family budgets for two parents, one child, 1999

State	Area name	Monthly expenses								Annual total
		Housing	Food	Child care	Trans.	Health care	Other necess.	Taxes	Total	
ME	Bangor	543	388	408	222	477	289	375	2,701	32,416
ME	Lewiston-Auburn	495	388	408	222	477	274	350	2,614	31,364
ME	Portland	641	388	408	222	477	319	429	2,884	34,606
ME	Portsmouth-Rochester (Maine portion)	710	388	408	222	477	340	467	3,012	36,147
ME	Rural	543	388	408	277	477	289	398	2,780	33,360
MI	Ann Arbor	698	388	470	226	203	337	434	2,756	33,074
MI	Benton Harbor	497	388	470	222	203	274	335	2,390	28,674
MI	Detroit	634	388	470	221	203	317	401	2,634	31,607
MI	Flint	521	388	470	208	203	282	342	2,414	28,971
MI	Grand Rapids-Muskegon-Holland	559	388	470	240	203	294	372	2,525	30,302
MI	Jackson	502	388	470	222	203	276	337	2,398	28,781
MI	Kalamazoo-Battle Creek	530	388	470	208	203	285	346	2,430	29,163
MI	Lansing-East Lansing	597	388	470	208	203	305	378	2,550	30,605
MI	Saginaw-Bay City-Midland	502	388	470	208	203	276	332	2,380	28,561
MI	Rural	433	388	470	277	203	254	324	2,350	28,196
MN	Duluth-Superior (Minn. portion)	459	388	588	222	262	263	277	2,458	29,499
MN	Minneapolis-St. Paul (Minn. portion)	666	388	588	240	262	327	395	2,866	34,392
MN	Rochester	569	388	588	222	262	297	339	2,664	31,968
MN	St. Cloud	491	388	588	222	262	273	285	2,508	30,098
MN	Fargo-Moorhead (Minn. portion)	550	388	588	222	262	291	329	2,629	31,553
MN	Grand Forks (Minn. portion)	536	388	588	222	262	287	316	2,598	31,179
MN	La Crosse (Minn. portion)	461	388	588	222	262	263	278	2,462	29,541
MN	Rural	444	388	588	277	262	258	287	2,504	30,044
MO	Columbia	475	388	343	222	208	268	233	2,136	25,637
MO	Joplin	388	388	343	222	208	241	140	1,930	23,158
MO	Kansas City (Mo. portion)	534	388	343	240	208	286	295	2,293	27,520
MO	St. Joseph	393	388	343	222	208	242	145	1,942	23,299
MO	St. Louis (Mo. portion)	501	388	343	240	208	276	275	2,231	26,769
MO	Springfield	435	388	343	208	208	255	183	2,021	24,246
MO	Rural	368	388	343	277	208	234	163	1,981	23,777
MS	Biloxi-Gulfport-Pascagoula	479	388	282	208	235	269	165	2,025	24,305
MS	Hattiesburg	398	388	282	222	235	244	95	1,863	22,352
MS	Jackson	504	388	282	208	235	277	189	2,082	24,989
MS	Memphis (Miss. portion)	530	388	282	240	235	285	241	2,199	26,393
MS	Rural	375	388	282	277	235	237	111	1,905	22,854
MT	Billings	501	388	361	222	295	276	317	2,360	28,321
MT	Great Falls	491	388	361	222	295	273	312	2,342	28,104
MT	Missoula	504	388	361	222	295	277	319	2,366	28,387
MT	Rural	470	388	361	277	295	266	323	2,381	28,575
NC	Asheville	538	388	325	222	259	287	295	2,314	27,770
NC	Charlotte-Gastonia-Rock Hill (N.C. portion)	551	388	325	240	259	291	312	2,366	28,393
NC	Fayetteville	476	388	325	208	259	268	235	2,160	25,919
NC	Goldsboro	429	388	325	222	259	253	191	2,068	24,810
NC	Greensboro--Winston-Salem--High Point	550	388	325	240	259	291	311	2,364	28,371
NC	Greenville	525	388	325	222	259	283	288	2,290	27,485
NC	Hickory-Morganton	488	388	325	208	259	272	252	2,192	26,303
NC	Jacksonville	460	388	325	222	259	263	229	2,146	25,754
NC	Raleigh-Durham-Chapel Hill	645	388	325	240	259	320	361	2,539	30,464
NC	Rocky Mount	429	388	325	222	259	253	191	2,068	24,810
NC	Wilmington	602	388	325	222	259	307	332	2,435	29,214
NC	Norfolk-Va Beach-Newpt News (N.C. portion)	576	388	325	240	259	299	325	2,412	28,943
NC	Rural	428	388	325	277	259	253	242	2,173	26,070
ND	Bismarck	503	388	377	222	216	276	269	2,251	27,012
ND	Fargo-Moorhead (N.D. portion)	550	388	377	222	216	291	295	2,339	28,062
ND	Grand Forks (N.D. portion)	536	388	377	222	216	287	286	2,311	27,735
ND	Rural	274	388	377	277	216	205	88	1,825	21,895
NE	Lincoln	525	388	313	226	217	283	186	2,139	25,671
NE	Omaha (Neb. portion)	578	388	313	226	217	300	247	2,269	27,229
NE	Sioux City (Neb. portion)	509	388	313	222	217	278	168	2,095	25,139
NE	Rural	405	388	313	277	217	246	91	1,936	23,236
NH	Manchester	677	388	480	222	343	330	359	2,800	33,596
NH	Nashua	774	388	480	222	343	360	397	2,964	35,568
NH	Portsmouth-Rochester (N.H. portion)	710	388	480	222	343	340	372	2,856	34,266

TABLE A4.4 Basic family budgets for two parents, one child, 1999

State	Area name	Housing	Food	Child care	Trans.	Health care	Other necess.	Taxes	Total	Annual total
NH	Boston (N.H. portion)	906	388	480	221	343	401	447	3,186	38,236
NH	Lawrence (N.H. portion)	708	388	480	208	343	340	367	2,835	34,018
NH	Lowell (N.H. portion)	737	388	480	208	343	349	378	2,884	34,607
NH	Rural	683	388	480	277	343	332	378	2,881	34,575
NJ	Atlantic-Cape May	739	388	438	208	265	349	393	2,780	33,359
NJ	Bergen-Passaic	878	388	438	240	265	393	462	3,062	36,747
NJ	Jersey City	776	388	438	226	265	361	414	2,868	34,414
NJ	Middlesex-Somerset-Hunterdon	960	388	438	240	265	418	496	3,204	38,453
NJ	Monmouth-Ocean	879	388	438	240	265	393	462	3,064	36,768
NJ	Newark	820	388	438	240	265	375	437	2,962	35,541
NJ	Trenton	810	388	438	208	265	371	423	2,903	34,835
NJ	Vineland-Millville-Bridgeton	692	388	438	222	265	335	377	2,716	32,593
NJ	Philadelphia (N.J. portion)	722	388	438	221	265	344	390	2,767	33,204
NM	Albuquerque	584	388	341	226	275	301	298	2,415	28,975
NM	Las Cruces	436	388	341	222	275	256	195	2,113	25,359
NM	Santa Fe	740	388	341	222	275	350	369	2,685	32,222
NM	Rural	427	388	341	277	275	253	230	2,192	26,303
NV	Las Vegas (Nev. portion)	693	388	405	240	270	335	328	2,659	31,906
NV	Reno	708	388	405	208	270	340	324	2,644	31,724
NV	Rural	623	388	405	277	270	313	312	2,589	31,062
NY	Albany-Schenectady-Troy	601	388	654	226	273	307	399	2,848	34,179
NY	Binghamton	498	388	654	222	273	275	347	2,657	31,880
NY	Buffalo-Niagara Falls	507	388	654	240	273	278	358	2,697	32,369
NY	Dutchess County	877	388	654	208	273	392	531	3,323	39,878
NY	Elmira	490	388	654	222	273	272	344	2,642	31,707
NY	Glens Falls	565	388	654	222	273	295	380	2,777	33,325
NY	Jamestown	480	388	654	222	273	269	339	2,624	31,492
NY	Nassau-Suffolk	1,105	388	654	240	273	463	718	3,841	46,088
NY	New York	891	388	654	221	273	397	599	3,422	41,061
NY	Newburgh (N.Y. portion)	712	388	654	208	273	341	447	3,023	36,279
NY	Rochester	606	388	654	240	273	308	407	2,876	34,506
NY	Syracuse	569	388	654	226	273	297	384	2,791	33,488
NY	Utica-Rome	489	388	654	208	273	272	338	2,622	31,465
NY	Rural	541	388	654	277	273	288	389	2,810	33,725
OH	Akron	554	388	358	226	194	292	267	2,279	27,351
OH	Canton-Massillon	472	388	358	208	194	267	177	2,064	24,762
OH	Cincinnati (Ohio portion)	531	388	358	240	194	285	261	2,256	27,077
OH	Cleveland-Lorain-Elyria	594	388	358	240	194	304	294	2,372	28,461
OH	Columbus	553	388	358	240	194	292	272	2,296	27,546
OH	Dayton-Springfield	542	388	358	226	194	288	262	2,258	27,094
OH	Hamilton-Middletown	566	388	358	208	194	296	266	2,276	27,312
OH	Lima	448	388	358	222	194	259	164	2,033	24,391
OH	Mansfield	433	388	358	222	194	255	145	1,994	23,930
OH	Steubenville-Weirton (Ohio portion)	419	388	358	222	194	250	132	1,963	23,552
OH	Toledo	528	388	358	226	194	284	252	2,230	26,758
OH	Youngstown-Warren	439	388	358	226	194	256	159	2,020	24,241
OH	Huntington-Ashland (Ohio portion)	437	388	358	208	194	256	140	1,980	23,762
OH	Parkersburg-Marietta (Ohio portion)	417	388	358	222	194	250	130	1,958	23,498
OH	Wheeling (Ohio portion)	419	388	358	222	194	250	132	1,963	23,552
OH	Rural	428	388	358	277	194	253	186	2,084	25,004
OK	Enid	398	388	313	222	228	244	153	1,945	23,341
OK	Lawton	469	388	313	222	228	266	232	2,117	25,406
OK	Oklahoma City	468	388	313	240	228	265	245	2,147	25,767
OK	Tulsa	520	388	313	226	228	282	293	2,250	27,001
OK	Fort Smith (Okla. portion)	404	388	313	222	228	246	159	1,959	23,511
OK	Rural	364	388	313	277	228	233	161	1,963	23,561
OR	Eugene-Springfield	597	388	410	208	293	305	413	2,615	31,383
OR	Medford-Ashland	601	388	410	222	293	307	447	2,668	32,013
OR	Portland-Vancouver (Ore. portion)	645	388	410	222	293	320	472	2,750	33,005
OR	Salem	568	388	410	208	293	296	396	2,561	30,728
OR	Rural	522	388	410	277	293	282	400	2,573	30,873
PA	Allentown-Bethlehem-Easton	669	388	514	226	195	328	423	2,743	32,919
PA	Altoona	431	388	514	222	195	254	313	2,316	27,793

TABLE A4.4 Basic family budgets for two parents, one child, 1999

State	Area name	Housing	Food	Child care	Trans.	Health care	Other necess.	Taxes	Total	Annual total
PA	Erie	441	388	514	208	195	257	313	2,316	27,789
PA	Harrisburg-Lebanon-Carlisle	559	388	514	226	195	294	374	2,550	30,600
PA	Johnstown	439	388	514	222	195	256	316	2,330	27,962
PA	Lancaster	576	388	514	208	195	299	376	2,556	30,668
PA	Philadelphia (Pa. portion)	722	388	514	221	195	344	445	2,829	33,947
PA	Pittsburgh	495	388	514	240	195	274	350	2,455	29,465
PA	Reading	544	388	514	208	195	289	361	2,499	29,993
PA	Scranton--Wilkes-Barre--Hazelton	480	388	514	226	195	269	339	2,411	28,933
PA	Sharon	439	388	514	222	195	256	316	2,330	27,962
PA	State College	624	388	514	222	195	314	402	2,658	31,895
PA	Williamsport	441	388	514	222	195	257	317	2,334	28,008
PA	York	544	388	514	208	195	289	361	2,499	29,993
PA	Newburgh (Pa. portion)	712	388	514	208	195	341	437	2,795	33,536
PA	Rural	458	388	514	277	195	262	346	2,440	29,282
RI	Providence-Fall River-Warwick (R.I. portion)	662	388	530	240	346	326	446	2,938	35,253
RI	New London-Norwich (R.I. portion)	723	388	530	208	346	344	463	3,004	36,048
RI	Rural	828	388	530	277	346	377	538	3,286	39,428
SC	Charleston-North Charleston	534	388	312	226	217	286	228	2,192	26,302
SC	Columbia	544	388	312	226	217	289	239	2,215	26,584
SC	Florence	470	388	312	222	217	266	155	2,030	24,358
SC	Greenville-Spartanburg-Anderson	483	388	312	226	217	270	171	2,068	24,815
SC	Myrtle Beach	549	388	312	222	217	291	240	2,219	26,627
SC	Sumter	433	388	312	222	217	255	114	1,941	23,288
SC	Augusta-Aiken (S.C. portion)	503	388	312	208	217	276	178	2,083	24,994
SC	Charlotte-Gastonia-Rock Hill (S.C. portion)	551	388	312	240	217	291	254	2,253	27,040
SC	Rural	425	388	312	277	217	252	152	2,022	24,269
SD	Rapid City	553	388	342	222	255	292	243	2,295	27,534
SD	Sioux Falls	591	388	342	222	255	304	260	2,362	28,338
SD	Rural	435	388	342	277	255	255	190	2,142	25,705
TN	Chattanooga (Tenn. portion)	510	388	341	208	223	278	188	2,137	25,642
TN	Clarksville-Hopkinsville (Tenn. portion)	443	388	341	222	223	258	141	2,016	24,189
TN	Jackson	462	388	341	222	223	264	157	2,056	24,673
TN	Johnson City-Kingsport-Bristol (Tenn. portion)	447	388	341	208	223	259	133	1,999	23,990
TN	Knoxville	468	388	341	226	223	265	165	2,076	24,917
TN	Memphis (Tenn. portion)	530	388	341	240	223	285	228	2,234	26,807
TN	Nashville	626	388	341	240	223	314	269	2,401	28,814
TN	Rural	365	388	341	277	223	233	108	1,936	23,227
TX	Abilene	479	388	316	222	264	269	181	2,119	25,433
TX	Amarillo	443	388	316	222	264	258	152	2,043	24,510
TX	Austin-San Marcos	699	388	316	240	264	337	302	2,546	30,554
TX	Beaumont-Port Arthur	474	388	316	208	264	267	169	2,087	25,043
TX	Brazoria	619	388	316	222	264	312	266	2,388	28,651
TX	Brownsville-Harlingen-San Benito	532	388	316	208	264	285	220	2,214	26,569
TX	Bryan-College Station	553	388	316	222	264	292	238	2,273	27,278
TX	Corpus Christi	552	388	316	208	264	291	234	2,254	27,049
TX	Dallas	718	388	316	221	264	343	304	2,554	30,648
TX	El Paso	527	388	316	226	264	284	227	2,233	26,793
TX	Fort Worth-Arlington	588	388	316	240	264	303	259	2,358	28,299
TX	Galveston-Texas City	562	388	316	222	264	295	242	2,288	27,461
TX	Houston	601	388	316	221	264	307	259	2,356	28,271
TX	Killeen-Temple	522	388	316	208	264	282	212	2,193	26,312
TX	Laredo	485	388	316	222	264	271	186	2,132	25,586
TX	Longview-Marshall	439	388	316	222	264	256	148	2,034	24,409
TX	Lubbock	499	388	316	222	264	275	198	2,162	25,946
TX	McAllen-Edinburg-Mission	418	388	316	226	264	250	131	1,994	23,923
TX	Odessa-Midland	469	388	316	222	264	266	173	2,098	25,177
TX	San Angelo	437	388	316	222	264	256	147	2,030	24,358
TX	San Antonio	554	388	316	240	264	292	244	2,298	27,578
TX	Sherman-Denison	466	388	316	222	264	265	171	2,092	25,100
TX	Texarkana (Texas portion)	458	388	316	222	264	262	164	2,075	24,894
TX	Tyler	476	388	316	222	264	268	179	2,113	25,356
TX	Victoria	446	388	316	222	264	259	154	2,049	24,587
TX	Waco	495	388	316	222	264	274	195	2,154	25,843

TABLE A4.4 Basic family budgets for two parents, one child, 1999

State	Area name	Housing	Food	Child care	Trans.	Health care	Other necess.	Taxes	Total	Annual total
					Monthly expenses					
TX	Wichita Falls	456	388	316	222	264	262	162	2,070	24,845
TX	Rural	396	388	316	277	264	243	148	2,033	24,397
UT	[HUD FMR] Kane County	470	388	358	222	262	266	296	2,262	27,146
UT	Provo-Orem	553	388	358	208	262	292	338	2,399	28,792
UT	Salt Lake City-Ogden	635	388	358	240	262	317	395	2,595	31,141
UT	Flagstaff (Utah portion)	594	388	358	222	262	304	366	2,494	29,927
UT	Rural	503	388	358	277	262	276	339	2,403	28,838
VA	Charlottesville	645	388	433	222	239	320	393	2,640	31,679
VA	Danville	431	388	433	222	239	254	283	2,250	26,996
VA	Lynchburg	440	388	433	222	239	257	287	2,266	27,192
VA	Norfolk-Va Beach-Newpt News (Va. portion)	576	388	433	240	239	299	365	2,540	30,479
VA	Richmond-Petersburg	620	388	433	226	239	313	382	2,601	31,211
VA	Roanoke	475	388	433	222	239	268	305	2,329	27,952
VA	Washington (Va. portion)	820	388	433	221	239	375	481	2,956	35,475
VA	Johnson City-Kingsport-Bristol (Va. portion)	447	388	433	208	239	259	286	2,260	27,121
VA	Rural	446	388	433	277	239	258	314	2,355	28,262
VT	Burlington	692	388	363	222	445	335	424	2,868	34,419
VT	Rural	601	388	363	226	445	307	383	2,712	32,541
WA	Bellingham	682	388	451	222	349	332	354	2,778	33,335
WA	Bremerton	620	388	451	222	349	313	331	2,673	32,075
WA	Olympia	655	388	451	222	349	323	344	2,732	32,787
WA	Richland-Kennewick-Pasco	675	388	451	222	349	330	352	2,766	33,193
WA	Seattle-Bellevue-Everett	736	388	451	240	349	349	380	2,893	34,712
WA	Spokane	519	388	451	208	349	281	288	2,485	29,815
WA	Tacoma	586	388	451	226	349	302	319	2,621	31,455
WA	Yakima	543	388	451	222	349	289	301	2,543	30,511
WA	Portland-Vancouver (Wash. portion)	645	388	451	222	349	320	340	2,715	32,583
WA	Rural	518	388	451	277	349	281	308	2,572	30,862
WI	Appleton-Oshkosh-Neenah	495	388	423	208	203	274	333	2,325	27,899
WI	Eau Claire	488	388	423	222	203	272	335	2,331	27,972
WI	Green Bay	530	388	423	222	203	285	362	2,412	28,948
WI	Janesville-Beloit	545	388	423	222	203	289	370	2,440	29,285
WI	Kenosha	577	388	423	222	203	299	388	2,500	30,002
WI	La Crosse (Wis. portion)	461	388	423	222	203	263	320	2,281	27,367
WI	Madison	658	388	423	208	203	324	428	2,633	31,593
WI	Milwaukee-Waukesha	605	388	423	240	203	308	411	2,578	30,940
WI	Racine	535	388	423	222	203	286	364	2,422	29,060
WI	Sheboygan	475	388	423	222	203	268	328	2,307	27,681
WI	Wausau	480	388	423	222	203	269	331	2,316	27,791
WI	Duluth-Superior (Wis. portion)	459	388	423	222	203	263	319	2,277	27,320
WI	Minneapolis-St. Paul (Wis. portion)	666	388	423	240	203	327	446	2,693	32,310
WI	Rural	430	388	423	277	203	254	327	2,302	27,626
WV	[HUD FMR] Berkeley County	504	388	316	222	231	277	283	2,221	26,657
WV	Charleston	490	388	316	208	231	272	256	2,163	25,951
WV	Huntington-Ashland (W.Va. portion)	437	388	316	208	231	256	205	2,042	24,499
WV	[HUD FMR] Jefferson County	556	388	316	222	231	293	313	2,319	27,831
WV	Parkersburg-Marietta (W.Va. portion)	417	388	316	222	231	250	195	2,019	24,232
WV	Wheeling (W.Va. portion)	419	388	316	222	231	250	197	2,024	24,288
WV	Washington (W.Va. portion)	820	388	316	221	231	375	443	2,794	33,525
WV	Cumberland (W.Va. portion)	497	388	316	222	231	274	277	2,206	26,466
WV	Steubenville-Weirton (W.Va. portion)	419	388	316	222	231	250	197	2,024	24,288
WV	Rural	375	388	316	277	231	237	195	2,019	24,233
WY	Casper	468	388	364	222	288	265	221	2,216	26,590
WY	Cheyenne	598	388	364	222	288	306	279	2,445	29,334
WY	Rural	445	388	364	277	288	258	234	2,254	27,047

Source: Author's calculations (see Appendix A)

TABLE A4.5 Basic family budgets for two parents, two children, 1999

State	Area name	Housing	Food	Child care	Trans.	Health care	Other necess.	Taxes	Total	Annual total
AK	Anchorage	$ 773	$ 510	$ 989	$ 208	$ 283	$ 398	$ 420	$ 3,581	$42,972
AK	Rural	783	510	989	277	283	401	444	3,687	44,249
AL	Anniston	381	510	552	222	366	276	290	2,596	31,155
AL	Birmingham	481	510	552	226	366	307	338	2,780	33,360
AL	Decatur	436	510	552	222	366	293	315	2,693	32,316
AL	Dothan	394	510	552	222	366	280	295	2,618	31,412
AL	Florence	429	510	552	222	366	291	312	2,681	32,167
AL	Gadsden	364	510	552	222	366	271	287	2,571	30,849
AL	Huntsville	518	510	552	208	366	319	349	2,822	33,859
AL	Mobile	482	510	552	226	366	307	339	2,782	33,381
AL	Montgomery	496	510	552	208	366	312	339	2,782	33,386
AL	Tuscaloosa	482	510	552	222	366	307	337	2,776	33,306
AL	Columbus (Ala. portion)	464	510	552	208	366	302	323	2,725	32,698
AL	Rural	360	510	552	277	366	270	299	2,633	31,594
AR	Fayetteville-Springdale-Rogers	506	510	525	208	236	315	237	2,537	30,444
AR	Fort Smith (Ark. portion)	404	510	525	222	236	283	176	2,355	28,263
AR	Jonesboro	397	510	525	222	236	281	171	2,341	28,097
AR	Little Rock-North Little Rock	497	510	525	226	236	312	240	2,546	30,555
AR	Pine Bluff	450	510	525	222	236	297	207	2,447	29,358
AR	Memphis (Ark. portion)	530	510	525	240	236	322	251	2,613	31,360
AR	Texarkana (Ark. portion)	458	510	525	222	236	300	212	2,462	29,546
AR	Rural	368	510	525	277	236	272	180	2,368	28,415
AZ	Flagstaff	594	510	555	222	235	342	259	2,716	32,587
AZ	Phoenix-Mesa	634	510	555	240	235	354	283	2,810	33,721
AZ	Tucson	603	510	555	226	235	345	265	2,738	32,852
AZ	Yuma	563	510	555	222	235	332	245	2,661	31,932
AZ	Las Vegas (Ariz. portion)	693	510	555	240	235	373	310	2,914	34,966
AZ	Rural	495	510	555	277	235	312	234	2,616	31,396
CA	Bakersfield	508	510	786	226	224	315	247	2,816	33,797
CA	Chico-Paradise	564	510	786	222	224	333	267	2,905	34,862
CA	Fresno	500	510	786	226	224	313	244	2,803	33,634
CA	Los Angeles-Long Beach	749	510	786	221	224	390	352	3,232	38,780
CA	Merced	538	510	786	222	224	325	257	2,861	34,335
CA	Modesto	572	510	786	208	224	335	266	2,902	34,818
CA	Oakland	861	510	786	240	224	425	412	3,457	41,489
CA	Orange County	871	510	786	240	224	428	417	3,475	41,702
CA	Redding	519	510	786	222	224	319	250	2,829	33,948
CA	Riverside-San Bernardino	597	510	786	221	224	343	280	2,960	35,521
CA	Sacramento	613	510	786	240	224	348	294	3,014	36,173
CA	Salinas	746	510	786	208	224	389	346	3,209	38,511
CA	San Diego	729	510	786	240	224	384	349	3,222	38,659
CA	San Francisco	1,167	510	786	240	224	520	566	4,012	48,138
CA	San Jose	1,139	510	786	240	224	511	551	3,960	47,520
CA	San Luis Obispo-Atascadero-Paso Robles	727	510	786	222	224	383	342	3,194	38,323
CA	Santa Barbara-Santa Maria-Lompoc	867	510	786	208	224	427	404	3,425	41,104
CA	Santa Cruz-Watsonville	954	510	786	222	224	454	450	3,599	43,187
CA	Santa Rosa	829	510	786	208	224	415	386	3,357	40,289
CA	Stockton-Lodi	592	510	786	226	224	341	279	2,959	35,505
CA	Vallejo-Fairfield-Napa	753	510	786	208	224	391	350	3,222	38,661
CA	Ventura	793	510	786	226	224	404	375	3,318	39,814
CA	Visalia-Tulare-Porterville	506	510	786	208	224	315	241	2,790	33,476
CA	Yolo	664	510	786	222	224	364	312	3,081	36,972
CA	Yuba City	488	510	786	222	224	309	238	2,777	33,319
CA	Rural	564	510	786	277	224	333	284	2,977	35,725
CO	Boulder-Longmont	766	510	819	208	260	395	479	3,437	41,246
CO	Colorado Springs	623	510	819	208	260	351	408	3,179	38,148
CO	Denver	664	510	819	240	260	364	440	3,296	39,556
CO	Fort Collins-Loveland	656	510	819	222	260	361	430	3,257	39,085
CO	Grand Junction	515	510	819	222	260	318	360	3,003	36,033
CO	Greeley	582	510	819	222	260	338	393	3,124	37,482
CO	Pueblo	540	510	819	222	260	325	372	3,048	36,574
CO	Rural	567	510	819	277	260	334	407	3,173	38,081
CT	Bridgeport	703	510	968	208	236	376	414	3,414	40,968

TABLE A4.5 Basic family budgets for two parents, two children, 1999

State	Area name	Housing	Food	Child care	Trans.	Health care	Other necess.	Taxes	Total	Annual total
CT	Danbury	905	510	968	222	236	438	517	3,794	45,531
CT	Hartford	692	510	968	240	236	372	423	3,439	41,273
CT	New Haven-Meriden	785	510	968	226	236	401	463	3,588	43,056
CT	New London-Norwich (Conn. portion)	723	510	968	208	236	382	426	3,452	41,422
CT	Stamford-Norwalk	1,106	510	968	208	236	501	616	4,143	49,718
CT	Waterbury	735	510	968	222	236	386	439	3,494	41,932
CT	Worcester (Conn. portion)	632	510	968	208	236	354	378	3,285	39,420
CT	Rural	705	510	968	277	236	377	445	3,516	42,192
DC	Washington (D.C. portion)	820	510	1,042	221	329	412	768	4,102	49,218
DE	Dover	613	510	645	222	343	348	349	3,029	36,346
DE	Wilmington-Newark (Del. portion)	671	510	645	226	343	366	382	3,142	37,700
DE	Rural	579	510	645	277	343	337	354	3,044	36,527
FL	Daytona Beach	580	510	501	208	306	338	210	2,652	31,829
FL	Fort Lauderdale	698	510	501	240	306	374	264	2,893	34,715
FL	Fort Myers-Cape Coral	578	510	501	208	306	337	209	2,649	31,789
FL	Fort Pierce-Port St. Lucie	657	510	501	208	306	362	240	2,783	33,395
FL	Fort Walton Beach	500	510	501	222	306	313	194	2,545	30,538
FL	Gainesville	536	510	501	222	306	324	199	2,597	31,164
FL	Jacksonville	569	510	501	240	306	334	215	2,674	32,093
FL	Lakeland-Winter Haven	479	510	501	208	306	306	177	2,487	29,848
FL	Melbourne-Titusville-Palm Bay	566	510	501	208	306	333	205	2,629	31,545
FL	Miami	702	510	501	240	306	376	266	2,900	34,796
FL	Naples	732	510	501	222	306	385	272	2,927	35,127
FL	Ocala	500	510	501	222	306	313	194	2,545	30,538
FL	Orlando	678	510	501	240	306	368	257	2,859	34,308
FL	Panama City	500	510	501	222	306	313	194	2,545	30,538
FL	Pensacola	500	510	501	208	306	313	188	2,526	30,313
FL	Punta Gorda	616	510	501	222	306	349	228	2,731	32,769
FL	Sarasota-Bradenton	654	510	501	226	306	361	244	2,801	33,613
FL	Tallahassee	603	510	501	208	306	345	219	2,692	32,298
FL	Tampa-St. Petersburg-Clearwater	584	510	501	240	306	339	221	2,700	32,398
FL	West Palm Beach-Boca Raton	715	510	501	240	306	380	271	2,922	35,060
FL	Rural	514	510	501	277	306	317	205	2,630	31,560
GA	Albany	431	510	661	222	270	292	283	2,667	32,001
GA	Athens	517	510	661	222	270	318	328	2,825	33,896
GA	Atlanta	688	510	661	221	270	371	417	3,137	37,648
GA	Augusta-Aiken (Ga. portion)	503	510	661	208	270	314	315	2,780	33,362
GA	Columbus (Ga. portion)	464	510	661	208	270	302	294	2,709	32,502
GA	Macon	504	510	661	208	270	314	316	2,782	33,385
GA	Savannah	524	510	661	208	270	320	326	2,819	33,825
GA	Chattanooga (Ga. portion)	510	510	661	208	270	316	319	2,793	33,516
GA	Rural	429	510	661	277	270	291	304	2,740	32,881
HI	Honolulu	863	510	668	226	232	425	509	3,434	41,205
HI	Rural	955	510	668	277	232	454	584	3,680	44,165
IA	Cedar Rapids	494	510	651	222	233	311	265	2,686	32,229
IA	Davenport-Moline-Rock Island (Iowa portion)	477	510	651	208	233	306	252	2,637	31,638
IA	Des Moines	551	510	651	208	233	329	289	2,770	33,244
IA	Dubuque	455	510	651	222	233	299	246	2,615	31,384
IA	Iowa City	567	510	651	222	233	334	302	2,818	33,812
IA	Sioux City (Iowa portion)	509	510	651	222	233	316	273	2,713	32,553
IA	Waterloo-Cedar Falls	430	510	651	222	233	291	239	2,576	30,910
IA	Omaha (Iowa portion)	578	510	651	226	233	337	309	2,844	34,128
IA	Rural	419	510	651	277	233	288	249	2,626	31,511
ID	Boise City	540	510	693	208	306	325	305	2,887	34,645
ID	Pocatello	417	510	693	222	306	287	242	2,677	32,121
ID	Rural	450	510	693	277	306	297	284	2,817	33,801
IL	Bloomington-Normal	551	510	722	222	277	329	352	2,962	35,545
IL	Champaign-Urbana	589	510	722	222	277	341	370	3,029	36,348
IL	Chicago	737	510	722	221	277	386	436	3,289	39,464
IL	Decatur	447	510	722	222	277	297	305	2,779	33,346
IL	Kankakee	546	510	722	222	277	327	350	2,953	35,439
IL	Peoria-Pekin	553	510	722	208	277	329	349	2,948	35,372
IL	Rockford	559	510	722	208	277	331	352	2,958	35,499

TABLE A4.5 Basic family budgets for two parents, two children, 1999

State	Area name	Housing	Food	Child care	Trans.	Health care	Other necess.	Taxes	Total	Annual total
IL	Davenport-Moline-Rock Island (Ill. portion)	477	510	722	208	277	306	314	2,814	33,765
IL	St. Louis (Ill. portion)	501	510	722	240	277	313	336	2,898	34,779
IL	Springfield	510	510	722	222	277	316	334	2,890	34,678
IL	Rural	392	510	722	277	277	279	300	2,756	33,075
IN	Bloomington	631	510	637	222	228	354	365	2,945	35,345
IN	Elkhart-Goshen	533	510	637	222	228	323	320	2,772	33,260
IN	Evansville-Henderson (Ind. portion)	489	510	637	208	228	310	295	2,676	32,107
IN	Fort Wayne	501	510	637	208	228	313	300	2,697	32,363
IN	Gary	620	510	637	226	228	350	362	2,932	35,185
IN	Indianapolis	545	510	637	240	228	327	332	2,817	33,807
IN	Kokomo	525	510	637	222	228	321	316	2,757	33,089
IN	Lafayette	583	510	637	222	228	339	343	2,860	34,323
IN	Muncie	434	510	637	222	228	292	276	2,598	31,175
IN	South Bend	556	510	637	208	228	330	326	2,794	33,532
IN	Terre Haute	427	510	637	222	228	290	275	2,588	31,051
IN	Louisville (Ind. portion)	498	510	637	226	228	312	305	2,716	32,591
IN	Cincinnati (Ind. portion)	531	510	637	240	228	323	325	2,793	33,511
IN	Rural	420	510	637	277	228	288	287	2,647	31,762
KS	Lawrence	541	510	693	222	301	326	302	2,893	34,720
KS	Topeka	494	510	693	222	301	311	280	2,810	33,721
KS	Wichita	521	510	693	226	301	319	294	2,864	34,368
KS	Kansas City (Kan. portion)	534	510	693	240	301	323	305	2,905	34,863
KS	Rural	408	510	693	277	301	285	260	2,733	32,793
KY	[HUD FMR] Gallatin County	429	510	567	222	286	291	282	2,586	31,028
KY	[HUD FMR] Grant County	404	510	567	222	286	283	276	2,547	30,564
KY	Lexington	521	510	567	208	286	319	321	2,732	32,779
KY	Louisville (Ky. portion)	498	510	567	226	286	312	316	2,715	32,574
KY	Owensboro	406	510	567	222	286	284	277	2,551	30,608
KY	[HUD FMR] Pendleton County	399	510	567	222	286	282	273	2,537	30,444
KY	Evansville-Henderson (Ky. portion)	489	510	567	208	286	310	304	2,673	32,073
KY	Cincinnati (Ky. portion)	531	510	567	240	286	323	339	2,794	33,527
KY	Clarksville-Hopkinsville (Ky. portion)	443	510	567	222	286	295	285	2,607	31,285
KY	Huntington-Ashland (Ky. portion)	437	510	567	208	286	293	281	2,582	30,986
KY	Rural	374	510	567	277	286	274	279	2,566	30,787
LA	Alexandria	438	510	558	222	283	294	214	2,517	30,200
LA	Baton Rouge	467	510	558	226	283	303	226	2,572	30,860
LA	Houma	413	510	558	222	283	286	199	2,470	29,634
LA	Lafayette	400	510	558	208	283	282	186	2,426	29,108
LA	Lake Charles	553	510	558	222	283	329	257	2,711	32,530
LA	Monroe	451	510	558	222	283	298	221	2,541	30,497
LA	New Orleans	520	510	558	240	283	319	248	2,677	32,120
LA	[HUD FMR] St James Parish	414	510	558	222	283	286	200	2,471	29,657
LA	Shreveport-Bossier City	486	510	558	208	283	309	227	2,579	30,951
LA	Rural	370	510	558	277	283	273	199	2,468	29,613
MA	Barnstable-Yarmouth	831	510	984	222	387	416	664	4,014	48,162
MA	Boston (Mass. portion)	906	510	984	221	387	439	703	4,150	49,795
MA	Brockton	695	510	984	208	387	373	588	3,746	44,949
MA	Fitchburg-Leominster	614	510	984	222	387	348	551	3,616	43,395
MA	Lawrence (Mass. portion)	708	510	984	208	387	377	595	3,770	45,236
MA	Lowell (Mass. portion)	737	510	984	208	387	386	610	3,823	45,872
MA	New Bedford	628	510	984	222	387	353	558	3,642	43,701
MA	Pittsfield	560	510	984	222	387	332	523	3,517	42,207
MA	Springfield	649	510	984	226	387	359	571	3,687	44,240
MA	Worcester (Mass. portion)	632	510	984	208	387	354	555	3,631	43,566
MA	Providence-Fall River-Warwick (Mass. portion)	662	510	984	240	387	363	583	3,729	44,751
MA	Rural	697	510	984	277	387	374	616	3,846	46,155
MD	Baltimore	628	510	794	240	240	353	473	3,237	38,839
MD	[HUD FMR] Columbia	885	510	794	222	240	432	611	3,693	44,319
MD	Cumberland (Md. portion)	497	510	794	222	240	312	391	2,965	35,579
MD	Hagerstown	495	510	794	222	240	311	390	2,961	35,533
MD	Washington (Md. portion)	820	510	794	221	240	412	574	3,570	42,839
MD	Wilmington-Newark (Md. portion)	671	510	794	226	240	366	492	3,298	39,578
MD	Rural	565	510	794	277	240	333	453	3,172	38,058

TABLE A4.5 Basic family budgets for two parents, two children, 1999

State	Area name	Housing	Food	Child care	Trans.	Health care	Other necess.	Taxes	Total	Annual total
ME	Bangor	543	510	625	222	477	326	331	3,033	36,394
ME	Lewiston-Auburn	495	510	625	222	477	311	304	2,943	35,320
ME	Portland	641	510	625	222	477	357	385	3,215	38,583
ME	Portsmouth-Rochester (Maine portion)	710	510	625	222	477	378	423	3,344	40,126
ME	Rural	543	510	625	277	477	326	354	3,112	37,338
MI	Ann Arbor	698	510	687	226	218	374	402	3,115	37,381
MI	Benton Harbor	497	510	687	222	218	312	303	2,748	32,980
MI	Detroit	634	510	687	221	218	354	369	2,993	35,914
MI	Flint	521	510	687	208	218	319	310	2,773	33,276
MI	Grand Rapids-Muskegon-Holland	559	510	687	240	218	331	340	2,884	34,609
MI	Jackson	502	510	687	222	218	314	306	2,757	33,088
MI	Kalamazoo-Battle Creek	530	510	687	208	218	322	314	2,789	33,469
MI	Lansing-East Lansing	597	510	687	208	218	343	347	2,909	34,912
MI	Saginaw-Bay City-Midland	502	510	687	208	218	314	301	2,739	32,867
MI	Rural	433	510	687	277	218	292	292	2,709	32,502
MN	Duluth-Superior (Minn. portion)	459	510	1,066	222	291	300	364	3,211	38,532
MN	Minneapolis-St. Paul (Minn. portion)	666	510	1,066	240	291	364	464	3,600	43,199
MN	Rochester	569	510	1,066	222	291	334	407	3,398	40,775
MN	St. Cloud	491	510	1,066	222	291	310	380	3,269	39,231
MN	Fargo-Moorhead (Minn. portion)	550	510	1,066	222	291	328	397	3,363	40,359
MN	Grand Forks (Minn. portion)	536	510	1,066	222	291	324	392	3,340	40,082
MN	La Crosse (Minn. portion)	461	510	1,066	222	291	301	365	3,215	38,574
MN	Rural	444	510	1,066	277	291	296	378	3,260	39,122
MO	Columbia	475	510	605	222	220	305	268	2,603	31,241
MO	Joplin	388	510	605	222	220	278	224	2,446	29,356
MO	Kansas City (Mo. portion)	534	510	605	240	220	323	304	2,735	32,820
MO	St. Joseph	393	510	605	222	220	280	228	2,456	29,476
MO	St. Louis (Mo. portion)	501	510	605	240	220	313	287	2,675	32,102
MO	Springfield	435	510	605	208	220	293	250	2,520	30,240
MO	Rural	368	510	605	277	220	272	240	2,490	29,880
MS	Biloxi-Gulfport-Pascagoula	479	510	459	208	248	306	177	2,388	28,651
MS	Hattiesburg	398	510	459	222	248	281	132	2,250	27,005
MS	Jackson	504	510	459	208	248	314	193	2,436	29,232
MS	Memphis (Miss. portion)	530	510	459	240	248	322	224	2,533	30,395
MS	Rural	375	510	459	277	248	274	145	2,288	27,456
MT	Billings	501	510	619	222	360	313	331	2,855	34,260
MT	Great Falls	491	510	619	222	360	310	326	2,837	34,042
MT	Missoula	504	510	619	222	360	314	332	2,860	34,325
MT	Rural	470	510	619	277	360	304	337	2,876	34,513
NC	Asheville	538	510	498	222	275	325	221	2,589	31,069
NC	Charlotte-Gastonia-Rock Hill (N.C. portion)	551	510	498	240	275	329	232	2,635	31,618
NC	Fayetteville	476	510	498	208	275	306	184	2,457	29,482
NC	Goldsboro	429	510	498	222	275	291	158	2,383	28,597
NC	Greensboro--Winston-Salem--High Point	550	510	498	240	275	328	232	2,633	31,595
NC	Greenville	525	510	498	222	275	321	219	2,569	30,833
NC	Hickory-Morganton	488	510	498	208	275	309	192	2,481	29,772
NC	Jacksonville	460	510	498	222	275	301	180	2,445	29,344
NC	Raleigh-Durham-Chapel Hill	645	510	498	240	275	358	281	2,807	33,687
NC	Rocky Mount	429	510	498	222	275	291	158	2,383	28,597
NC	Wilmington	602	510	498	222	275	345	252	2,703	32,439
NC	Norfolk-Va Beach-Newpt News (N.C. portion)	576	510	498	240	275	337	245	2,681	32,168
NC	Rural	428	510	498	277	275	291	187	2,465	29,585
ND	Bismarck	503	510	680	222	223	314	281	2,732	32,788
ND	Fargo-Moorhead (N.D. portion)	550	510	680	222	223	328	305	2,818	33,820
ND	Grand Forks (N.D. portion)	536	510	680	222	223	324	298	2,793	33,514
ND	Rural	274	510	680	277	223	243	182	2,389	28,665
NE	Lincoln	525	510	539	226	229	321	216	2,565	30,782
NE	Omaha (Neb. portion)	578	510	539	226	229	337	229	2,647	31,765
NE	Sioux City (Neb. portion)	509	510	539	222	229	316	211	2,534	30,406
NE	Rural	405	510	539	277	229	283	146	2,388	28,654
NH	Manchester	677	510	840	222	394	368	376	3,386	40,628
NH	Nashua	774	510	840	222	394	398	413	3,550	42,600
NH	Portsmouth-Rochester (N.H. portion)	710	510	840	222	394	378	389	3,442	41,299

TABLE A4.5 Basic family budgets for two parents, two children, 1999

State	Area name	Monthly expenses								Annual total
		Housing	Food	Child care	Trans.	Health care	Other necess.	Taxes	Total	
NH	Boston (N.H. portion)	906	510	840	221	394	439	464	3,772	45,268
NH	Lawrence (N.H. portion)	708	510	840	208	394	377	384	3,421	41,051
NH	Lowell (N.H. portion)	737	510	840	208	394	386	395	3,470	41,641
NH	Rural	683	510	840	277	394	370	395	3,467	41,607
NJ	Atlantic-Cape May	739	510	641	208	272	387	356	3,113	37,352
NJ	Bergen-Passaic	878	510	641	240	272	430	425	3,395	40,742
NJ	Jersey City	776	510	641	226	272	399	377	3,201	38,408
NJ	Middlesex-Somerset-Hunterdon	960	510	641	240	272	456	459	3,537	42,446
NJ	Monmouth-Ocean	879	510	641	240	272	430	425	3,397	40,762
NJ	Newark	820	510	641	240	272	412	400	3,295	39,535
NJ	Trenton	810	510	641	208	272	409	386	3,236	38,831
NJ	Vineland-Millville-Bridgeton	692	510	641	222	272	372	340	3,049	36,588
NJ	Philadelphia (N.J. portion)	722	510	641	221	272	382	353	3,100	37,199
NM	Albuquerque	584	510	650	226	299	339	304	2,911	34,928
NM	Las Cruces	436	510	650	222	299	293	234	2,642	31,701
NM	Santa Fe	740	510	650	222	299	387	379	3,186	38,227
NM	Rural	427	510	650	277	299	290	249	2,701	32,410
NV	Las Vegas (Nev. portion)	693	510	605	240	292	373	289	3,000	35,999
NV	Reno	708	510	605	208	292	377	285	2,985	35,816
NV	Rural	623	510	605	277	292	351	273	2,930	35,155
NY	Albany-Schenectady-Troy	601	510	975	226	273	344	361	3,289	39,473
NY	Binghamton	498	510	975	222	273	312	307	3,096	37,149
NY	Buffalo-Niagara Falls	507	510	975	240	273	315	318	3,137	37,646
NY	Dutchess County	877	510	975	208	273	430	609	3,881	46,567
NY	Elmira	490	510	975	222	273	310	303	3,081	36,976
NY	Glens Falls	565	510	975	222	273	333	341	3,218	38,612
NY	Jamestown	480	510	975	222	273	307	298	3,063	36,760
NY	Nassau-Suffolk	1,105	510	975	240	273	500	741	4,343	52,114
NY	New York	891	510	975	221	273	434	621	3,924	47,085
NY	Newburgh (N.Y. portion)	712	510	975	208	273	379	522	3,578	42,933
NY	Rochester	606	510	975	240	273	346	369	3,317	39,804
NY	Syracuse	569	510	975	226	273	334	345	3,231	38,775
NY	Utica-Rome	489	510	975	208	273	310	297	3,061	36,734
NY	Rural	541	510	975	277	273	326	350	3,251	39,014
OH	Akron	554	510	692	226	204	330	273	2,788	33,460
OH	Canton-Massillon	472	510	692	208	204	304	228	2,618	31,418
OH	Cincinnati (Ohio portion)	531	510	692	240	204	323	267	2,766	33,187
OH	Cleveland-Lorain-Elyria	594	510	692	240	204	342	296	2,878	34,531
OH	Columbus	553	510	692	240	204	329	277	2,805	33,655
OH	Dayton-Springfield	542	510	692	226	204	326	267	2,767	33,204
OH	Hamilton-Middletown	566	510	692	208	204	333	272	2,785	33,422
OH	Lima	448	510	692	222	204	297	224	2,596	31,148
OH	Mansfield	433	510	692	222	204	292	221	2,573	30,881
OH	Steubenville-Weirton (Ohio portion)	419	510	692	222	204	288	219	2,553	30,633
OH	Toledo	528	510	692	226	204	322	261	2,742	32,905
OH	Youngstown-Warren	439	510	692	226	204	294	223	2,588	31,050
OH	Huntington-Ashland (Ohio portion)	437	510	692	208	204	293	220	2,564	30,771
OH	Parkersburg-Marietta (Ohio portion)	417	510	692	222	204	287	218	2,550	30,599
OH	Wheeling (Ohio portion)	419	510	692	222	204	288	219	2,553	30,633
OH	Rural	428	510	692	277	204	291	232	2,634	31,606
OK	Enid	398	510	570	222	242	281	227	2,450	29,397
OK	Lawton	469	510	570	222	242	303	267	2,583	30,996
OK	Oklahoma City	468	510	570	240	242	303	270	2,602	31,229
OK	Tulsa	520	510	570	226	242	319	292	2,679	32,153
OK	Fort Smith (Okla. portion)	404	510	570	222	242	283	231	2,462	29,543
OK	Rural	364	510	570	277	242	271	232	2,466	29,586
OR	Eugene-Springfield	597	510	610	208	293	343	387	2,948	35,372
OR	Medford-Ashland	601	510	610	222	293	344	447	3,026	36,313
OR	Portland-Vancouver (Ore. portion)	645	510	610	222	293	358	472	3,109	37,306
OR	Salem	568	510	610	208	293	334	370	2,893	34,719
OR	Rural	522	510	610	277	293	320	374	2,905	34,862
PA	Allentown-Bethlehem-Easton	669	510	791	226	208	365	421	3,190	38,285
PA	Altoona	431	510	791	222	208	292	313	2,766	33,193

TABLE A4.5 Basic family budgets for two parents, two children, 1999

State	Area name	Housing	Food	Child care	Trans.	Health care	Other necess.	Taxes	Total	Annual total
PA	Erie	441	510	791	208	208	295	313	2,766	33,188
PA	Harrisburg-Lebanon-Carlisle	559	510	791	226	208	331	372	2,997	35,965
PA	Johnstown	439	510	791	222	208	294	317	2,780	33,360
PA	Lancaster	576	510	791	208	208	337	373	3,003	36,034
PA	Philadelphia (Pa. portion)	722	510	791	221	208	382	443	3,276	39,312
PA	Pittsburgh	495	510	791	240	208	311	348	2,902	34,829
PA	Reading	544	510	791	208	208	327	359	2,947	35,359
PA	Scranton--Wilkes-Barre--Hazelton	480	510	791	226	208	307	337	2,858	34,299
PA	Sharon	439	510	791	222	208	294	317	2,780	33,360
PA	State College	624	510	791	222	208	351	399	3,105	37,260
PA	Williamsport	441	510	791	222	208	295	318	2,784	33,402
PA	York	544	510	791	208	208	327	359	2,947	35,359
PA	Newburgh (Pa. portion)	712	510	791	208	208	379	434	3,242	38,901
PA	Rural	458	510	791	277	208	300	344	2,887	34,648
RI	Providence-Fall River-Warwick (R.I. portion)	662	510	878	240	386	363	459	3,498	41,972
RI	New London-Norwich (R.I. portion)	723	510	878	208	386	382	477	3,564	42,766
RI	Rural	828	510	878	277	386	415	552	3,846	46,147
SC	Charleston-North Charleston	534	510	612	226	229	323	209	2,643	31,720
SC	Columbia	544	510	612	226	229	327	215	2,662	31,939
SC	Florence	470	510	612	222	229	304	191	2,537	30,442
SC	Greenville-Spartanburg-Anderson	483	510	612	226	229	308	196	2,563	30,758
SC	Myrtle Beach	549	510	612	222	229	328	215	2,664	31,972
SC	Sumter	433	510	612	222	229	292	172	2,469	29,625
SC	Augusta-Aiken (S.C. portion)	503	510	612	208	229	314	197	2,572	30,864
SC	Charlotte-Gastonia-Rock Hill (S.C. portion)	551	510	612	240	229	329	224	2,693	32,316
SC	Rural	425	510	612	277	229	290	190	2,531	30,371
SD	Rapid City	553	510	538	222	277	329	206	2,635	31,618
SD	Sioux Falls	591	510	538	222	277	341	221	2,699	32,389
SD	Rural	435	510	538	277	277	293	185	2,514	30,168
TN	Chattanooga (Tenn. portion)	510	510	607	208	237	316	198	2,586	31,028
TN	Clarksville-Hopkinsville (Tenn. portion)	443	510	607	222	237	295	178	2,492	29,901
TN	Jackson	462	510	607	222	237	301	189	2,527	30,323
TN	Johnson City-Kingsport-Bristol (Tenn. portion)	447	510	607	208	237	297	175	2,480	29,765
TN	Knoxville	468	510	607	226	237	303	194	2,544	30,531
TN	Memphis (Tenn. portion)	530	510	607	240	237	322	211	2,656	31,873
TN	Nashville	626	510	607	240	237	352	248	2,819	33,826
TN	Rural	365	510	607	277	237	271	160	2,426	29,110
TX	Abilene	479	510	556	222	281	306	195	2,548	30,574
TX	Amarillo	443	510	556	222	281	295	176	2,482	29,780
TX	Austin-San Marcos	699	510	556	240	281	375	273	2,933	35,195
TX	Beaumont-Port Arthur	474	510	556	208	281	305	187	2,520	30,239
TX	Brazoria	619	510	556	222	281	350	238	2,774	33,292
TX	Brownsville-Harlingen-San Benito	532	510	556	208	281	323	200	2,610	31,315
TX	Bryan-College Station	553	510	556	222	281	329	212	2,662	31,949
TX	Corpus Christi	552	510	556	208	281	329	208	2,644	31,722
TX	Dallas	718	510	556	221	281	381	275	2,941	35,289
TX	El Paso	527	510	556	226	281	321	204	2,624	31,493
TX	Fort Worth-Arlington	588	510	556	240	281	340	231	2,745	32,940
TX	Galveston-Texas City	562	510	556	222	281	332	216	2,678	32,133
TX	Houston	601	510	556	221	281	344	230	2,743	32,912
TX	Killeen-Temple	522	510	556	208	281	320	199	2,595	31,137
TX	Laredo	485	510	556	222	281	308	196	2,557	30,681
TX	Longview-Marshall	439	510	556	222	281	294	173	2,474	29,691
TX	Lubbock	499	510	556	222	281	313	197	2,577	30,919
TX	McAllen-Edinburg-Mission	418	510	556	226	281	288	164	2,442	29,308
TX	Odessa-Midland	469	510	556	222	281	303	189	2,530	30,354
TX	San Angelo	437	510	556	222	281	293	172	2,471	29,648
TX	San Antonio	554	510	556	240	281	330	218	2,687	32,249
TX	Sherman-Denison	466	510	556	222	281	302	188	2,524	30,288
TX	Texarkana (Texas portion)	458	510	556	222	281	300	183	2,509	30,110
TX	Tyler	476	510	556	222	281	306	193	2,542	30,509
TX	Victoria	446	510	556	222	281	296	177	2,487	29,846
TX	Waco	495	510	556	222	281	311	197	2,571	30,852

TABLE A4.5 Basic family budgets for two parents, two children, 1999

State	Area name	Housing	Food	Child care	Trans.	Health care	Other necess.	Taxes	Total	Annual total
									Monthly expenses	
TX	Wichita Falls	456	510	556	222	281	299	182	2,506	30,066
TX	Rural	396	510	556	277	281	281	173	2,474	29,682
UT	[HUD FMR] Kane County	470	510	560	222	262	304	273	2,600	31,198
UT	Provo-Orem	553	510	560	208	262	329	311	2,733	32,798
UT	Salt Lake City-Ogden	635	510	560	240	262	355	368	2,929	35,148
UT	Flagstaff (Utah portion)	594	510	560	222	262	342	339	2,828	33,934
UT	Rural	503	510	560	277	262	314	312	2,737	32,845
VA	Charlottesville	645	510	681	222	250	358	373	3,038	36,455
VA	Danville	431	510	681	222	250	292	266	2,650	31,805
VA	Lynchburg	440	510	681	222	250	294	271	2,667	32,000
VA	Norfolk-Va Beach-Newpt News (Va. portion)	576	510	681	240	250	337	346	2,938	35,254
VA	Richmond-Petersburg	620	510	681	226	250	350	363	2,999	35,987
VA	Roanoke	475	510	681	222	250	305	288	2,730	32,760
VA	Washington (Va. portion)	820	510	681	221	250	412	461	3,354	40,252
VA	Johnson City-Kingsport-Bristol (Va. portion)	447	510	681	208	250	297	269	2,661	31,929
VA	Rural	446	510	681	277	250	296	295	2,753	33,038
VT	Burlington	692	510	592	222	445	372	380	3,212	38,548
VT	Rural	601	510	592	277	445	344	357	3,125	37,499
WA	Bellingham	682	510	734	222	349	369	334	3,200	38,398
WA	Bremerton	620	510	734	222	349	350	310	3,095	37,138
WA	Olympia	655	510	734	222	349	361	324	3,154	37,851
WA	Richland-Kennewick-Pasco	675	510	734	222	349	367	331	3,188	38,256
WA	Seattle-Bellevue-Everett	736	510	734	240	349	386	360	3,315	39,775
WA	Spokane	519	510	734	208	349	319	268	2,907	34,878
WA	Tacoma	586	510	734	226	349	340	299	3,043	36,519
WA	Yakima	543	510	734	222	349	326	281	2,964	35,573
WA	Portland-Vancouver (Wash. portion)	645	510	734	222	349	358	320	3,137	37,646
WA	Rural	518	510	734	277	349	319	287	2,994	35,925
WI	Appleton-Oshkosh-Neenah	495	510	710	208	215	311	360	2,809	33,713
WI	Eau Claire	488	510	710	222	215	309	362	2,816	33,787
WI	Green Bay	530	510	710	222	215	322	386	2,894	34,729
WI	Janesville-Beloit	545	510	710	222	215	327	394	2,922	35,067
WI	Kenosha	577	510	710	222	215	337	412	2,982	35,784
WI	La Crosse (Wis. portion)	461	510	710	222	215	301	347	2,765	33,180
WI	Madison	658	510	710	208	215	362	452	3,114	37,373
WI	Milwaukee-Waukesha	605	510	710	240	215	345	435	3,060	36,720
WI	Racine	535	510	710	222	215	324	388	2,903	34,841
WI	Sheboygan	475	510	710	222	215	305	355	2,791	33,495
WI	Wausau	480	510	710	222	215	307	358	2,801	33,606
WI	Duluth-Superior (Wis. portion)	459	510	710	222	215	300	346	2,761	33,135
WI	Minneapolis-St. Paul (Wis. portion)	666	510	710	240	215	364	470	3,174	38,091
WI	Rural	430	510	710	277	215	291	353	2,787	33,440
WV	[HUD FMR] Berkeley County	504	510	602	222	246	314	291	2,688	32,259
WV	Charleston	490	510	602	208	246	310	279	2,645	31,740
WV	Huntington-Ashland (W.Va. portion)	437	510	602	208	246	293	263	2,560	30,717
WV	[HUD FMR] Jefferson County	556	510	602	222	246	330	316	2,781	33,375
WV	Parkersburg-Marietta (W.Va. portion)	417	510	602	222	246	287	260	2,544	30,525
WV	Wheeling (W.Va. portion)	419	510	602	222	246	288	261	2,548	30,571
WV	Washington (W.Va. portion)	820	510	602	221	246	412	444	3,255	39,058
WV	Cumberland (W.Va. portion)	497	510	602	222	246	312	287	2,676	32,107
WV	Steubenville-Weirton (W.Va. portion)	419	510	602	222	246	288	261	2,548	30,571
WV	Rural	375	510	602	277	246	274	260	2,544	30,526
WY	Casper	468	510	528	222	314	303	191	2,534	30,413
WY	Cheyenne	598	510	528	222	314	343	231	2,745	32,939
WY	Rural	445	510	528	277	314	296	196	2,565	30,777

Source: Author's calculations (see Appendix A)

TABLE A4.6 Basic family budgets for two parents, three children, 1999

State	Area name	Monthly expenses								Annual total
		Housing	Food	Child care	Trans.	Health care	Other necess.	Taxes	Total	
AK	Anchorage	$ 1,075	$ 647	$ 1,363	$ 208	$ 305	$ 440	$ 579	$ 4,617	$ 55,406
AK	Rural	1,053	647	1,363	277	305	444	593	4,681	56,172
AL	Anniston	532	647	809	222	401	319	417	3,347	40,166
AL	Birmingham	653	647	809	226	401	350	475	3,562	42,738
AL	Decatur	564	647	809	222	401	336	435	3,414	40,972
AL	Dothan	542	647	809	222	401	323	423	3,366	40,397
AL	Florence	535	647	809	222	401	334	424	3,372	40,459
AL	Gadsden	472	647	809	222	401	314	393	3,258	39,095
AL	Huntsville	690	647	809	208	401	361	486	3,603	43,236
AL	Mobile	649	647	809	226	401	350	474	3,556	42,676
AL	Montgomery	675	647	809	208	401	354	478	3,573	42,878
AL	Tuscaloosa	663	647	809	222	401	350	477	3,569	42,831
AL	Columbus (Ala. portion)	607	647	809	208	401	345	449	3,467	41,599
AL	Rural	471	647	809	277	401	312	413	3,330	39,960
AR	Fayetteville-Springdale-Rogers	684	647	724	208	252	358	341	3,214	38,566
AR	Fort Smith (Ark. portion)	540	647	724	222	252	326	277	2,988	35,859
AR	Jonesboro	547	647	724	222	252	324	279	2,995	35,939
AR	Little Rock-North Little Rock	688	647	724	226	252	355	348	3,241	38,887
AR	Pine Bluff	568	647	724	222	252	340	294	3,047	36,565
AR	Memphis (Ark. portion)	736	647	724	240	252	365	376	3,340	40,082
AR	Texarkana (Ark. portion)	604	647	724	222	252	343	309	3,100	37,205
AR	Rural	491	647	724	277	252	315	276	2,982	35,786
AZ	Flagstaff	797	647	757	222	248	385	355	3,411	40,927
AZ	Phoenix-Mesa	882	647	757	240	248	397	395	3,566	42,794
AZ	Tucson	839	647	757	226	248	388	372	3,477	41,727
AZ	Yuma	782	647	757	222	248	375	346	3,377	40,527
AZ	Las Vegas (Ariz. portion)	965	647	757	240	248	415	430	3,703	44,433
AZ	Rural	495	647	757	277	248	354	260	3,038	36,461
CA	Bakersfield	706	647	1,097	226	224	358	360	3,619	43,428
CA	Chico-Paradise	773	647	1,097	222	224	376	389	3,728	44,733
CA	Fresno	695	647	1,097	226	224	356	356	3,601	43,207
CA	Los Angeles-Long Beach	1,011	647	1,097	221	224	433	508	4,140	49,683
CA	Merced	743	647	1,097	222	224	367	376	3,676	44,110
CA	Modesto	797	647	1,097	208	224	378	395	3,746	44,952
CA	Oakland	1,180	647	1,097	240	224	468	597	4,452	53,427
CA	Orange County	1,212	647	1,097	240	224	471	611	4,501	54,017
CA	Redding	722	647	1,097	222	224	362	366	3,639	43,671
CA	Riverside-San Bernardino	829	647	1,097	221	224	386	415	3,819	45,829
CA	Sacramento	850	647	1,097	240	224	391	434	3,882	46,585
CA	Salinas	1,038	647	1,097	208	224	432	513	4,159	49,912
CA	San Diego	1,014	647	1,097	240	224	427	514	4,162	49,947
CA	San Francisco	1,601	647	1,097	240	224	562	809	5,180	62,161
CA	San Jose	1,561	647	1,097	240	224	554	787	5,110	61,318
CA	San Luis Obispo-Atascadero-Paso Robles	1,009	647	1,097	222	224	426	504	4,129	49,551
CA	Santa Barbara-Santa Maria-Lompoc	1,207	647	1,097	208	224	469	596	4,449	53,385
CA	Santa Cruz-Watsonville	1,326	647	1,097	222	224	496	660	4,672	56,065
CA	Santa Rosa	1,153	647	1,097	208	224	458	570	4,357	52,279
CA	Stockton-Lodi	823	647	1,097	226	224	384	415	3,816	45,795
CA	Vallejo-Fairfield-Napa	1,045	647	1,097	208	224	434	517	4,172	50,066
CA	Ventura	1,055	647	1,097	226	224	446	533	4,229	50,746
CA	Visalia-Tulare-Porterville	706	647	1,097	208	224	358	354	3,594	43,124
CA	Yolo	920	647	1,097	222	224	407	461	3,977	47,726
CA	Yuba City	680	647	1,097	222	224	352	347	3,569	42,826
CA	Rural	779	647	1,097	277	224	375	414	3,813	45,761
CO	Boulder-Longmont	1,067	647	1,187	208	278	438	687	4,512	54,148
CO	Colorado Springs	868	647	1,187	208	278	394	595	4,177	50,127
CO	Denver	922	647	1,187	240	278	407	632	4,312	51,748
CO	Fort Collins-Loveland	911	647	1,187	222	278	404	620	4,269	51,227
CO	Grand Junction	693	647	1,187	222	278	360	521	3,909	46,902
CO	Greeley	807	647	1,187	222	278	381	572	4,094	49,128
CO	Pueblo	727	647	1,187	222	278	368	537	3,966	47,593
CO	Rural	765	647	1,187	277	278	377	575	4,106	49,272
CT	Bridgeport	878	647	1,367	208	249	419	616	4,385	52,616
CT	Danbury	1,194	647	1,367	222	249	481	790	4,951	59,411
CT	Hartford	868	647	1,367	240	249	415	623	4,409	52,911

TABLE A4.6 Basic family budgets for two parents, three children, 1999

State	Area name	Housing	Food	Child care	Trans.	Health care	Other necess.	Taxes	Total	Annual total
CT	New Haven-Meriden	1,005	647	1,367	226	249	444	692	4,631	55,568
CT	New London-Norwich (Conn. portion)	905	647	1,367	208	249	425	633	4,435	53,215
CT	Stamford-Norwalk	1,482	647	1,367	208	249	544	963	5,460	65,521
CT	Waterbury	917	647	1,367	222	249	429	643	4,474	53,691
CT	Worcester (Conn. portion)	789	647	1,367	208	249	397	563	4,221	50,648
CT	Rural	952	647	1,367	277	249	419	682	4,593	55,120
DC	Washington (D.C. portion)	1,118	647	1,434	221	329	455	1,045	5,248	62,979
DE	Dover	795	647	877	222	373	391	465	3,770	45,234
DE	Wilmington-Newark (Del. portion)	911	647	877	226	373	409	515	3,959	47,504
DE	Rural	761	647	877	277	373	380	469	3,784	45,411
FL	Daytona Beach	770	647	663	208	330	380	275	3,273	39,281
FL	Fort Lauderdale	971	647	663	240	330	417	353	3,621	43,453
FL	Fort Myers-Cape Coral	807	647	663	208	330	380	285	3,320	39,845
FL	Fort Pierce-Port St. Lucie	854	647	663	208	330	404	306	3,413	40,954
FL	Fort Walton Beach	678	647	663	222	330	356	244	3,140	37,677
FL	Gainesville	734	647	663	222	330	367	264	3,227	38,719
FL	Jacksonville	752	647	663	240	330	377	277	3,286	39,435
FL	Lakeland-Winter Haven	594	647	663	208	330	349	214	3,005	36,064
FL	Melbourne-Titusville-Palm Bay	758	647	663	208	330	376	270	3,252	39,027
FL	Miami	965	647	663	240	330	418	352	3,615	43,380
FL	Naples	1,018	647	663	222	330	428	365	3,672	44,067
FL	Ocala	657	647	663	222	330	356	238	3,113	37,350
FL	Orlando	891	647	663	240	330	411	328	3,510	42,116
FL	Panama City	638	647	663	222	330	356	233	3,088	37,055
FL	Pensacola	669	647	663	208	330	356	238	3,111	37,328
FL	Punta Gorda	855	647	663	222	330	392	307	3,415	40,980
FL	Sarasota-Bradenton	841	647	663	226	330	403	307	3,418	41,018
FL	Tallahassee	788	647	663	208	330	388	282	3,306	39,671
FL	Tampa-St. Petersburg-Clearwater	776	647	663	240	330	382	286	3,323	39,880
FL	West Palm Beach-Boca Raton	950	647	663	240	330	422	349	3,601	43,208
FL	Rural	648	647	663	277	330	360	253	3,179	38,145
GA	Albany	588	647	943	222	285	334	412	3,432	41,182
GA	Athens	706	647	943	222	285	361	470	3,635	43,616
GA	Atlanta	916	647	943	221	285	414	576	4,002	48,024
GA	Augusta-Aiken (Ga. portion)	683	647	943	208	285	357	454	3,578	42,931
GA	Columbus (Ga. portion)	607	647	943	208	285	345	419	3,454	41,449
GA	Macon	695	647	943	208	285	357	459	3,595	43,136
GA	Savannah	707	647	943	208	285	363	466	3,620	43,444
GA	Chattanooga (Ga. portion)	659	647	943	208	285	359	445	3,547	42,564
GA	Rural	559	647	943	277	285	334	422	3,467	41,606
HI	Honolulu	1,167	647	917	226	232	468	714	4,372	52,459
HI	Rural	1,252	647	917	277	232	497	787	4,609	55,307
IA	Cedar Rapids	688	647	843	222	243	354	440	3,437	41,240
IA	Davenport-Moline-Rock Island (Iowa portion)	617	647	843	208	243	349	360	3,267	39,205
IA	Des Moines	715	647	843	208	243	371	452	3,480	41,762
IA	Dubuque	581	647	843	222	243	342	349	3,226	38,715
IA	Iowa City	787	647	843	222	243	376	488	3,606	43,272
IA	Sioux City (Iowa portion)	635	647	843	222	243	358	377	3,325	39,898
IA	Waterloo-Cedar Falls	573	647	843	222	243	334	343	3,204	38,452
IA	Omaha (Iowa portion)	758	647	843	226	243	380	480	3,577	42,922
IA	Rural	534	647	843	277	243	330	348	3,222	38,665
ID	Boise City	750	647	1,075	208	306	368	505	3,859	46,307
ID	Pocatello	568	647	1,075	222	306	330	414	3,562	42,740
ID	Rural	604	647	1,075	277	306	340	459	3,708	44,498
IL	Bloomington-Normal	765	647	1,010	222	292	371	486	3,794	45,522
IL	Champaign-Urbana	808	647	1,010	222	292	383	504	3,867	46,406
IL	Chicago	922	647	1,010	221	292	429	559	4,081	48,972
IL	Decatur	604	647	1,010	222	292	339	419	3,534	42,404
IL	Kankakee	697	647	1,010	222	292	370	462	3,700	44,400
IL	Peoria-Pekin	735	647	1,010	208	292	372	471	3,736	44,833
IL	Rockford	703	647	1,010	208	292	374	460	3,695	44,345
IL	Davenport-Moline-Rock Island (Ill. portion)	617	647	1,010	208	292	349	422	3,546	42,547
IL	St. Louis (Ill. portion)	652	647	1,010	240	292	356	448	3,645	43,739
IL	Springfield	679	647	1,010	222	292	359	452	3,661	43,929
IL	Rural	515	647	1,010	277	292	322	401	3,465	41,581

TABLE A4.6 Basic family budgets for two parents, three children, 1999

State	Area name	Monthly expenses								Annual total
		Housing	Food	Child care	Trans.	Health care	Other necess.	Taxes	Total	
IN	Bloomington	876	647	880	222	241	396	499	3,761	45,133
IN	Elkhart-Goshen	682	647	880	222	241	366	420	3,458	41,493
IN	Evansville-Henderson (Ind. portion)	612	647	880	208	241	352	386	3,327	39,919
IN	Fort Wayne	646	647	880	208	241	356	399	3,378	40,530
IN	Gary	778	647	880	226	241	393	465	3,630	43,563
IN	Indianapolis	682	647	880	240	241	370	427	3,487	41,845
IN	Kokomo	675	647	880	222	241	363	416	3,445	41,339
IN	Lafayette	811	647	880	222	241	381	471	3,653	43,839
IN	Muncie	588	647	880	222	241	335	376	3,289	39,468
IN	South Bend	694	647	880	208	241	373	422	3,466	41,586
IN	Terre Haute	533	647	880	222	241	333	356	3,212	38,540
IN	Louisville (Ind. portion)	687	647	880	226	241	355	419	3,456	41,473
IN	Cincinnati (Ind. portion)	712	647	880	240	241	365	436	3,522	42,261
IN	Rural	541	647	880	277	241	331	377	3,295	39,539
KS	Lawrence	752	647	917	222	326	368	417	3,650	43,799
KS	Topeka	668	647	917	222	326	354	382	3,516	42,196
KS	Wichita	704	647	917	226	326	362	400	3,583	42,993
KS	Kansas City (Kan. portion)	739	647	917	240	326	366	418	3,654	43,843
KS	Rural	528	647	917	277	326	327	343	3,366	40,387
KY	[HUD FMR] Gallatin County	538	647	831	222	286	334	391	3,248	38,976
KY	[HUD FMR] Grant County	564	647	831	222	286	326	398	3,274	39,282
KY	Lexington	711	647	831	208	286	362	467	3,512	42,140
KY	Louisville (Ky. portion)	687	647	831	226	286	355	461	3,493	41,919
KY	Owensboro	545	647	831	222	286	327	391	3,248	38,974
KY	[HUD FMR] Pendleton County	501	647	831	222	286	324	372	3,183	38,196
KY	Evansville-Henderson (Ky. portion)	612	647	831	208	286	352	423	3,359	40,309
KY	Cincinnati (Ky. portion)	712	647	831	240	286	365	481	3,561	42,735
KY	Clarksville-Hopkinsville (Ky. portion)	605	647	831	222	286	338	420	3,348	40,175
KY	Huntington-Ashland (Ky. portion)	557	647	831	208	286	336	394	3,259	39,112
KY	Rural	484	647	831	277	286	316	384	3,225	38,701
LA	Alexandria	607	647	790	222	302	336	313	3,218	38,611
LA	Baton Rouge	648	647	790	226	302	345	332	3,292	39,498
LA	Houma	574	647	790	222	302	329	298	3,163	37,951
LA	Lafayette	551	647	790	208	302	325	284	3,108	37,293
LA	Lake Charles	725	647	790	222	302	372	367	3,425	41,104
LA	Monroe	608	647	790	222	302	340	314	3,224	38,693
LA	New Orleans	708	647	790	240	302	362	364	3,413	40,955
LA	[HUD FMR] St James Parish	516	647	790	222	302	329	278	3,084	37,010
LA	Shreveport-Bossier City	650	647	790	208	302	351	328	3,278	39,333
LA	Rural	486	647	790	277	302	315	282	3,100	37,199
MA	Barnstable-Yarmouth	1,040	647	1,353	222	387	458	852	4,960	59,520
MA	Boston (Mass. portion)	1,132	647	1,353	221	387	482	898	5,120	61,438
MA	Brockton	865	647	1,353	208	387	416	761	4,638	55,654
MA	Fitchburg-Leominster	790	647	1,353	222	387	391	726	4,517	54,199
MA	Lawrence (Mass. portion)	885	647	1,353	208	387	420	770	4,671	56,055
MA	Lowell (Mass. portion)	924	647	1,353	208	387	429	789	4,739	56,862
MA	New Bedford	785	647	1,353	222	387	395	726	4,516	54,187
MA	Pittsfield	702	647	1,353	222	387	374	684	4,370	52,441
MA	Springfield	811	647	1,353	226	387	402	741	4,568	54,812
MA	Worcester (Mass. portion)	789	647	1,353	208	387	397	723	4,504	54,051
MA	Providence-Fall River-Warwick (Mass. portion)	831	647	1,353	240	387	406	755	4,620	55,436
MA	Rural	892	647	1,353	277	387	417	799	4,773	57,279
MD	Baltimore	831	647	1,148	240	254	395	673	4,188	50,259
MD	[HUD FMR] Columbia	1,170	647	1,148	222	254	475	846	4,762	57,148
MD	Cumberland (Md. portion)	657	647	1,148	222	254	355	572	3,855	46,259
MD	Hagerstown	649	647	1,148	222	254	354	568	3,842	46,109
MD	Washington (Md. portion)	1,118	647	1,148	221	254	455	815	4,658	55,892
MD	Wilmington-Newark (Md. portion)	911	647	1,148	226	254	409	707	4,303	51,633
MD	Rural	751	647	1,148	277	254	376	646	4,098	49,179
ME	Bangor	709	647	841	222	477	369	437	3,702	44,427
ME	Lewiston-Auburn	620	647	841	222	477	354	393	3,555	42,654
ME	Portland	802	647	841	222	477	399	489	3,878	46,532
ME	Portsmouth-Rochester (Maine portion)	910	647	841	222	477	421	544	4,062	48,738
ME	Rural	702	647	841	277	477	369	458	3,771	45,254
MI	Ann Arbor	915	647	903	226	233	417	513	3,856	46,266

TABLE A4.6 Basic family budgets for two parents, three children, 1999

				Monthly expenses					
State	Area name	Housing	Food	Child care	Trans.	Health care	Other necess.	Taxes	Total	Annual total
MI	Benton Harbor	622	647	903	222	233	355	380	3,363	40,353
MI	Detroit	793	647	903	221	233	397	459	3,654	43,845
MI	Flint	666	647	903	208	233	362	394	3,415	40,979
MI	Grand Rapids-Muskegon-Holland	701	647	903	240	233	374	423	3,522	42,263
MI	Jackson	628	647	903	222	233	356	383	3,373	40,479
MI	Kalamazoo-Battle Creek	664	647	903	208	233	365	395	3,416	40,992
MI	Lansing-East Lansing	780	647	903	208	233	386	445	3,603	43,240
MI	Saginaw-Bay City-Midland	628	647	903	208	233	356	378	3,355	40,258
MI	Rural	564	647	903	277	233	335	372	3,332	39,989
MN	Duluth-Superior (Minn. portion)	613	647	1,544	222	319	343	555	4,243	50,917
MN	Minneapolis-St. Paul (Minn. portion)	901	647	1,544	240	319	407	713	4,771	57,254
MN	Rochester	788	647	1,544	222	319	377	644	4,541	54,496
MN	St. Cloud	621	647	1,544	222	319	353	562	4,269	51,225
MN	Fargo-Moorhead (Minn. portion)	763	647	1,544	222	319	371	631	4,497	53,969
MN	Grand Forks (Minn. portion)	739	647	1,544	222	319	367	619	4,457	53,482
MN	La Crosse (Minn. portion)	617	647	1,544	222	319	344	557	4,250	50,995
MN	Rural	560	647	1,544	277	319	338	554	4,240	50,883
MO	Columbia	660	647	866	222	232	348	405	3,380	40,562
MO	Joplin	511	647	866	222	232	321	338	3,137	37,639
MO	Kansas City (Mo. portion)	739	647	866	240	232	366	450	3,540	42,477
MO	St. Joseph	496	647	866	222	232	322	333	3,118	37,417
MO	St. Louis (Mo. portion)	652	647	866	240	232	356	412	3,405	40,861
MO	Springfield	601	647	866	208	232	336	373	3,263	39,154
MO	Rural	480	647	866	277	232	315	345	3,161	37,934
MS	Biloxi-Gulfport-Pascagoula	668	647	637	208	262	349	272	3,044	36,527
MS	Hattiesburg	534	647	637	222	262	324	218	2,844	34,132
MS	Jackson	670	647	637	208	262	357	276	3,057	36,688
MS	Memphis (Miss. portion)	736	647	637	240	262	365	315	3,202	38,422
MS	Rural	483	647	637	277	262	317	217	2,841	34,086
MT	Billings	673	647	877	222	391	356	468	3,634	43,607
MT	Great Falls	639	647	877	222	391	353	453	3,582	42,980
MT	Missoula	649	647	877	222	391	357	458	3,601	43,215
MT	Rural	620	647	877	277	391	346	465	3,624	43,488
NC	Asheville	701	647	672	222	292	367	301	3,202	38,429
NC	Charlotte-Gastonia-Rock Hill (N.C. portion)	726	647	672	240	292	371	320	3,269	39,223
NC	Fayetteville	659	647	672	208	292	348	271	3,098	37,173
NC	Goldsboro	552	647	672	222	292	334	227	2,946	35,354
NC	Greensboro--Winston-Salem--High Point	758	647	672	240	292	371	333	3,314	39,762
NC	Greenville	708	647	672	222	292	363	302	3,207	38,480
NC	Hickory-Morganton	615	647	672	208	292	352	255	3,041	36,495
NC	Jacksonville	638	647	672	222	292	343	266	3,080	36,962
NC	Raleigh-Durham-Chapel Hill	866	647	672	240	292	401	400	3,518	42,211
NC	Rocky Mount	568	647	672	222	292	334	234	2,969	35,622
NC	Wilmington	823	647	672	222	292	387	368	3,412	40,942
NC	Norfolk-Va Beach-Newpt News (N.C. portion)	803	647	672	240	292	379	364	3,398	40,771
NC	Rural	559	647	672	277	292	333	252	3,033	36,400
ND	Bismarck	700	647	983	222	230	357	435	3,574	42,891
ND	Fargo-Moorhead (N.D. portion)	763	647	983	222	230	371	467	3,684	44,211
ND	Grand Forks (N.D. portion)	739	647	983	222	230	367	455	3,644	43,728
ND	Rural	498	647	983	277	230	286	344	3,265	39,182
NE	Lincoln	697	647	764	226	240	363	301	3,240	38,874
NE	Omaha (Neb. portion)	758	647	764	226	240	380	330	3,347	40,158
NE	Sioux City (Neb. portion)	635	647	764	222	240	358	273	3,141	37,686
NE	Rural	519	647	764	277	240	326	239	3,013	36,161
NH	Manchester	846	647	1,199	222	394	411	485	4,204	50,448
NH	Nashua	1,053	647	1,199	222	394	441	555	4,511	54,126
NH	Portsmouth-Rochester (N.H. portion)	910	647	1,199	222	394	421	507	4,300	51,599
NH	Boston (N.H. portion)	1,132	647	1,199	221	394	482	590	4,664	55,973
NH	Lawrence (N.H. portion)	885	647	1,199	208	394	420	496	4,250	50,994
NH	Lowell (N.H. portion)	924	647	1,199	208	394	429	510	4,312	51,739
NH	Rural	903	647	1,199	277	394	412	519	4,352	52,220
NJ	Atlantic-Cape May	926	647	845	208	279	430	439	3,774	45,292
NJ	Bergen-Passaic	1,170	647	845	240	279	473	542	4,196	50,347
NJ	Jersey City	986	647	845	226	279	441	468	3,893	46,713
NJ	Middlesex-Somerset-Hunterdon	1,304	647	845	240	279	498	593	4,407	52,878

TABLE A4.6 Basic family budgets for two parents, three children, 1999

State	Area name	Housing	Food	Child care	Trans.	Health care	Other necess.	Taxes	Total	Annual total
									Monthly expenses	
NJ	Monmouth-Ocean	1,168	647	845	240	279	473	541	4,193	50,319
NJ	Newark	1,033	647	845	240	279	455	492	3,991	47,887
NJ	Trenton	1,097	647	845	208	279	452	501	4,030	48,355
NJ	Vineland-Millville-Bridgeton	862	647	845	222	279	415	418	3,688	44,258
NJ	Philadelphia (N.J. portion)	903	647	845	221	279	424	434	3,754	45,042
NM	Albuquerque	805	647	958	226	322	382	462	3,801	45,616
NM	Las Cruces	598	647	958	222	322	336	364	3,446	41,351
NM	Santa Fe	993	647	958	222	322	430	555	4,126	49,514
NM	Rural	567	647	958	277	322	333	371	3,475	41,700
NV	Las Vegas (Nev. portion)	965	647	805	240	313	415	388	3,772	45,269
NV	Reno	986	647	805	208	313	420	386	3,765	45,180
NV	Rural	845	647	805	277	313	394	357	3,638	43,652
NY	Albany-Schenectady-Troy	754	647	1,296	226	273	387	620	4,203	50,431
NY	Binghamton	634	647	1,296	222	273	355	557	3,983	47,799
NY	Buffalo-Niagara Falls	634	647	1,296	240	273	358	565	4,012	48,149
NY	Dutchess County	1,140	647	1,296	208	273	473	803	4,840	58,075
NY	Elmira	621	647	1,296	222	273	353	551	3,962	47,539
NY	Glens Falls	707	647	1,296	222	273	376	595	4,115	49,376
NY	Jamestown	621	647	1,296	222	273	349	550	3,957	47,487
NY	Nassau-Suffolk	1,537	647	1,296	240	273	543	1,060	5,596	67,151
NY	New York	1,114	647	1,296	221	273	477	799	4,827	57,919
NY	Newburgh (N.Y. portion)	903	647	1,296	208	273	421	686	4,434	53,207
NY	Rochester	777	647	1,296	240	273	389	635	4,256	51,067
NY	Syracuse	726	647	1,296	226	273	377	604	4,149	49,793
NY	Utica-Rome	621	647	1,296	208	273	352	545	3,942	47,309
NY	Rural	705	647	1,296	277	273	368	613	4,179	50,149
OH	Akron	693	647	1,027	226	214	372	427	3,607	43,284
OH	Canton-Massillon	590	647	1,027	208	214	347	375	3,408	40,900
OH	Cincinnati (Ohio portion)	712	647	1,027	240	214	365	436	3,641	43,695
OH	Cleveland-Lorain-Elyria	755	647	1,027	240	214	385	458	3,726	44,713
OH	Columbus	702	647	1,027	240	214	372	435	3,637	43,644
OH	Dayton-Springfield	700	647	1,027	226	214	369	428	3,612	43,338
OH	Hamilton-Middletown	708	647	1,027	208	214	376	427	3,608	43,296
OH	Lima	571	647	1,027	222	214	340	370	3,391	40,687
OH	Mansfield	541	647	1,027	222	214	335	331	3,317	39,799
OH	Steubenville-Weirton (Ohio portion)	535	647	1,027	222	214	331	327	3,303	39,631
OH	Toledo	680	647	1,027	226	214	364	420	3,579	42,942
OH	Youngstown-Warren	552	647	1,027	226	214	337	364	3,367	40,407
OH	Huntington-Ashland (Ohio portion)	557	647	1,027	208	214	336	332	3,322	39,860
OH	Parkersburg-Marietta (Ohio portion)	541	647	1,027	222	214	330	329	3,310	39,718
OH	Wheeling (Ohio portion)	535	647	1,027	222	214	331	327	3,303	39,631
OH	Rural	550	647	1,027	277	214	333	380	3,429	41,148
OK	Enid	554	647	827	222	257	324	361	3,192	38,304
OK	Lawton	651	647	827	222	257	346	411	3,361	40,327
OK	Oklahoma City	651	647	827	240	257	346	418	3,386	40,628
OK	Tulsa	724	647	827	226	257	362	449	3,493	41,914
OK	Fort Smith (Okla. portion)	540	647	827	222	257	326	356	3,175	38,099
OK	Rural	487	647	827	277	257	313	352	3,160	37,925
OR	Eugene-Springfield	833	647	809	208	293	386	591	3,768	45,218
OR	Medford-Ashland	835	647	809	222	293	387	598	3,792	45,504
OR	Portland-Vancouver (Ore. portion)	897	647	809	222	293	401	660	3,929	47,151
OR	Salem	782	647	809	208	293	377	565	3,682	44,185
OR	Rural	723	647	809	277	293	362	563	3,676	44,113
PA	Allentown-Bethlehem-Easton	871	647	1,068	226	235	408	554	4,009	48,113
PA	Altoona	562	647	1,068	222	235	334	421	3,490	41,878
PA	Erie	569	647	1,068	208	235	337	420	3,485	41,825
PA	Harrisburg-Lebanon-Carlisle	704	647	1,068	226	235	374	485	3,740	44,875
PA	Johnstown	569	647	1,068	222	235	337	424	3,502	42,029
PA	Lancaster	752	647	1,068	208	235	379	497	3,787	45,442
PA	Philadelphia (Pa. portion)	903	647	1,068	221	235	424	568	4,067	48,802
PA	Pittsburgh	620	647	1,068	240	235	354	454	3,618	43,420
PA	Reading	679	647	1,068	208	235	369	469	3,676	44,108
PA	Scranton--Wilkes-Barre--Hazelton	599	647	1,068	226	235	349	441	3,566	42,792
PA	Sharon	569	647	1,068	222	235	337	424	3,502	42,029
PA	State College	818	647	1,068	222	235	394	529	3,914	46,962

TABLE A4.6 Basic family budgets for two parents, three children, 1999

State	Area name	Monthly expenses								Annual total
		Housing	Food	Child care	Trans.	Health care	Other necess.	Taxes	Total	
PA	Williamsport	569	647	1,068	222	235	337	425	3,503	42,040
PA	York	678	647	1,068	208	235	369	468	3,674	44,093
PA	Newburgh (Pa. portion)	903	647	1,068	208	235	421	563	4,046	48,553
PA	Rural	600	647	1,068	277	235	343	456	3,627	43,519
RI	Providence-Fall River-Warwick (R.I. portion)	831	647	1,226	240	426	406	610	4,386	52,635
RI	New London-Norwich (R.I. portion)	905	647	1,226	208	426	425	633	4,470	53,643
RI	Rural	1,056	647	1,226	277	426	457	725	4,815	57,778
SC	Charleston-North Charleston	710	647	911	226	241	366	334	3,436	41,227
SC	Columbia	719	647	911	226	241	369	339	3,453	41,432
SC	Florence	587	647	911	222	241	346	272	3,227	38,718
SC	Greenville-Spartanburg-Anderson	609	647	911	226	241	350	285	3,270	39,240
SC	Myrtle Beach	686	647	911	222	241	371	324	3,402	40,819
SC	Sumter	592	647	911	222	241	335	270	3,217	38,609
SC	Augusta-Aiken (S.C. portion)	683	647	911	208	241	357	311	3,358	40,298
SC	Charlotte-Gastonia-Rock Hill (S.C. portion)	726	647	911	240	241	371	348	3,485	41,814
SC	Rural	543	647	911	277	241	332	271	3,223	38,671
SD	Rapid City	752	647	735	222	295	372	282	3,305	39,656
SD	Sioux Falls	748	647	735	222	295	384	284	3,315	39,776
SD	Rural	577	647	735	277	295	335	236	3,102	37,226
TN	Chattanooga (Tenn. portion)	659	647	874	208	250	359	274	3,272	39,260
TN	Clarksville-Hopkinsville (Tenn. portion)	605	647	874	222	250	338	256	3,192	38,308
TN	Jackson	639	647	874	222	250	344	268	3,244	38,927
TN	Johnson City-Kingsport-Bristol (Tenn. portion)	581	647	874	208	250	339	246	3,146	37,747
TN	Knoxville	624	647	874	226	250	346	265	3,233	38,794
TN	Memphis (Tenn. portion)	736	647	874	240	250	365	308	3,420	41,037
TN	Nashville	853	647	874	240	250	395	351	3,610	43,315
TN	Rural	480	647	874	277	250	314	229	3,071	36,852
TX	Abilene	646	647	796	222	298	349	262	3,220	38,635
TX	Amarillo	618	647	796	222	298	338	251	3,169	38,027
TX	Austin-San Marcos	970	647	796	240	298	417	382	3,750	44,998
TX	Beaumont-Port Arthur	628	647	796	208	298	348	253	3,177	38,124
TX	Brazoria	862	647	796	222	298	393	338	3,555	42,659
TX	Brownsville-Harlingen-San Benito	666	647	796	208	298	366	269	3,249	38,993
TX	Bryan-College Station	771	647	796	222	298	372	306	3,411	40,931
TX	Corpus Christi	752	647	796	208	298	372	296	3,369	40,422
TX	Dallas	994	647	796	221	298	423	386	3,764	45,168
TX	El Paso	730	647	796	226	298	364	293	3,353	40,240
TX	Fort Worth-Arlington	820	647	796	240	298	383	328	3,511	42,137
TX	Galveston-Texas City	780	647	796	222	298	375	309	3,426	41,113
TX	Houston	837	647	796	221	298	387	329	3,514	42,171
TX	Killeen-Temple	726	647	796	208	298	362	286	3,323	39,876
TX	Laredo	606	647	796	222	298	351	251	3,170	38,044
TX	Longview-Marshall	599	647	796	222	298	337	245	3,143	37,713
TX	Lubbock	695	647	796	222	298	355	279	3,291	39,492
TX	McAllen-Edinburg-Mission	522	647	796	226	298	330	222	3,041	36,488
TX	Odessa-Midland	652	647	796	222	298	346	263	3,223	38,680
TX	San Angelo	600	647	796	222	298	336	245	3,143	37,720
TX	San Antonio	771	647	796	240	298	372	311	3,435	41,214
TX	Sherman-Denison	595	647	796	222	298	345	246	3,148	37,781
TX	Texarkana (Texas portion)	604	647	796	222	298	343	248	3,157	37,882
TX	Tyler	660	647	796	222	298	348	266	3,237	38,838
TX	Victoria	619	647	796	222	298	339	252	3,172	38,058
TX	Waco	659	647	796	222	298	354	268	3,243	38,914
TX	Wichita Falls	607	647	796	222	298	342	249	3,160	37,920
TX	Rural	533	647	796	277	298	324	238	3,111	37,335
UT	[HUD FMR] Kane County	630	647	762	222	262	346	374	3,243	38,920
UT	Provo-Orem	766	647	762	208	262	372	436	3,453	41,433
UT	Salt Lake City-Ogden	884	647	762	240	262	398	507	3,699	44,391
UT	Flagstaff (Utah portion)	797	647	762	222	262	385	459	3,533	42,398
UT	Rural	670	647	762	277	262	356	418	3,393	40,712
VA	Charlottesville	857	647	929	222	259	401	515	3,829	45,948
VA	Danville	578	647	929	222	259	334	380	3,348	40,181
VA	Lynchburg	578	647	929	222	259	337	381	3,352	40,226
VA	Norfolk-Va Beach-Newpt News (Va. portion)	803	647	929	240	259	379	493	3,749	44,989
VA	Richmond-Petersburg	863	647	929	226	259	393	516	3,833	45,996

TABLE A4.6 Basic family budgets for two parents, three children, 1999

State	Area name	Monthly expenses								Annual total
		Housing	Food	Child care	Trans.	Health care	Other necess.	Taxes	Total	
VA	Roanoke	610	647	929	222	259	348	398	3,412	40,942
VA	Washington (Va. portion)	1,118	647	929	221	259	455	639	4,267	51,200
VA	Johnson City-Kingsport-Bristol (Va. portion)	581	647	929	208	259	339	378	3,341	40,088
VA	Rural	600	647	929	277	259	339	412	3,462	41,546
VT	Burlington	943	647	821	222	445	415	502	3,995	47,940
VT	Rural	789	647	821	226	445	387	438	3,753	45,037
WA	Bellingham	942	647	1,018	222	349	412	448	4,038	48,452
WA	Bremerton	838	647	1,018	222	349	393	412	3,878	46,540
WA	Olympia	901	647	1,018	222	349	404	433	3,974	47,686
WA	Richland-Kennewick-Pasco	940	647	1,018	222	349	410	446	4,032	48,387
WA	Seattle-Bellevue-Everett	1,022	647	1,018	240	349	429	481	4,186	50,232
WA	Spokane	705	647	1,018	208	349	362	359	3,649	43,782
WA	Tacoma	815	647	1,018	226	349	382	403	3,841	46,091
WA	Yakima	728	647	1,018	222	349	369	372	3,705	44,462
WA	Portland-Vancouver (Wash. portion)	897	647	1,018	222	349	401	431	3,965	47,576
WA	Rural	685	647	1,018	277	349	361	374	3,711	44,527
WI	Appleton-Oshkosh-Neenah	625	647	996	208	228	354	507	3,566	42,792
WI	Eau Claire	626	647	996	222	228	352	512	3,583	43,001
WI	Green Bay	736	647	996	222	228	365	565	3,760	45,114
WI	Janesville-Beloit	682	647	996	222	228	370	544	3,689	44,264
WI	Kenosha	794	647	996	222	228	380	598	3,865	46,374
WI	La Crosse (Wis. portion)	617	647	996	222	228	344	505	3,559	42,702
WI	Madison	914	647	996	208	228	405	656	4,055	48,654
WI	Milwaukee-Waukesha	758	647	996	240	228	388	593	3,851	46,209
WI	Racine	691	647	996	222	228	367	546	3,697	44,364
WI	Sheboygan	593	647	996	222	228	348	496	3,531	42,366
WI	Wausau	654	647	996	222	228	349	523	3,620	43,439
WI	Duluth-Superior (Wis. portion)	613	647	996	222	228	343	503	3,552	42,625
WI	Minneapolis-St. Paul (Wis. portion)	901	647	996	240	228	407	665	4,085	49,016
WI	Rural	553	647	996	277	228	334	497	3,533	42,394
WV	[HUD FMR] Berkeley County	629	647	888	222	261	357	402	3,406	40,867
WV	Charleston	673	647	888	208	261	353	411	3,442	41,300
WV	Huntington-Ashland (W.Va. portion)	557	647	888	208	261	336	362	3,260	39,120
WV	[HUD FMR] Jefferson County	723	647	888	222	261	373	443	3,557	42,681
WV	Parkersburg-Marietta (W.Va. portion)	541	647	888	222	261	330	359	3,248	38,973
WV	Wheeling (W.Va. portion)	535	647	888	222	261	331	357	3,241	38,886
WV	Washington (W.Va. portion)	1,118	647	888	221	261	455	621	4,211	50,532
WV	Cumberland (W.Va. portion)	657	647	888	222	261	355	411	3,441	41,294
WV	Steubenville-Weirton (W.Va. portion)	535	647	888	222	261	331	357	3,241	38,886
WV	Rural	485	647	888	277	261	317	354	3,228	38,741
WY	Casper	642	647	692	222	340	346	242	3,130	37,558
WY	Cheyenne	764	647	692	222	340	386	290	3,340	40,075
WY	Rural	594	647	692	277	340	339	242	3,130	37,560

Source: Author's calculations (see Appendix A)